# CLASS NOTES

*Posing As Politics and Other
Thoughts on the American Scene*

ADOLPH REED, JR.

THE NEW PRESS   NEW YORK

To Anthony Mazzocchi, Katherine Isaac, and the memory of Bob Kasen, and to Noel Beasley, Richard Berg, Howard Botwinick, Bob Brown, Ed Bruno, Dave Campbell, Robert L. Clark, Kit Costello, Beth Gonzalez, Stephanie Karamitsos, Michael Kaufman, David Klein, Les Leopold, Laura McClure, Rich Monje, Cecelia Perry, Carl Rosen, Frank Rosen, Leo Seidlitz, Tom Verdone, and Gerald Zero, as well as the many others who are working to build our Labor Party.

Requests for permission to reproduce selections from this book should be mailed to: Permissions Department, The New Press, 120 Wall Street, 31st floor, New York, NY 10005.

Grateful acknowledgment is made to the following:

"Martyrs and False Populists," "Tokens of the White Left," letter to the editor in "The Underclass Myth," "Pimping Poverty, Then and Now," "Kiss the Family Good-bye," "Token Equality," "The Battle of Liberty Monument," "Looking Back at *Brown*," "Sectarians on the Prowl," and "Building Solidarity" are reprinted by permission of the *Progressive*, 409 E. Main Street, Madison, WI 53703.

"'Fayettenam,' 1969" was originally published in the *Objector*, the journal of the Central Committee for Conscientious Objectors.

"Why Is There No Black Political Movement?," "The Curse of 'Community,'" "Romancing Jim Crow," "Have We Exhaled Yet?," "We Were Framed," "What Color Is Anti-Semitism?," "Triumph of the Tuskegee Will," "'What Are the Drums Saying, Booker?': The Curious Role of the Black Public Intellectual," "Liberals, I Do Despise," "A Polluted Debate," "Nasty Habits," "A Livable Wage," "Skin Deep," "The Content of Our Cardiovascular," "Posing As Politics," and "The Longer March" originally appeared in the *Village Voice*.

"The Rise of Louis Farrakhan" by Adolph Reed, Jr. from the January 28, 1999 issue of the *Nation*.

"Looking Backward" by Adolph Reed, Jr. from the November 28, 1994 issue of the *Nation*.

Originally published in the United States by The New Press, New York, 2000
This paperback edition published by The New Press, 2001

CIP data available
ISBN 978-1-56584-482-7 (hc.)
ISBN 978-1-56584-675-3 (pb.)

Distributed by Perseus Distribution

The New Press publishes books that promote and enrich public discussion and understanding of the issues vital to our democracy and to a more equitable world. These books are made possible by the enthusiasm of our readers; the support of a committed group of donors, large and small; the collaboration of our many partners in the independent media and the not-for-profit sector; booksellers, who often hand-sell New Press books; librarians; and above all by our authors.

www.thenewpress.com

Printed in the United States of America

# —Contents

# —Preface

The final stages of preparing this book for publication have been marked by a singular tragedy. Joe Wood, the editor who guided the project from its inception, disappeared— last seen while hiking on Mt. Rainier outside Seattle.

Joe has been more than this book's editor. His ear, voice, and hand are present throughout it, and this presence extends far beyond his capacity with The New Press. It was Joe who nagged me for more than a year to write for the *Village Voice* when he was an editor there; specifically, he prodded me first to undertake a critical assessment of the "black public intellectual" phenomenon and then to do a regular column in the *Voice*. Since we met in 1991, he also read practically everything I wrote for the *Voice*, the *Progressive*, the *Nation* and elsewhere. In fact, we read most of each other's work in draft, and we talked at length about nearly all of it. I have valued his ear, eye, and insight; he has been one of the smallest handful of readers I imagine when I write.

Going through these last preparations against the stark reality of Joe's absence, therefore, is an experience that is simultaneously eerie and ultimately indescribable. He has been a confidant, collaborator, comrade, and crony; a younger brother, fellow searcher, and pal. It's all of a piece: enjoying and appreciating his clear prose, in its spareness and quiet clarity evoking haiku and Thelonious Monk (comparisons which have met with his somewhat embarrassed appreciation as well); long, widely ranging conversations on the phone, in bars, watching ball games, sitting around listening to a potpourri of music, walking all over Manhattan; variously productive and uniquely mirthful evenings at the Algonquin, Pampy's, the Checkerboard, the Green Mill, and the Jazz Showcase; observing in conspiratorial invisibility (behind boots, jeans, parkas, and a cap) the bizarre human comedy enacted beneath the surface of dazzle at B. Smith's; outlining a journal project at the Mello Yello Cafe and polishing off the success at Jimmy's Woodlawn Tap; kvetching, commiserating, and advising about the personal and the political; sharing gossip, info, and speculations about the many crosscutting domains of mutual concern; learning and engaging around facets of each other's biographies and family stories; comparing impressions of the complexities of the South, both past and present; his genuine pleasure and sense of vindication at my sudden, totally unexpected rebirth in '96 as a Yankees fan after a lifetime of automatic and un-equivocal Yankee-hating; his irrational animus toward Michael Jordan and the Chicago Bulls and equally irrational commitment to the ridiculously overhyped mediocrity that is the Ewing-era Knicks; our bonding around high regard for Thomas Mann and Ellison and astonishment at the absurdities of both New Jack basketball and the ideology of cultural politics.

Joe was young when he disappeared, not yet thirty-five. Most of his life's work certainly lay ahead of him when he took that day trip onto Mt. Rainier to decompress and bird-watch. If he's gone, many of us are pained and diminished by the loss, but I know that he would insist that his demise should be seen, except within his world of intimates, as no more tragic—notwithstanding his impressive accomplishments, his even greater promise, his visibility, and Yale pedigree—than that of anyone else who meets an untimely or unfair end. His striving to maintain that kind of balance of perspective and honesty stands out as part of the core of his beauty as a person.

Yet within that world of intimates, part of the difficulty no doubt for all those who loved him, is the indeterminacy of it all, the per-sisting hope that somewhere, somehow he's still among us. As that smoldering hope threatens to dim, I at least can take some small solace that, in addition to his editorial hand, encouragement, and critical judgment, Joe is present in this book in all the aspects and quirks of our friendship, and he always will be.

*September 1999*

# —Introduction

This book is built on commentary about current issues and events in American politics over most of the 1990s. As such, it expresses an on-going attempt to make sense of contemporary American political life from a critical perspective. Most of the essays published here appeared originally in substantially the same form in my regular columns in *The Progressive* and *The Village Voice*, or in similar venues. Writing in those venues presents a special challenge—to convey complex, perhaps unconventional ideas clearly and concisely to a general audience. I've found this challenge very useful partly because I work out my own views on many issues by writing about them; to that extent, these essays are much less a set of didactic pronouncements than a sustained attempt to think things through, and the obligation to communicate those views effectively to others encourages preciseness and clarity. Having to ask constantly, "What would this formulation mean to someone outside my own head or outside a narrowly specialized community of discourse?" imposes a requirement to bring abstractions down to the ground, to imagine how—if at all—they appear in, explain or bear upon the daily world we inhabit and reproduce. The challenge is more important, though, as a corrective to the flight from concreteness that has increasingly beset left theorizing and social criticism, and as a result political practice, in the U.S. in recent decades.

This flight has taken at least two distinct forms, both fueled by the decline of popular activism after the 1960s. One route led directly from activists' deepening isolation in the 1970s and was driven by a failure to adapt to the new political situation. The other was charted by university-based leftists' accommodations to their environment during the 1970s and 1980s.

These tendencies, of course, were not the 1960s' only radical legacy. Many activists dug in and persisted in the labor movement and other terrains of organizing, advocacy, and constituency-based politics, adapting to political realities and the requirements of building a real base for action while not losing sight of larger principles and goals. More than a few did so after or through periods of sectarian affiliation, often drawing usefully on the discipline learned in such political organizations while discarding the immobilizing sectarian baggage. One of the most encouraging aspects of the current period is that a good many of those people have become solid, well-rooted leaders in trade unions and other popularly grounded political institutions.

It is no accident that this legacy of 1960s radicalism goes largely unnoticed in public discussion around the state of the left. Even in what passes for a left public sphere there is little sense of creating a movement as an activity that rests on organizing, working actually to build support and solidarity among real people in real places around concrete objectives that they perceive as concerns—people who may not, indeed probably do not, all start from commitment to what is generally understood as a left political perspective or identification with issues that leftists see as highly symbolic. Instead, the more gestural approaches to politics associated with the flight from concreteness have been much more prominent and visible, and tend to monopolize public discourse about the left. That results mainly, I suspect, from the circumstance that the left public sphere itself is sharply slanted toward the social world and sensibilities of disconnected left intellectuals and political celebrities and, to that extent, reflects the symbiosis of defeatist thinking and wish fulfillment that have come to shape political thinking in such quarters.

This book proceeds from a different view, one neatly summarized in the Labor Party's model of an "organizing approach to politics." From this perspective, the key fact is that we do not have the popularly based, institutionalized, mass political movement that we need to realize any meaningful progressive agenda in the United States. Therefore, the principal task should be building an active membership base for such a movement. Strategic political thinking and critique should be harnessed to that goal as the normative and pragmatic linchpin of analysis. Finally, the movement we need cannot be convoked magically overnight or by proxy. It cannot be galvanized through proclamations, press conferences, symbolic big events, resolutions or quixotic electoral candidacies; it can be built only through connecting with large numbers of people in cities and towns and workplaces all over the country who can be brought together around a political agenda that speaks directly and clearly to their needs and aspirations as they perceive them. This, like all organizing, is a painstaking, slow and time-consuming process, and it promises no guarentees of ultimate victory or even shorter-term success. But there are no alternatives other than fraud, pretense or certain failure.

This viewpoint has always seemed to me to be simple common sense. The twists and turns of the self-identified left, both activist and intellectual varieties, from the Carter years through Clinton—including more than a decade of responding to the Reaganite onslaught by focusing on international solidarity work and serving as prop soldiers in Jesse Jackson's Potemkin army, never admitting what his game so clearly is—underscore just how great a toll the legacy of defeat has taken on strategic will and clarity within our ranks. For that reason, I think it is helpful to reconstruct the two main roads that led to this situation.

One strain of those activists who found themselves cut off from ready access to any broader audience or dialogue were left talking to no one but one another. Their isolation was reinforced by a largely honorable rejection of pressures to abjure radicalism. Practical expressions of that rejection, however, were often naïvely catechistic and misguided strategically. Radicalism's proceeding marginalization heightened fears that attempts to compensate would slide into an opportunistic betrayal of fundamental radical commitments. Those fears set in motion a dynamic of intensifying ideological vigilance and purification. As a consequence, many who took that route succumbed to the temptation to retreat into arcane debates, ever further removed from issues and concerns that resonate with the lives of people outside the self-conscious left. They produced a pattern of left discourse that centers on fitting aspects of contemporary social relations into one or another pre-scripted narrative of global revolution or noble resistance. Thus a current of activist radicalism dribbled off into scholastic, albeit bizarrely intense (and often intensely bizarre), debates over what "stage" of capitalism or imperialism the current moment represented, to what extent which populations in the United States or elsewhere enacted generic roles assigned to them in a given potted narrative, or which mundane political actions or events indicated impending revolutionary ferment or proper revolutionary consciousness.

The more isolated this radicalism became, the more insular and idiosyncratic became its language and critiques. The more it was removed from connection to palpable constituencies or membership outside the ranks of the already faithful, the less constrained it was by pragmatic or strategic thinking. The more solipsistic it became, the less capable it was of distnguishing matters of principle, strategy and tactics, and the less dependent theoretical arguments were on any test of practical efficacy. And throughout this spiral a flamboyant and self-righteous rhetoric combined with interpretations of current events and popular behavior—without regard to the expressed understandings and objectives of those who enact such events and behaviors—as proxy evidence for radicals' pet theories, a combination that has worked to paper over the reality of marginalization.

Characterizing a rent strike, say, or a group of neighbors' challenge to an eviction as, *in effect*, a rejection of capitalist imperatives in the provision of housing, or representing a protest against an instance of police brutality as the equivalent of a demand for self-determination camouflages radicals' inability to win adherents for their programs. Such representations accommodate marginalization through a form of denial. Redefining such political expressions as deeply, intrinsically, substantively, or implicitly radical enables a sleight-of-hand that imputes support for the radicals' broader programs by association, without the test of persuasion. This is what underlies sectarian newspapers' penchant for running photographs of members displaying signs with radical slogans at union picket lines or other sorts of more broadly based demonstrations and rallies. Moreover, because this politics is propelled by illusion and a Humpty Dumpty-like use of language, it can wildly inflate the meaning of the most modest or conventional actions or events without reservation. It also has built-in mechanisms for avoiding critical self-reflection on practice and acknowledgement of failure. I recall from my graduate school years a particularly outrageous illustration of the lengths to which this kind of reasoning can go to invert reality.

In the immediate aftermath of Pinochet's brutal coup against Salvador Allende's government in Chile, a colleague of mine pronounced the coup "progressive" because it had taught the Chilean left the futility of the electoral option. To the objections that the left was being liquidated even as he spoke, he responded that it was possible to "kill the individuals but not the tendency."

Substituting fanciful taxonomy for strategic analysis and assessment (for example, portraying the Million Man March as a general strike) also made it possible to tag along with whatever motion appears to have some visibility or popular support. Worse, precisely because its operative logic ("has a similar effect as = might as well be = is") generates protean capacities for projecting its illusions onto the behavior of others, this politics can rationalize quite disreputable and opportunistic associations, simply by defining them formalistically as something loftier. After all, anything can mean anything if you get to stipulate the conditions of meaning without constraint by the mundane facts of an external world, such as the perceptions and objectives of others. In recent years one of the clearest instances of this tendency on the national stage has been so many leftists' persistence in tailing after Jesse Jackson's political charade and minimizing or justifying his dubious, often obviously and crudely self-serving, programmatic twists and turns. For many this commitment has extended even to accepting the preposterous formula that defines the character of media and official attention to Jackson's person—the rhetoric, resonant with the presumptions of an absolutist Sovereign, centered on whether he has been treated with "respect"—as identical with recognition of progressive interests. In some cases, to be sure, this will to believe stems from political romanticism and naïveté, racial patriotism or guilty racial liberalism. In many others, however, it rests on doomed hope that association with Jackson will confer popular legitimacy or otherwise provide access to a popular constituency. That association and the desperate hope undergirding it are poignant evidence of the legacy of defeat.

A second form of the left's flight from concreteness is distinct from, but grew organically within the defeatist environment prepared by, the first. The notions of cultural politics that acquired currency over the 1980s and 1990s developed most immediately in university circles. Intellectually, this tendency's proximate sources derived from the structuralist and poststructuralist turns in left academic discourse that had become increasingly prominent during the 1970s and 1980s. This strain as well originated from entirely reasonable, even politically laudable concerns. Leftist scholars, particularly in the social sciences and humanties, who entered the professoriat from the activism of the 1960s were generally concerned to find ways to harmonize their intellectual and political interests and to secure a place for left perspectives in mainstream academic discourses.

Structuralist Marxism, a 1970s theoretical import either directly from France or via the British, *New Left Review*, appealed to those concerns. In emphasizing the causal significance of durable social forces in shaping social systems and constraining behavior, structuralism provided a common conceptual frame of reference for radical and nonradical—or Marxist and non-Marxist—scholars interested in examining the ways that societies change or remain stable. This common frame of reference promised to open lines of communication between radical and nonradical tendencies and thereby to soften the ideological and institutional barriers that marginalized radical critiques within conventional academic disciplines.

The greater legitimacy came at a price that became both less noticeable and more consequential as extramural activism receded toward the vanishing point in the historical rearview mirror. Pursuit of respectability in mainstream academic disciplines required shelving the idea of class struggle as an orienting principle of inquiry and debate. Pressures to do so came from several sources. Maintaining a community of discourse with nonradicals meant suspending premises the latter found unacceptable. Contemporary academic norms regard obvious political engagement—that is, linking inquiry to unconventional or controversial political programs and interpretations—as inconsistent with scholarly distance and integrity. Those norms operate at the individual level as career imperatives as well. And the atrophy of radical activism outside the university fed this process by eroding possibilities for anchoring left scholarly activity in strategic dialogue with coherent political movements.

Structuralism's departure from the vantage point of class struggle supported a tendency to understate the space for meaningful human intervention in politics. The result was a form of theoretical narrative emphasizing the power of entrenched patterns of relations and institutions and discounting the possibilities for systemic change. A structuralist perspective is biased toward predicting continuities; structural forces move inertially. However, political interventions that can disrupt that inertia are volatile and usually unpredictable. To the extent that structuralist Marxism lost its moorings in the commitment to grounding inquiry and interpretation in the objective of strategic intervention in class struggle—or any other program of transformative practical action—this turn produced a radical scholarship that more than mirrored the decline of the left outside the university; it also often rationalized that decline and sanctified it in the language of scientific law.

A curious parallel to ultraleft sectarianism developed in academic life: a logic of radical one-upmanship in which the winning arguments were those that purportedly demonstrated that capitalist or ruling class power was so great that any specific action attempting to challenge it was destined to fail. Like left sectarianism, the discourse of structuralist Marxism failed to see the processual, dialectical character of political action, its contingent open-endedness. Much as left sectarians are immobilized by their conviction that it is not possible to change anything until everything is changed, the vantage point of structuralist Marxism similarly immobilizes by its tendency to view the configuration of power relations existing at a given moment as identical to the limits of possibility. They equally fail to recognize that putting the ball in play can suddenly change the alignment of forces in the field and create openings that could not have been predicted. Both forget, that is, what Marx recognized more than a century and a half ago: that, although constrained by structures (which in turn are not active, insuperable things, but the congealed effect of "circumstances directly encountered, given and transmitted from the past"), the course of history is dynamic and open-ended, that *people* actually do make history, even if not "just as they please, under circumstances chosen by themselves." Sectarians respond to their immobilization with apocalyptic rhetoric, opportunism and wish-fulfillment; structuralist-Marxist academics tend to respond with melancholy and an almost sentimental pessimism—the highly theorized retreat to a world-weary, sometimes agonizedly disappointed quietism that presumes the privilege of secure, middle to upper-middle class employment with good benefits.

In the early 1980s left academic theorizing took a turn at least suggestive of explicit political engagement. Originating primarily in the humanities, a self-consciously radical scholarly discourse formed around the interpretive programs and intellectual sensibility represented by such labels as poststructuralism, deconstruction and postmodernism. This sensibility converged on reaction against large-scale social theories of any kind and rejection of any form of centralizing power or notion of objective truth. As a politics, this translates into: 1) a focus on the supposedly liberatory significance of communities and practices defined by their marginality in relation to systems of entrenched power or institutions, 2) a preference for strategies of "resistance" to imperatives of institutions and "transgression" of conventions rather than strategies aimed at transformation of institutions and social relations, and 3) a conviction that the basic units of a radical politics should be groups formed around ascriptive identities that relate to one another on a principle of recognizing and preserving the integrity of their various differences.

This politics has a dual institutional foundation in academic life. Theoretically, it emerged from the turn in literary studies to linguistic analysis that sought to destabilize conventional understandings of the relation between signifiers and signified, text and world. It also no doubt seemed attractive to some left-inclined scholars and students who wanted to overcome structuralism's denial of possibilities for transformative political action. Sociologically, it struck a responsive chord in those academic networks concerned with advancing the status of women, blacks and other minorities as students, faculty, and subject matter, particularly at elite colleges and universities. The new academic radicalism appealed to faculty and

students struggling, against an often bigoted skepticism and orthodoxy, to establish footholds of institutional legitimacy for women's
studies, black studies, and other specialty areas associated with the
democratization and expanded purview of American academic life
since the 1960s. Its immersion in Continental European philosophy
and rarefied critical theory give it a high intellectuality that legitimizes studies of "marginal discourses" in conventionally profes-
sionalistic academic terms—by vesting them with the raiments of
technical sophistication and the authority of a canon of Greats.

Because it is formulated at high levels of theoretical abstraction,
the postmodernist / poststructuralist sensibility is broadly gauged
enough to provide a common critical frame of reference for practitioners and advocates of the various marginal discourses and, indeed, has been partly responsible for constituting them as such a
group. In that sense, as a practical academic politics this radicalism
has functioned in ironic contrast to its theoretical commitments to
"decentering" and suspicion of "totalizing" projects; it has operated rather more like a language of nation-building or, at a minimum, interest-group aggregation. The various specialty areas still
compete with one another for resources and visibility, and the status
of postmodernism and poststructuralism within each is contested,
sometimes sharply, as in African American studies. However, an
apparatus of journals, colloquia, anthologies, and conferences has
helped to create a community of discourse and institutional networks that unite adherents across fields. The emergence of "cultural studies" as a rubric is an expression, and an instrument, of
that process.

The new sensibility's critique of the conventional disciplines'
ideological partiality and arbitrary exclusivism in their focal preoc-
cupations was an obvious source of its attractiveness in those insurgent academic precincts that would come together affirmatively
around the rhetoric of cultural studies, multiculturalism, or diversity, and that have shared the frustrating condition of being ignored
or assigned inferior status in disciplines, departments, and budgets.
In taking "difference," marginality, and fragmentation as guiding
theoretical principles and in orienting inquiry around specification
of an expanding mulitiplicity of "voices" and discrete group per-

spectives, the postmodernist / poststructuralist sensibility is congenial to arguments for enhancing the institutional and intellectual
status of those new fields and practitioners within them.

Formulations such as "standpoint theory" recast the insight that
perception is shaped by social position—articulated by Marx and
a long-available, uncontroversial first premise of the sociology of
knowledge—and elevate it into a major interpretive departure and a
theory of knowledge and research program in its own right. Asserting the primary importance of "positionality" in shaping perception
and grounding knowledge has two programmatic implications that
buttress the institutional programs of the new fields. First, in establishing a rationale for reading coherent group perspective unprob-
lematically from common identity, that assertion solidifies field
boundaries by giving them an elaborate theoretical foundation. If
group identity is a fundamental ingredient of perception, then organizing academic programs and discourses around identity-group
studies is all the more appropriate. Second, its premise that a shared
identity confers a special interpretive authority reinforces, more or
less subtly, a proprietary advantage for practitioners and interpretations able to claim that authority. As a guild move, this arguably
mitigates the ethnocentric bias that partly defines mainstream lines
of academic prestige, status, and interpretive priority dominated by
white, heterosexual men. It does so, however, at the price of at least
opening the door to the proposition that being classified as an X by
definition gives one special insight to interpreting the X, a proposition that is indefensible and potentially poisonous both intellectually and politically.

The hefty theoretical apparatus obscures the fact that those
claims, and the larger arguments elevating positionality, rest on
badly flawed, at least implicitly essentialist views about group consciousness. Formulations such as "the experience or perspective of
the X" depend logically on presumption of a universal, consensual
or somehow otherwise singularly definitive and authentic state of
X-ness. The abstract and hermetic language of positionality, difference, and otherness fixes the interpretive lens at a point so remote
from the ways that people live their lives and form themselves in the
everyday world we all share—the world of seeking, working, or

worrying about a job, finding and consuming healthcare, forming and maintaining personal attachments, paying bills, raising children, playing, fretting about the future, shopping for furniture, trying to make sense of current events—that it never confronts very mundane questions that expose the inadequacy of essentializing notions of identity. How is it plausible to project such singular perspectives as "the standpoint of the X" onto populations consisting of individuals whose lives and social positions are not reducible to a single category, whose individual histories of experience differ enormously and whose points of view and interests are likely to be shaped in complex and idiosyncratic ways? Of the multiple identities that can be gleaned from the life of a given individual—student, worker, parent, manager, child, stamp collector, fantasy baseball enthusiast, precinct captain, deacon, veteran, homeowner, landlord, nurse, developer, teacher, electrician—why should we assume that perspective is endowed *fundamentally* by race, gender, or sexual orientation?

A common response to the last question is that those identities stand out because they are the ones through which populations in this society are marked for marginalization. True enough, but those are not the only categories of people marginalized in the society; the more than forty-three million with no healthcare access, the hundreds of thousands of permanently displaced steelworkers and mineworkers, the millions of homeless and near homeless people, the so called urban underclass, residents of low-income public housing, low-wage workers in sweatshops and the consumer service sector are among the most obvious. Those categories crosscut race, gender, and sexual orientation, and for individuals many of them overlap. Nonwhites and women are disproportionately present within nearly all of them, but they are not reducible to race or gender. And it is by no means a foregone conclusion that, say, a displaced black steelworker, who is a single parent working an insecure, low-wage job with no benefits and trying to negotiate the metropolitan crisis in affordable housing, will experience her daily life and social position, fashion her dreams and expectations, or interpret her concerns and grievances primarily or typically through perceptions of racial or gender identity over the other categories that reflect pertinent facets of her practical life. That response also does not clearly enough distinguish a claim of moral obligation (that we should privilege race, gender, and sexual orientation because those are the terms under which people are sorted hierarchically and oppressed) and an empirical one (that we should privilege those categories because they are the ones through which—perhaps because of their centrality in the system of social hierarchy—people primarily understand themselves).

Attempts within postmodernist sensibility to account for the multiplicity and variety of individuals' identities center on the notion of "hybridity," the blending or mixture of identities to form new ones. However, this notion emerges from a discourse centered on specifying "difference"; unsurprisingly, therefore, its accommodation is formalistic and reified. Hybridity, much like scientific racialist notions of dual consciousness and atavism in the Victorian era, presumes the merger or pastiche of distinct identities, a curiously mechanistic view of how human beings are formed and form themselves. Such constructions as "the subject position of the black gay male," as presumably distinguishable from the white gay male, black straight male, etc., do not overcome the problem of essentializing views of identity. They only compound it by extending the logic of fragmentation to break down larger essentialisms into congeries of smaller ones, mapping ever more precise combinations of identity positions.

The fetish of precision in specifying identities relates ironically both to this intellectual movement's general critical project and its self-image of cultural radicalism. Although the impulse probably stems most immediately from theoretical and moral or ideological concern with acknowledging marginalization or unrepresented "voices," the attempt to follow through on this concern assumes an unproblematic ability to map and detail the bases of human action that is reminiscent of the most naïve positivist faith in the possibility of scientific certainty. This assumption can be sustained only by arbitrarily limiting the universe of pertinent identities to the handful of privileged "standpoints."

This idealist pretense, though, is subject to pressure, consistent with the natural logic of the discourse of difference, further to elaborate the universe of privileged identities. We might, therefore, imagine an effort to define *the* subject position of *the* black, heterosexual, single mother, displaced steelworker, low-wage worker with inadequate healthcare and poor access to affordable housing. That is doubtful, however, and not least because undertaking the effort would demonstrate the folly of the entire enterprise. There is, after all, no such single subject position, not even in the life of a given individual who might occupy all the categories. And even if there were such a least common denominator position, it would hardly be accessible through a method of adding up reified notions of a bunch of discrete "identities."

Despite its affective packaging, the disposition to catalogue and aggregate neatly rounded-off identities is in no meaningful way radical. Not only is it evocative of nineteenth-century essentialisms, it also reproduces the mindset of the mass information industry, which, through public opinion and market research, sorts the population into the demographic equivalent of sound bites — market shares, taste communities — all in service to the corporate sales effort and management of the national political agenda.

Within progressive politics, this mode of argument has precedents in the allegations of black workers' double oppression that appeared in some quarters of left debate in the 1970s and of black women's double or triple oppression that gained currency within the women's movement perhaps a bit later. Implicit in both formulations was a presumption that greater oppression assigned a group greater insight or gave its claims moral priority. To the extent that the proliferating specification of identity positions follows a similar logic it betrays the grain of truth beneath conservatives' ugly dismissals of the new academic specialties as "oppression studies." The right-wing smear aims to discredit successes in broadening the composition of faculties and student bodies and to reinstate the narrow, sanitized, and parochial orthodoxies that had been hegemonic in the social sciences and humanities. However, it is a sinisterly motivated exaggeration of a nonetheless real tendency to invoke language that inflates the political and moral urgency of what are ultimately insular academic debates.

Any intellectual movement that develops a following will do so because it gains institutional and ideological, as well as theoretical, traction. The new academic radicalism, whatever its other attributes, meshes well with a sort of interest-group politics that has developed out of the democratization of university culture during the 1970s and 1980s. This development has accompanied and helped to solidify a marked improvement over the parochialism that previously defined much of academic life. Its accomplishments, though, can be limited and distorted by succumbing to its own ideological mystifications just as the narrow, self-centered pufferies of a generation ago passed for universal truth.

For example, the idea that the social world in general can be read as one would literary texts is a staple of the poststructuralist / postmodernist sensibility. This idea has made a very useful intellectual contribution. In particular, it has been important in focusing critical attention on the extent to which accounts of natural and social events and phenomena are narratives and display properties common that form, which means, among other things, that they are strategically organized and not pure or passive expressions of those phenomena.

The insight that the world can be read as a text, however, easily slides into the reverse—a claim that interpreting literary texts is identical with interpreting the wider world. This reversal is an attractive fiction partly because it invests studies of literary and other forms of cultural production with an aura of political importance they would not otherwise possess. It is understandable that scholars who generally see themselves as committed to progressive or activist interests would be inclined to locate and emphasize political significance in their work. However, the leap that equates, for instance, the practices of textual interpretation or the production and analysis of forms of popular culture with direct challenges to power relations—such as conducting a strike, electing or defeating a legislator, mobilizing against NAFTA, fighting against segregation or for national healthcare—takes that inclination to the point of solipsism. And it empties the idea of political action of any substantive meaning.

Assertions of political significance also add rhetorical force in the struggle for position and competition for resources in institutional politics. Equating the particularistic objectives of an academic program and a global struggle against injustice rehearses a common ploy in liberal discourse, one that originates in the dramaturgy of War on Poverty and Great Society politics in the 1960s. It is a standard move in the interest-group negotiation that is the default mode of American liberal politics.

This compatibility with interest-group pluralism may be a cornerstone of the material and ideological foundation of the postmodern / poststructuralist sensibility's cachet as a style of political expression. The interest-group model depends on a form of elite brokerage, centered on a relation between governing elites and entities or individuals recognized as representatives of designated groups. The heart of the relation is negotiation of policies, programs, and patterns of distribution of resources that presumably protect and advance the interests of the pertinent groups, but safely—in ways that harmonize them with the governing elite's priorities. What we now understand as identity politics emerged as a rhetorical and programmatic vehicle for incorporating an appropriate notion of black interests into this arrangement, in response to popular mobilizations associated with civil rights and black power activism. Feminist, other nonwhite minority group, and gay interests subsequently have been incorporated on the same model.

The new academic radicalism has attained currency partly because it ratifies what already exists; beneath all the theoretical pyrotechnics, it both packages the world in familiar ways and reinforces prevailing conceptual and organizational arrangements of liberal politics—both inside the university and as it looks at the society in general. More specifically, the style of pluralist identity politics it endorses and enacts assigns a privileged place to academic interpreters of the interests and perspectives—the "positionality"—of the designated identity groups. The essentialist underpinnings of these notions of group identity define away the contradiction of a scholarly and political discourse that purports to articulate perceptions and intentions of populations without evidence of the latter's explicit participation in communicating those perceptions and intentions. This is what the "politics of recognition" that arises from the postmodernist / poststructuralist sensibility boils down to—a call to accept the authority of cultural theorists as articulators of the voices of populations who are presumed by the theory to be incapable of speaking clearly for themselves in public, explicit ways.

This is the rational core within the absurd nattering about whether the "subaltern" can speak. It also underlies the popularity of the notion of "cultural politics," which I discuss at length in the first two essays in Part Three. Its basic premise is that the authentic forms of political expression among marginalized groups are not made directly or through regular, institutional channels of political action. Their authentic expressions are instead surreptitious or indirect—in "hidden transcripts," covert acts of "resistance," and "resistive" cultural practices (for example, dancing, hanging out in the club scene, wearing unconventional fashion). This argument, requires disregarding much dramatically courageous, acutely articulate and self-conscious activity as at least implicitly inauthentic, and it ultimately renders those populations mute and reinforces the intermediary role of the academic interpreters.

From this vantage point, recent debates that juxtapose identity politics or cultural politics to class politics are miscast. Cultural politics and identity politics *are* class politics. They are manifestations within the political economy of academic life and the left-liberal public sphere—journals and magazines, philanthropic foundations, the world of "public intellectuals"—of the petit bourgeois, brokerage politics of interest-group pluralism. Postmodernist and poststructuralist theorizing lays a radical-sounding patina over this all-too-familiar worldview and practice.

As it moves beyond the academic arena, the limitations of this approach to politics become all the more striking. Insofar as identity politics insists on recognizing difference as the central truth of political life, it undercuts establishing a broad base as a goal of organizing. Its reflex is to define ever more distinct voices and to approach collective action from an attitude more like suspicion than solidarity. Not unlike left sectarianism, its tendency is to demand that a movement be born fully formed, that all its participants possess an evenly developed, comprehensive progressive critique from the outset. This stance typically requires demonstrating knowledge of and appropriate gestures of respect for the differences and "perspectives" of a broad range of potential participants as prerequisite to acting in concert; this is how the "politics of recognition" takes shape as a practice. Whites must demonstrate their antiracism; heterosexuals must prove their opposition to homophobia; men must establish their antisexism; each nonwhite group must convincingly show its appreciation and respect for the perspectives of the others—all *before* strategic consideration of possible points of mutual concern. Also as with sectarianism, managing the internal politics of the movement comes easily to take precedence over externally focused action.

Anyone with experience in left-of-center activist politics in the last thirty years has been exposed to the dynamic. The standards of proof vary, not only with the specific context, but also with the mood, personal and political idiosyncrasies, and sincerity of the participants. Because there is no such thing as "the perspective of the X" apart from the pronouncements of those who claim privileged access to it, no one can ever be fully certain not to be committing disrespect. (Just as in mainstream interest-group politics, the ironic truth underlying this style is that it requires the good will of those who are presumed to be insensitive; otherwise, they would feel no guilt or concern to prove themselves.) In such conditions, opportunists or wackos can deploy the language of distrust with the destructive effect of provocateurs.

Because identity politics does not grow from a coherent vision of how the society should work, it cannot build broad unity around a coherent common program. Instead, its model of movement-building revolves around constructing and imposing formal images of representativeness. This approach reduces political criticism to scrutinizing the official composition of a movement to ascertain which "voices" are present in what proportions and with what prominence, and which are not. The tendency, therefore, is to subordinate consideration of a movement's or organization's program, goals, and strategies to the appearance of its freeze-frame photo. A standard form of intervention from the mindset of identity politics illustrates this limitation.

A predictable moment in progressive meetings of virtually any sort, even at incipient stages of an organizing effort, is when someone—more or less piously, more or less smugly, always self-righteously—rises to introduce the concern that, "As I look around the room, I don't see enough of the X, the Y or the Z present" and to issue the standard calls for inclusiveness and for making greater effort to reach out, etc. This intervention has a pro forma, gestural quality. It is a ritual act that seems automatic and obligatory. Like a mantra or a Catholic prayer of ejaculation, its purpose seems more therapeutic and aesthetic than instructive. It is typically offered as a self-sufficient commentary, seldom accompanied by specific proposals for correcting the perceived imbalances. Sometimes, in the unfolding of a meeting or event, it is possible even to notice identitarians surveying the room, seemingly with only scant regard to the progress of the meeting's agenda, doing an inventory of the groups arguably *not* represented—in preparation for tailoring the predetermined intervention to the specific gathering.

Almost no one ever disagrees with it on principle, and the typical response is a round of nods of assent and a return to the business at hand. Occasionally, though, it does provoke rebukes for presumptuousness, most likely when the intervention comes from newcomers to the initiative that prompted the meeting, whose incautious and uninformed enthusiasm all too frequently ensues in their comeuppance. Self-righteousness, though, can insulate against the embarrassment of making a fool of oneself in public. I witnessed one such instance during a Chicago-wide conference of labor and community activists and progressive elected officials, when an earnest neophyte, armed with the arrogant self-assurance that can arise only from ignorant true belief, interrupted the flow of the discussion to protest what she perceived to be the absence of some significant identity categories among the participants. On being informed brusquely of the inaccuracy of her perception and chastised for impertinence by a longtime South Side activist, she responded with indignation at not having been apprised of the situation sooner.

This kind of political intervention is fundamentally counter-solidaristic. Its default posture is accusation; it is propelled by presumption of others' bad faith. In its narrowness and self-righteousness it parallels left sectarianism in yet another way. Yet this intervention has an opportunist quality that also displays marks of its ancestor in black power-era racial politics. A political stance that pivots on accusations of exclusion or disrespect sets up a role for the accuser as either a special conduit to—or a proxy for—the excluded or overlooked constituencies. As I argue in the last two essays in Part One, this motif underlies a pattern of racially opportunistic practice within predominantly white liberal and progressive organizations.

The combination of lack of a coherent critical, strategic vision and the conviction that generic ascriptive categories are the fundamental units of political consciousness and action produces a view of a political program as primarily a vehicle for demonstrating recognition of pertinent identity groups. This means that programs tend to become simply laundry lists of designer issues. The logic of identity as an ideological position impels toward defining issues narrowly enough to fasten them to specific groups. (Apropos of this mindset, a student recently argued in my seminar, and with passionate resolve, that the material gains that black Americans experienced through the New Deal do not count as improvement of blacks' social condition because they were not designated for blacks specifically!) That logic also leads to proliferation of the groups thus recognized, if only by virtue of ever more precise specifying of identities. The result is an inertial tendency for the list to expand in number and to become steadily more diffuse as a totality.

At the same time, the commitment to gross, reified categories as the foundation of political authenticity turns symbols of recognition into the least-common-denominator issues held to represent the concerns of specified groups as singular collectivities. But because they are so general, such issues—for example, opposition to English-only requirements, defense of affirmative action, support for Mumia Abu-Jamal—are not likely to animate the great bulk of people to whom they are presumed to appeal, people whose felt concerns are much more immediate and mundane. The high-profile, generic issues are much more meaningful to activists and progressives (you know, the few hundred of us anywhere who show up for one another's events and actions) than to anyone else.

This is not to argue that those issues are trivial, just as noting the wrongheadedness of the identitarian rhetoric of inclusiveness is not to deny either the importance of building an inclusive politics or the fact that doing so may require special effort. The point is that these characteristics of identity politics militate against mobilizing a popular base broad and large enough to hope to have any significant effect in advancing democratic and egalitarian interests. In fact, insofar as politics is about the effort to mobilize an effective base for concerted public action, it may be improper to call the ideology and rhetoric of identity a politics at all. Its focus on who is not in the room certainly does not facilitate strategic discussion of how best to deploy the resources of those who *are* in the room, and its fixation on organizing around difference overtaxes any attempt to sustain concerted action.

The prominence of identity politics and cultural politics is less the harbinger of new types of social movements befitting postmodern times, as a group of scholars of and many propagandists for these approaches would have it, than it is evidence of demoralization, defeat, historical amnesia, and class insularity within elements of the left. Cultural politics in particular in some ways strikingly approximates the Reaganite/Thatcherite view of the world. It devalues political institutions and processes and elevates private, individual acts over public, collective engagement. Within its purview, as in Thatcher's apothegm, there is no such thing as society, "only individuals and their families." Exaltation of "everyday acts of resistance" is a don't worry, be happy politics. If all is resistance, there is no need for concern with mobilizing collective action, especially because in this view public institutions are inauthentic or corrupting.

The perspectives of both identity politics and cultural politics also diminish the structuring role of political-economic and class forces in shaping the social order, including its shifting forms and constellations of identity. Notwithstanding potted disclaimers to the contrary, both reject organizing on an explicit class basis as a strategy for building a movement capable of fighting for a just and egalitarian society; in doing so, they embrace a different class base implicitly. In fact, in reducing politics to gestures and poses, both imagine a social movement without a foundation in willful, painstaking, highly labor-intensive organizing of any sort.

Defenders of identity politics would argue, rightly, that class is itself an identity and that class politics is, therefore, also an identity politics. The crucial distinction is not that class is in some way more real or authentic than other identities, though it is certainly possible to argue that in this society class — as functional location in the system of social reproduction — is the social relation through which other identities are constituted and experienced within political economy. Even without elaborating that theoretical argument, however, there is a pragmatic justification that is sufficient for taking class as the identity around which to organize. The goal of building a mass movement — and there is no way other than such a movement to pursue progressive social transformation with any chance for even partial or contingent success — requires proceeding from those identities that unite as much of the society as possible around a vision and program that most directly challenge the current power relations. For the vast majority of people in this country — of all racial classifications or identities, all genders and sexual orientations — the common frame of reference is the employment relation, the fact of working, or being expected to work, a job. Moreover, the concerns and aspirations that are most widely shared are those that are rooted in the common experience of everyday life shaped and constrained by political economy — for example, finding, keeping or advancing in a job with a living wage, keeping or attaining access to decent healthcare, securing decent, affordable housing, pursuing education for oneself and intimates, being able to seek or keep the protection of a union, having time for quality of life, being able to care adequately for children and elders, having access to good quality public services and social infrastructure.

A politics focused on bringing people together around such concerns and the objective of collectively crafting a vehicle to address them is a politics that proceeds from what we have in common. It is a politics that, like trade unionism, presumes a concrete, material basis for solidarity — not gestures, guilt-tripping and idealist abstractions. To the extent that differences are real and meaningful, the best way to negotiate them is from a foundation of shared purpose and *practical* solidarity based on a pragmatic understanding of the old principle that an injury to one is an injury to all.

This is not simply a politics that attempts to build on a base in the working class; it is a politics that in the process can fashion a broadly inclusive class identity that clearly encompasses all sorts of working people—both employed and unemployed or on what remains of public assistance. This is the politics we so desperately need and have needed for all of our lifetimes and much longer. We cannot construct it with potted narratives, global abstractions, wish fulfillment or solipsism. We can create it only through direct organizing and mobilization within the class, at the level of the neighborhood, the workplace and the union, and it can be created only by recognizing that it does not yet exist. A truly popular politics of this stripe cannot be built, especially not in its early stages, mainly through big events. It grows much more from one-on-one interaction and with small groups of coworkers, neighbors, friends and other associates.

Part of the intellectual work of this kind of organizing is cultivation of an ongoing discussion, linked to practical political activity, around making collective sense of how the social order and its mystifications are reproduced on a daily basis. The essays collected in this book are episodic attempts to stimulate and contribute to that discussion. They cohere around a premise that understanding American politics, and organizing effectively to operate within it, requires recognizing the centrality of class forces and dynamics in shaping consciousness and establishing both lines of cleavage and possibilities for solidarity.

# Part One

# ISSUES IN BLACK PUBLIC LIFE

# —Why Is There No Black Political Movement?

The question itself, no doubt, is already a provocation. Even as I pose it, I can imagine loud objections to its obvious presumptions. It's easy to anticipate a list of examples to the contrary: from the hip-hop nation to the Million Man and Woman marches to the current plans to organize a Black Radical Congress; from the black women who mobilized in support of Anita Hill to Jesse Jackson's Rainbow Coalition, Inc., and Operation PUSH; from various local mobilizations to the Congressional Black Caucus, the Urban League, the Southern Christian Leadership Conference, and the NAACP; from a plethora of nominal (both single-issue and multipurpose) coalitions to independent parties and candidacies to nationalist and other sects. So, before going any further, I should clarify the presumptions and why I ask the question. The rub lies in what one means by a "political movement."

What I mean is a force that has shown a capability, over time, of mobilizing popular support for programs that expressly seek to alter the patterns of public policy or economic relations. There simply is no such entity in black American life at this point.

I can also imagine objections to this notion of politics—protestations that say it is too narrow; that it overlooks the deeper significance of what Robin Kelley, following political scientist James Scott, has usefully summarized as "infrapolitics": the region of "daily confrontations, evasive actions, and stifled thoughts." Hogwash. Twenty years after Reaganism took hold and twenty-three years after Maynard Jackson, Atlanta's first black mayor, summarily fired nearly 2000 striking black sanitation workers with no rooted opposition from the black community, it's time for us to face some brute realities.

Sure, there's infrapolitics—there always is, and there always will be; wherever there's oppression, there's resistance. That's one of the oldest slogans on the left. But it's also a simple fact of life. People don't like being oppressed or exploited, and they respond in ways that reflect that fact. That and a buck fifty will get you on the subway. "Daily confrontations" are to political movements as carbon, water, and oxygen are to life on this planet. They are the raw material for movements of political change, and expressions of dissatisfaction that reflect the need for change, but their presence says nothing more about the potential for such a movement to exist, much less its actuality.

At best, those who romanticize "everyday resistance" or "cultural politics" read the evolution of political movements teleologically; they presume that those conditions necessarily, or even typically, lead to political action. They don't. Not any more than the presence of carbon and water necessarily leads to the evolution of Homo sapiens. Think about it: infrapolitics is ubiquitous, developed political movements are rare.

At worst, and more commonly, defenders of infrapolitics treat it as politically consequential in its own right. This idealism may stem from a romantic confusion, but it's also an evasive acknowledgment of the fact that there is no real popular political movement. Further, it's a way of pretending that the missing movement is not a problem—that everyday, apolitical social practices are a new, maybe even more "authentic," form of politics.

This evasive tendency links up with much deeper and broader reflexes in black political life and masks a defeatist strain in black activism.

This defeatism stems from an impossible position that black organizers have locked themselves into for nearly all of this century: the "brokerage" model of politics. Under this strategy, political action centers on the claim to express the unified interests of black Americans as a single, corporate entity. It's ultimately a form of high-level negotiation; its main practice is assuming the voice of a putatively coherent black community and projecting it toward policy makers.

This political style emerged at a time in which disfranchisement and white supremacy severely limited possibilities for popular participation. However, its origins in the black elite made it easy to overlook the significance of that limitation. The strategy was accompanied by a highborn sense of duty among the elite—a responsibility to guide a rank-and-file population thought to be in need of uplift as much as opportunity. And there was no shortage of energetic, middle-class "Race Leaders" prepared to accept the burden of speaking for the mute masses. Thus the old quip that any black person with a clean suit and five dollars in his pocket imagined himself a Negro leader. This form of politics reigns across the black ideological spectrum. It defines the terms of debate along that left-right axis—a debate propelled by claims to legitimacy of spokesmanship shaped within a rhetoric of authenticity (claims, it should be said, that are directed largely at a white audience). Criticism of Ward Connerly, Clarence Thomas, or the Harvard Afro-American Studies Dream Team, for instance, focuses at least as much on their supposed distance from "the community" as on the substance of their ideas.

This is a corporatist argument—born of brokerage-style politics—not a populist one. Even as it comes dressed in invocations of "the people" or "the masses," this is not an approach that leads to popular mobilization. Rather, the Race Leader principle—and its pursuit of a vague notion of black unity—undercuts the discussion that could actually help stimulate a genuine movement. The "people" don't get to speak; they are spoken for. This is true by definition because "the people" exist only as an idea.

What exists in reality, though, is a broad variety of black individuals with an array of concerns and interests that converge and diverge, crosscut and overlap from issue to issue. A politics that insists on unity, and representation of an idealized collective, hinders mobilization precisely because its reflex is to diminish the significance of these differences.

Instead, the current activist model subordinates debate over political diversity in favor of establishing "unity." This, in turn, means generating political programs that combine laundry lists of issues that bow to arbitrarily defined constituencies, and sets of least-common-denominator particulars that symbolize generically racial interests and outrages—such as church burnings and police brutality—that demonstrate the persistence and extent of racism.

But the concerns that the vast majority of black people experience the vast majority of the time are not about those outrages and large, symbolic issues (for instance, defense of affirmative action and majority-minority legislative districts). This is not to say that people don't care about those issues or that they aren't important. They are not, however, the kinds of issues on which a sustained popular movement can be built. They are too remote from ordinary individuals' daily experience to generate either intense, active support over time or the kind of dialogue that fuels political education.

The result is a notion of black leadership — "authentic" leadership — that substitutes for popular mobilization. It's a model that assumes categories of leader and led. The myth of the organic black community, moreover, makes it unnecessary to be troubled over questions regarding democratic representation — such as how to achieve accountability of spokespersons; how to stimulate and safeguard open debate; how to define plausible constituencies. These and other such issues are entirely absent from a black political discourse that conceptualizes democracy only in corporatist terms — as a condition that exists between the black community and others, not as a matter of serious interest within black political life itself.

A telling indication of how far the existing black politics is from such concerns is the general unwillingness to anchor political action in the creation of membership organizations — that is, groups with clearly identified constituencies that are, at least in principle, empowered to pass and execute judgment on leaders' actions. Nationally, only the NAACP is governed by its membership. Operation PUSH and the National Rainbow Coalition are mere banners for Jesse Jackson to speak in front of. Even the main products of the high period of political activism in the 1960s — the Student Nonviolent Coordinating Committee, Congress on Racial Equality, and Southern Christian Leadership Conference — were not mass-membership organizations.

My point is not that those specific groups should have structured themselves on a popular membership basis; they did the work they were created to do in epic political circumstances and did it effectively. However, the limitations of a politics — especially a movement politics — that doesn't take account of the need to stimulate popular participation have come home to roost dramatically in the subsequent history of the SCLC, the only one of those organizations to survive visibly into the present. That has been a story of decline, spiraling ever further downward into nostalgia and nepotism.

More radical, even avowedly Marxist or revolutionary, organizations have been no more inclined to concentrate on organizing concrete constituencies into membership organizations. Groups from the 1960s and '70s—the Black Panther Party, Black Workers Congress, National Black Assembly, African Liberation Support Committee—and the more recent attempts to create black united fronts all have been either cadre organizations (organizations of organizers) or coalitions of such organizations. The latter, which amount to little more than stacks of letterhead, give the illusion of a broad, popular base by equating breadth of representation with the length of the list of paper organizations.

This politics creates a particular conundrum for radicals, for whom the idea of connectedness to a popular constituency is a paramount goal. Opportunism is often employed as a tactic to paper over the problem.

As a case in point, nationalist activists organized an Afro-Caribbean International Festival of Life held in Chicago's Washington Park, principal location for South Side cookouts and family reunions, on July 4. Ever since the Black Power era, black Americans' celebration of the Fourth has been something of a thorn in the side for radicals, an apparent indication of how little headway our theoretical critiques have made in the population. In that context there are two ways to read the International Festival. On the one hand, it could be a strategy for presenting an alternative to the Fourth of July imagery; staging a big event where people are congregating anyway seems like a reasonable way to distribute the message. On the other hand, the festival could be an attempt to claim to speak for a large gathering by jumping out in front of it and controlling the only microphone.

Kwanzaa, Maulana Ron Karenga's mid-60s invention, was perhaps the prototype of this self-deluding flimflam. For years, radicals had been trying to sell a critique of Christmas as a destructively consumerist and inappropriately Eurocentric celebration. Kwanzaa was an attempt to coopt the ritual of midwinter celebration that the majority of black Americans were unwilling to give up. Less obviously, it was an admission of failure to sell an alternative view of the world that would make Christmas unappealing. Instead, Kwanzaa merely creates a mythology that paints Christmas black without really upsetting conventional practices.

From this perspective Kwanzaa belongs to the same family of evasions as claims about infrapolitics and the brokerage school of political action. All of them rely on the pretension to express the concerns of people who don't have any say in the matter. In the 1980s, Jesse Jackson figured out how to work this pretense through the mass media. Louis Farrakhan pushed its evolution in the '90s with a strategy of giving speeches to packed civic auditoriums. Because in that format he is the only one empowered to speak, Farrakhan is able to claim that the lively, packed audiences both endorse his politics and represent a larger, mass base.

The Million Man March was this strategy's culminating moment, and radicals' defenses of this event underscore the proliferation of evasive politics. They also suggest its ultimate sources and why its seems so hard to break out of it. The defenses basically amount to a claim that the march should be separated from the man — that those who attended did so for multifarious reasons and didn't necessarily embrace Farrakhan's program.

The defense is hollow. The second claim is no doubt true, just as it was true of the 1963 March on Washington, anti-Vietnam War demos, and every other large gathering. The key fact about the MMM was that Farrakhan got to set the agenda, control the terms of discussion, and project himself as its leader. Those radicals who support and defend his rally dispute his claim by projecting other objectives onto the assembled throng. But even if one accepts this explanation, the throng remains an undifferentiated, mute mass — the repository of the interpretations of others who presume to speak on its behalf.

We'll never be able to create the kind of movement we need until we can break with the mystifications and opportunism that tie activism to the bankrupt brokerage model of politics. The only possibly successful strategy is one based on genuinely popular, deliberative processes and concrete, interest-based organizing that connects with people's daily lives.

# —The Curse of "Community"

I just got some Afrocentric hate mail from a guy in Dayton who castigates me as a race traitor Uncle Tom for criticizing Farrakhan and the Million Man March. The writer accuses me of not speaking for him, a charge that's absolutely accurate. He declares himself a nationalist and writes about how black people who disagree with him are mental defectives, dupes, or sellouts. He notes that the MMM, which he proudly says he attended, was for "real men," "real niggas" like himself.

I mention this letter because it highlights what I think is a central problem in black politics, a crucial internal obstacle to generating a popularly based progressive black political movement. This problem, ironically, is the notion of a "black community" and the rhetoric of authenticity that comes with it. I say ironic because the ideological force of the black community idea—which is now such an impediment to organizing—rests largely on the imagery of grassroots activism and mobilization. But, as the man said, "All that's apparent is not real."

Assertion of links to, roots in, messages from, or the wisdom of "the community" is more a way to end a conversation about politics than to begin one. It is often the big trump in a game of one-upmanship, an attempt to validate one's position or self by alleging privileged connection to the well-spring of authenticity, to preempt or curtail dissent by invoking the authority of that unassailable, primordial source of legitimacy.

But who exactly is "the community"? How can we assess the claims of those who purport to represent it? These questions are seldom raised, much less answered. A strain of Jeffersonian romanticism obscures them among the left, for whom community implies an organic entity animated by a collective mind and will. From that perspective we don't need to ask how the community makes its decisions, how it forms its will, because it reflects an immediate, almost mystical identity of interest and common feeling. In the Jeffersonian fantasy world, it is possible to imagine that formalistic democracy—that burdensome and imperfect apparatus—springs from the desire to approximate the informal, automatic popularity and transparent authenticity of the community's decision making. This idea of community is a mystification, however, and an antidemocratic one at that. All social units are comprised of discrete individuals whose perspectives and interests and alliances differ, and every unit's members are bound together through a combination of negotiation and coercion. The less attention is paid to cultivating and protecting the sphere of negotiation, the more the balance shifts to coercion. The rhetoric of community is impatient with the former, and its myth of authenticity rationalizes the latter.

We can see this rhetoric's antidemocratic face clearly among the so-called new communitarians, for whom the label is a warrant to enforce a conformist, punitive moralism. They attack divorce and abortion, and even civil rights: the American Alliance for Rights and Responsibilities—one of the communitarians' main organizations—went out of its way a couple of years ago to support the Chicago Housing Authority and its Battle of Algiers–like policy of putting housing projects on lock-down and conducting indiscriminate sweep searches, ostensibly seeking drugs and guns.

The community idea's undemocratic, antiparticipatory underside is less visible in black politics, partly because black political activity and rhetoric are articulated most forcefully against oppressive outside forces. The effect is to shift everyone's focus away from the internal dynamics that shape black political culture. But more insidious tendencies also blind observers to the black communitarian reflex's ugly foundation. Because whites by and large don't see black Americans as a complex population of differentiated individuals, the organic community imagery seems reasonable and natural to them. I cringe when I recollect the many occasions I've heard white activists rhapsodize about "the black community" coming in, with its particular clarity and moral force, to proffer its matter-of-fact, cut-to-the-chase wisdom, like the Ninth Cavalry of the Army of Righteousness.

Within black politics, of course, hustlers of one sort or another, high-toned and low, have always been willing to exploit that fundamentally racist mind-set, usually by giving whites with resources authentic-sounding doses of what they want to hear. More corrosive, however, is the fact that well-intentioned black activists themselves seem incapable of breaking out of the communitarian frame and its discourse of authenticity. This failure is a vestige of a style of class-based brokerage politics that prevailed among black Americans for most of this century, a style the 1965 Voting Rights Law should have eliminated. Now that black people have access to regular forms of civic participation, they should no longer have to depend on a politics in which white elites recognize and negotiate with nominal, ultimately unaccountable race "leaders." I suspect that black activists' continuing romance with political hustlers and demagogues ("Up with hope, down with dope!") stems from their seductive promise of connection to a real, mobilizable constituency—something that black activists haven't experienced in fact in more than twenty years, and then not for very long.

Whatever its appeal, the idea of a black community may do more harm than good at this point. And I do not in any way mean to endorse the black neocons' disingenuous jeremiads about a totalitarian reign of ideological terror in the Bantustan; the problem is rather the opposite. There are no significant forces on the ground in black politics attempting to generate any sort of popular, issue-based civic discourse, and the language of community is largely the reason.

Community presumes homogeneity of interest and perception, at least in principle. A politics stuck in its name is threatened by the heterogeneous tendencies put in motion by open debate. It is a politics that always has depended on narrowing the active black public and fastening the population as a whole to a middle-class–inflected program. But now that we have black people generating inegalitarian urban-redevelopment policies and victimized by them, black people both enforcing and demonized by underclass ideology, black people fighting for and opposing gender equality and openness with respect to sexual orientation, the hollowness and inadequacy of this politics is all the more striking.

Moreover, the game is becoming all the more dangerous. Not only does this essentially demobilizing political style not provide a basis for generating effective responses to the corporate reorganization of American life that promises to wreak particular havoc on black people, but we can see signs of the black communitarian rhetoric's appropriation for frightening ends—and not just at the hands of explicit reactionaries like Farrakhan and the agents of church-based black moral rearmament. The philanthropic foundations are joining hands in their own sly way with the right to undercut the basis for public, civic life by proclaiming the superiority of "community-based organizations," which are accountable only to them (a domestic version of the non-governmental organizations deployed to weaken governments in what used to be the Third World).

In Chicago, for instance, we've gotten a foretaste of the new breed of foundation-hatched black communitarian voices; one of them, a smooth Harvard lawyer with impeccable do-good credentials and vacuous-to-repressive neoliberal politics, has won a state senate seat on a base mainly in the liberal foundation and development worlds. His fundamentally bootstrap line was softened by a patina of the rhetoric of authentic community, talk about meeting in kitchens, small-scale solutions to social problems, and the predictable elevation of process over program—the point where identity politics converges with old-fashioned middle-class reform in favoring form over substance. I suspect that his ilk is the wave of the future in U.S. black politics here, as in Haiti and wherever the International Monetary Fund has sway. So far the black activist response hasn't been up to the challenge. We have to do better.

# —Romancing Jim Crow

Of course the Nazis' genocidal regime was terrible, and it's really good that it was defeated. Bad as it was, though, it certainly brought the Jews together. They were a united, mutually supportive community in the camps in a way that they haven't been since; they experienced a commonality that transcended class, gender, and other differences. It's ironic and a bit sad that Hitler's defeat came at the price of sacrificing the basis for that sense of community, so we should pause to celebrate and perhaps mourn the passage of that world of Jewish togetherness, lost with the liberation of the death camps.

Sounds outrageous, doesn't it? Of course, no one in their right mind would propose such a view seriously. Yet it isn't so different from what has lately become a conventional narrative about black Americans and the regime of racial segregation that prevailed in much of this country for most of this century. The Third Reich was a sui generis horror: a state resting on systematic mass murder as a central goal and organizational principle is a nightmare of almost unimaginable proportion. But as Michael Burleigh and Wolfgang Wipperman detail in *The Racial State 1933–1945*, the conceptual foundation of that all-too-real nightmare was a commitment to racial ideology as the lens through which to make sense of and to order social life.

From that perspective the difference between Nazi Germany and the Jim Crow South is one of degree rather than kind, a matter of having the impetus and capacity to follow the ideology to its logical conclusion. Noting that the Holocaust is a species within a larger genus in no way diminishes it as an unparalleled event. My point, rather, is to highlight why current nostalgia for the organic community black Americans supposedly lost with the success of the civil rights movement is so frighteningly shortsighted and dangerous.

That nostalgia is everywhere—in every major newspaper and excuse for a news magazine at the supermarket checkout line, in the classroom, in the local bar, across the dinner table, in cultural criticism, in foundation boardrooms and policy papers, on the talk show circuit. Political left, right, and center embrace it equally, and it's the staple hope of a burgeoning black memoir industry. Henry Louis Gates's *Colored People* is a reflection on the idyllic world of his Jim Crow youth in West Virginia, a yearning for a prelapsarian black communal order. Harold Cruse's *Plural But Equal* dresses this nostalgia up as social theory, arguing that it was mistaken for blacks to have fought to overturn the Jim Crow system precisely because its defeat unraveled community life. William Julius Wilson's *The Truly Disadvantaged* also trades on the Decline From Segregation narrative, though he ducks its implications by discussing only northern cities. Wilson conjures up images of a 1940s Harlem where people could pass hot summer nights sleeping safely on fire escapes, in contrast to the chaotic heart of darkness created when desegregation allowed the black middle class to escape inner-city ghettos, leaving the poor without stable institutions and role models for upward mobility.

This sort of nostalgic theory is dangerous on two counts: it falsifies the black past, and it serves reactionary and frankly racist interests in the present. Clifton Taulbert's *Once Upon a Time When We Were Colored* (originally published by a small press but reissued by Penguin), and television actor-director Tim Reid's feature-film adaptation of it, provide a good template for examining both problems. The inspirational memoir is this Once Upon a Time When We Were Segregated and Happy tale's natural home, where the cheery tones of personal triumph wash brightly over the backdrop of codified racial subordination.

*Once Upon a Time* recalls Taulbert's first seventeen years, spent in the Mississippi Delta town of Glen Allan. Taulbert's story is particularly resonant for me. He and I are about the same age, we graduated from high school in the same month. I don't know his hometown, and I doubt that I know the Delta region as intimately as he. I do know it, though, and my experiences of it roughly coincide in time with his. My father's family comes partly from that area, but on the other side of the river and therefore across the state line. Not that state lines mean much down there, in that zone of transhumance that laps across the northeast corner of Louisiana, southeast corner of Arkansas, and northwest Mississippi; Eudora, Arkansas, the town from which that branch of our family emanates, is eight miles from the Louisiana line and thirty miles from Greenville, Mississippi. As it was for Taulbert's Glen Allan, Greenville is Eudora's regional city where air travelers and mall shoppers go, and it seems to be about equidistant from the two towns.

Taulbert's book and Reid's film differ significantly and interestingly, but in ways that together flesh out the components of a shared ideology. Reid mutes black Glen Allan's status hierarchy, while Taulbert notes it matter-of-factly, exulting in his family's elevated position. Reid's vision so stresses fastidious morality that he goes out of his way to link the mildest deviation with mortification, even inventing a vignette in which the beloved great-aunt Ma Ponk makes a onetime visit to a hooch show only to pay by being absent from her mother's deathbed. In Reid's telling, elders counsel picnicking children not to drag an American flag on the ground because colored boys are dying in Korea to defend that flag. Taulbert recalls a quite different admonition: "Boy, don't you know if white folks see you messing with this here flag like this, they subject to kill you?" Poppa, the great-grandfather patriarch, is much more prominent in the movie than the book, as Reid responds to the yearning for patriarchal order that suffuses this new Up From Slavery narrative. Similarly, Reid reinvents Ma Ponk as a culinary wonder, while Taulbert says she was so little a cook that she relied on "plain store-bought cake and chicken fried by my mother" for her contribution to the big church function. Here, also, art imposes ideological order on a messy world.

Both Reid and Taulbert mistake the apparent simplicity of childhood for the simplicity of a social order, an elision that feeds aging black boomers' wistfulness about lost youth and innocence. It's propelled by a naive trope of modernization that presumes our world to be constantly increasing in complexity and divisiveness, contrasting it to a comfortingly static past. This vision authenticates itself by dipping into a common reservoir of experience. The scene in which the neighborhood gathers to view the Joe Louis–Rocky Marciano fight stimulated a Pavlovian recollection of my own experience of the fight in a different part of the country. We were at my uncle's house; my younger cousin and I were playing on the floor in front of the sofa, and I recall my father's lament that this would be our only memory of seeing Joe fight.

Some stimuli are generic: the first day of school, the doting (female) relative who dresses you like a geek for your own good, the excitement of little outings with an adored grandparent, the pleasures of running around with schoolyard pals. Some are more racially specific: first encounters with Jim Crow etiquette, truckloads of black people headed to the cotton fields, witnessing adults assert their contingent dignity in small encounters with whites. Instructively, though, it is only Reid who suggests these assertions. Taulbert recounts no such incidents; it was the Mississippi Delta, after all, and his folks weren't the sort to make waves.

Memory is a great liar. Sure, you're convinced that the strawberry floats tasted better then, but remember how much smaller your old room seemed the first time you returned in adulthood? The house didn't shrink, did it? Of course life was simpler then; we were kids, and its complexities were lost on us. Of course the world seems in retrospect to have been nurturing; as kids, being nurtured was our job description. Or rather, it was for some of us.

Although it has attained a nearly universal status in black public discourse, this nostalgic narrative is in crucial ways a class vision. My father used to say that the story of the lion hunt would be a different tale if the lion had a typewriter. And that prompts an insight into the pervasive romanticism about segregated black schools: those who recall the Jim Crow schools so fondly are those who most likely were nurtured and catered to in them. Think about it. Who goes on to publish well-marketed memoirs or otherwise speak into the public microphone besides those marked early for success, those who have been encouraged and attended to? And who, by and large, are they but the children of community notables and elites? Are we certain that the recollections of universally nurturing black schools don't generalize synecdochically from personal experience, which comes, after all, via the limited perspective of a child?

At any age, privilege tends to be recollected in the tranquility of oblivion, with no recognition that others weren't comparably entitled. Think of the class reunion in which former in-group members are genuinely shocked to learn what a radically different place the school had been for the outsiders. An example from a context not too unlike Taulbert's is suggestive. My mother taught for a time at a small Baton Rouge school run by an order of black nuns who came from the same social network and many of the same families as the students. As an outsider, she saw clearly how family standing influenced judgments about students. Expressions of good will and encouragement, assessment of talents, and allocation of awards and special opportunities — the concrete stuff of nurturance — were as likely as not shaped by personal attachments or vendettas and perceptions of family status. This pattern of invidious treatment was part of normal life, requiring neither justification nor explanation even when it extended to extraordinary interventions: "Let's just change a couple of these numbers so that the Patin girl can be valedictorian. She's such a lovely girl and comes from such a nice family."

Of course, this kind of behavior is hardly restricted to the world of Jim Crow. It's really an intraracial manifestation of the sort of class-based quotidian injustice that assumes racialized forms in integrated environments. Black people are neither more nor less capable of pettiness and class prejudice than anyone else. Race is just not an active category in the calculus of judgment in an all-black context, and black students, therefore, don't get the short end of the stick simply because they're black. However, the harsh facts of segregation mitigate that benefit. Skin tone, family connections, and even more arbitrary considerations all created fissures in the phantom unity of the pre-civil rights black community, just as they do today. And a situation defined by woefully inadequate resources breeds unfairness; there's not enough of anything to go around, so arbitrary criteria become necessary.

The white supremacist system made teaching one of the few avenues available for middle-class employment, increasing the likelihood that individual teachers were there by default and suffering with frustrated ambitions. The demoralizing effort of those limitations combined with the reality of "second-class citizenship" to support a communitarian excuse for an internal pecking order: we can wink at abstract principles of fairness in the community because it's just *us*, and those elevated notions don't really apply to dealing among the folk; we all know how it is. In these circumstances what can we expect to be the lot of the unattractive, timid, slightly slow, or sullen child of poorly regarded sharecroppers? What would her memories be of the Golden Age of segregation? We can find clues by sitting in classrooms or listening to teachers in today's under-funded inner-city schools.

Class ideology, in fact, permeates and drives the current nostal-gia. While it reflects a generic sentimentality about lost innocence, it is also black boomers' racially distinctive variant of a historically specific class yearning, one that appears among their white coun-terparts as wistful attachment to a mythical Victorian or Edwardian era, the collective dream on which PBS and the specialized home-improvement industry thrive. In both cases, it's about the wish for a world that is simpler and more settled, to be sure, but simpler and settled in ways that clarify and consolidate the status of the upper middle class as the social order's presumptive center. The vision—equally false as history in both color codings—is of an organic, face-to-face community in which everyone has a role, status markers are clear, and convivial, automatic deference and noblesse oblige are the social organism's lifeblood, the substance of its mutual regard.

Among whites this typically translates into images of a close-knit world of little shops where one is known and served cheerfully by contented proprietors and their energetic employees, where one is recognized naturally as the center of the community, the embodi-ment of its best values and aspirations, its pivotal consumer. The black vision is more folkish in its mythology, but no less aestheti-cized. Where white Fairfield County yuppies imagine themselves in a sleek Merchant-Ivory fantasy of a fin de siècle drawing room, their black neighbors may shoehorn themselves into a colorful, down-home juke joint sprung to life from the canvases of Varnette Hon-eywood or Ernie Barnes. The black vision includes as well being respected as a role model and natural leader of the race. Nostalgia for the Jim Crow black world, particularly when it masquerades as social science, keys its imagery of the Fall to the putative loss of petit bourgeois authority in the Bantustan—for example, in

William Julius Wilson's prattle about the middle class as a force for moral order and propriety among the poor. In a concocted scene in Reid's film, Poppa confronts the impoverished tenant farmer whose son has sired a child out of wedlock. When the farmer refuses any obligation to the young mother and baby, citing his inability to add two hungry mouths to his household, Poppa tells him sternly, "Having nothing don't mean you don't know what's right."

Taulbert is serenely candid about the class stratification of his cherished "place where people nurtured and protected and enjoyed each other." He establishes at the very beginning of his book that he is descended from black planters and recounts with loving pride how his elderly aunt showed him the records that verified their once-exalted status. His mother's family lost the plantation but retained elevated status in black Glen Allan. Poppa was "a well-known and respected Baptist preacher [who] was looked to for his wisdom and in many instances served as a go-between for the coloreds when problems arose involving the whites," and Taulbert points out that they owned "a large rambling house with separate bedrooms, a formal dining and living room with two screened-in sun rooms." He notes that Ma Ponk "always made it a point to talk with Miss Lottie because she was among the upper-class coloreds" and insisted on riding the train because she felt that "only the poor coloreds rode the bus."

None of this is unusual. Memoirists who pine for the lost community of Jim Crow tend to have middle-class parents, who typically strove to insulate their offspring from the regime's demeaning and dangerous realities, especially from contact with whites. Except in New Orleans, I can't recall having more than a couple of interactions with whites of any age in the South (not counting priests and nuns) until I was in high school. It is less commonly recalled that petit bourgeois parents worked equally hard to shield their kids from black social inferiors. The leveling effects of discrimination made the latter more difficult, but those dedicated to class insularity found ways to adapt. The Jack and Jill clubs existed to provide an explicitly class-conscious local and national social network for the black bourgeoisie's children in the same way that fraternities and sororities, the Links, the Girl Friends, the Boulé, and other such organizations did for adults. And only middle-class children who were protected from its social and institutional realities—or those who didn't live in it at all—could remember the segregated world so fondly, as a naive, communitarian metaphor. When it came time for Taulbert to negotiate the regime as an adult, he left, telling us only that "Glen Allan could not make my dreams come true." He never confronts the fact that what he knew and recalls as a warm, nurturing world was compensatory, an artifact of a hideously unjust social order that brutalized lives and crushed aspirations.

Although its wrongheadedness may seem merely misguided, this class-inflected nostalgia plays a decidedly sinister role in contemporary politics. Not only does it rest on sentimental notions of family that sanitize gender inequality, it naturalizes current class privilege by projecting it fantastically backward in time. PBS subscribers imagine their earlier lives in genteel domestic settings, not sweatshops or stockyards, and Afrocentrics don't envision themselves as less than, say, the pharaoh's majordomo or attaché. The black memoir strain goes one better: it draws the dots connecting present and past privilege and lauds the continuity as race pride. The ubiquitous grandmother in these narratives may have been a strong-proud-black-woman-race-leader-and-closeted-lesbian, but she was first of all a member in good standing of the Talented Tenth. The message is clear: our very bloodline is elite. We're just as authentically bourgeois—in our distinctively black way—as our white counterparts, *and* we're the race's natural aristocracy. Gates tells us of his maternal family's place in the local social order: "The Colemans were the first colored to own guns and hunt on white land, the first to become Eagle Scouts, the first to go to college, the first to own property."

This bias comes through in another of Reid's inventions. He has the good folk of Glen Allan decide to stand up to the white supremacist order, not for their citizenship rights or to challenge discrimination, lynching, or their exploitation in the cotton economy. In his vision, they assert themselves in defense of Taulbert's Uncle Cleve, the ice man supposedly being driven out of business unfairly by a big white firm from Greenville. Reid's townsfolk refuse to work the cotton fields in protest, noting Cleve's—and thus black entrepreneurship's—paramount symbolic importance to the entire black population; they cared more about his welfare than their own. (Taulbert says of his uncle, by the way, "Surely if my Uncle Cleve were alive today, he'd find a reason to be a black Republican." And the author himself is no leftist; he chortles at enforcement of child labor laws and expresses relief that his parents, despite tough times, were able to avoid becoming part of the welfare "system.") This is an absurdly self-serving image of petit bourgeois grandeur. I've filed it in my collection of Perverse Appropriations of Popular Insurgency, right next to that of a student who told me a few years ago that the ultimate goal of the civil rights movement was to make sure she could attend Yale and then go on to work at Morgan Stanley or Goldman Sachs. Sadly, this perversion captures the moment of bourgeois trimuphalism in black political life.

An insidious slippage between I and We drives black communication rhetoric and makes possible the bizarre claim that intraracial stratification is benign because it's organic. This view has no room for class tension or contradictions, because it disconnects class from position and role in the reproduction of the social system. Poppa "mediated" with the whites; he didn't occupy a managerial niche in the Jim Crow order. A family friend was a labor contractor for the white planters and acquired rental property originally built to house interned Japanese Americans during World War II. Taulbert never imagines that these business endeavors might have put him at odds with some of Glen Allan's black residents, or muses about the irony of a black man profiting from internment. Such ruminations aren't consonant with this narrative's objectives.

The point of the nostalgia narrative is that there *are* no internal tensions; there is no significant differentiation. Perhaps this yearning for a seamless black world partly reflects status anxiety within the current black middle class, an anxiety that can take several overlapping and even contradictory forms. It could express the famous guilt that middle-class blacks supposedly experience about the growing black poverty that contrasts with their success—though I've never seen a case of it in anyone over undergraduate age that wasn't a backhanded form of self-congratulation. It could also reflect just the opposite. Leveling the black experience also levels racial oppression and thereby equates the middle-class experience of racism ("I couldn't get a cab," "I got stopped by the cops on Metro-North," "My colleagues don't respect me," "I can't get a promotion") with the borderline genocidal regime tightening around the inner-city poor. One often hears the lament: we suffer, too. And the communitarian idyll can be emotional solace for those middle-class blacks who work and live in racially integrated environments, a dreamworld respite from racialized tension—the necessary, constant anticipation of affront that permeates their daily reality. An analogue is 1960s black cultural nationalism, which was largely the product of black students on white college campuses.

No matter what emotional needs it addresses, though, this communitarian nostalgia propounds a political message that what an increasingly fractured black "community" needs is to entrust itself to the loving care of its "natural" leadership. Some middle-class blacks opposed the Jim Crow order because it limited *their* options, constrained *their* career and social opportunities, and didn't make appropriate class distinctions among blacks. This criticism isn't necessarily hinged to a broader egalitarian social vision. Therefore, as the rightward thrust of national politics and the realities of the glass ceiling imperil possibilities for absorption—on black and proud terms, to be sure—into the mainstream elite, a latter-day accommodationism can seem consistent and attractive. Like Milton's Lucifer, many middle-class blacks are finding it more desirable to reign in the Bantustan than to be dissed outside, especially now that the basic accomplishments of the 1964 and 1965 civil rights legislation—guaranteeing the rudiments of equal citizenship—seem solidly established. This impulse supports an accommodationism that trades on the rhetoric of racial difference to assign the petite bourgeoisie a tutorial, agenda-setting position vis-à-vis the rest of the race. The Nurturing Black Community, therefore, rehearses an elitist communitarianism of lengthy pedigree (shared, for example by Booker T. Washington and the young Du Bois), and it secures a functional role for a separate-but-equal black middle-class: official management and administration of inequality. This includes, besides role modeling and running the institutions of public authority, directing public policy—in the form of "community revitalization"—to clear away suitable enclaves for the occupancy and consumption needs of the new uplifters.

A friend of mine remarked years ago, as we observed the rise of the first stratum of black public officials, that they generally presume that all that stuff about due process, participation, citizenship rights, equality, justice, and the rest stops at the entrance to the Bantustan. We didn't realize at the time that formalist democracy goes against the grain of the communitarian ideology on which black leadership grounds itself. Nor did we recognize that this antidemocratic impulse rests on a solid, pragmatic foundation in structurally rooted class interest.

# —Have We Exhaled Yet?

I recently had an e-mail conversation with an old friend who lamented in passing that she and a pal feel they've been suffering from "successful black woman syndrome" in their intimate lives with men. That observation, along with a dose of Terry McMillan and my own recent explorations of gender in the history of black political thought, set me thinking about just what that syndrome is.

Sexism doesn't stop at the boundaries of the Bantustan. And one of its more dubious black and proud forms is the "nationalism," fed by the Moynihan report, that defines black liberation as enabling men to control "their" women. Although much of the chatter these days about the black war between the sexes is banal psychodrama, there is a clear problem with men's expectations, and that's key to making sense of the real issue. Most men in this society have the same difficulty simply seeing women as human beings like themselves that whites have vis-à-vis the rest of us, and that's true across the color line. Women are either reified parts, or expressions of male power or status, or both. Either way women are property, and this relationship has been enforced historically through economic inequality. So financially independent women are desirable insofar as they're low maintenance, but threatening because they're, well, independent. The financial impact of racism further narrows the pool of black men who wouldn't be intimidated by female economic independence. And middle-class people, black as well as white, seem especially susceptible to a formalistic, home and hearth ideology that bristles at the fact that people, especially women, actually have things to do that they take seriously and like doing and therefore are committed to before all else, in an existentially self-defining way. Bottom line: It's tough out there for many women who yearn for intimate connection with men, and it's especially tough for black women. That's hardly news; this point is broadcast loudly from the Afrocentric self-help section of every bookstore that has one.

This also helps to explain that antelope-at-the-watering-hole feeling "statistically appropriate" black men sometimes complain about to black women; they feel impersonally targeted.

Understandably, they are. I mean, who wants to be lonely? What's interesting, though, is the extent to which the women who seek these men seem not to connect with them as particular human beings—which, from a male perspective, makes it all seem bizarre because it's often so clear that if any of the women bothered to take a closer look at these statistically appropriate specimens, she might find that she had no interest whatsoever. In those circumstances one wonders exactly what, if anything living at all, women see when they look.

Despite the Wayans family/*Def Comedy Jam* misogyny, however, middle-class black women in particular aren't necessarily looking for someone to supply financial security, do home repair, or "be my baby daddy." So why the objectifying fixation? The answer lies in the interplay of culture and political economy and one of its main artifacts, the mystified idea of "family." "Family" is at bottom an ideological construct; it sanctifies one particular form of household organization, treating it as a universal ideal—even to the extent of projecting it onto other species in nature shows and the idiocy of sociobiology. And the form is patriarchal, the nuclear body with a male head.

Why political economy? Because the realities of gendered economic discrimination mean that most women live "a man away from poverty." Therefore, economic dependence is built into the texture of "family" life at its foundation, and the ideal that the male "head" of household is the one who bears its financial responsibility only deepens female economic dependence. If the bastard leaves you for his fitness instructor, who hopes that she's young enough to be the last model traded for, you probably don't even have a pension or decent social security benefits to fall back on because you've been in and out of the labor force, following him around, doing the unpaid labor of raising the kids and maintaining the household to sustain his comfort and reputation as a solid citizen and person of substance.

Why culture? Because in this environment, women face a damned-if-you-do, damned-if-you-don't situation. If you try to live without a man, unless you're part of a statistically small minority fortunate enough to be financially independent, you wind up either impoverished or facing a constant grind to avoid impoverishment. If you marry your way into contingent economic security, the contingency is just as important as the security, because your dependence is your ticket. This becomes clearer with time, as you experience erosion of the two main features on which your spousal position rests when men have the resources to choose and women are objectified—youthful attractiveness and novelty. Thus the specter of the suburban matron who starts freaking out with the first wrinkles and goes on to support the growth of a vast cosmetic industry—from skin care fads to personal trainers to the physical mutilation of plastic surgery—in a desperate battle to, as Cher so aptly sings, hold back time.

What this means, among other things, is that for women from one end of the economic food chain to the other there's a hard material foundation for the idea that having a man is a necessary element of self-esteem and self-worth. It is not coincidental that the ranks of the poor and the nearly poor are crowded with households headed by single women. And having kids is not insurance against ejection from even the upper middle class; it seems that the more money men earn, the less likely they are to pay child support—another problem with the "irresponsible black male" stereotype of underclass theory. And even if you do get him to pay, there's always the danger that he'll resort to the O. J. option, which is much less rare than we might think—after all, it's only another logical outgrowth of the wife-and-kids-as-property principle that undergrinds the idea of family.

So it's not surprising that even within the autonomous discourse of women themselves, a man of one's own remains an important marker of personal completeness even in the absence of pressing financial need. This is not simply a matter of benighted romanticism or, as the current cliché has it, "low self-esteem"; for sound material reasons, women recognize one another partly by that standard. The human desire for companionship and intimacy inevitably gets enmeshed in this dynamic. Thus the socially driven compulsion to "have a man" becomes the general expression of a yearning that requires a much more specific response, the desire for intimate connection with *someone*. This very real status anxiety is especially acute for black women, inflaming the debate over intermarriage, as some take the "loss" of black men to nonblack women in the abstract as an act of profound personal betrayal. This is an interesting reversal of the property claim, in effect defining generic black men as the exclusive property of generic black women. In theory, at least, there's a delicious irony about this, as there is with the antelope-at-the-watering-hole sensation; both turn male objectification on its head. But in practice the irony has no savor because men still hold the trumps. And their patter shows it: "Yeah, man, I don't understand why women just always want to have 'relationships.' I say, 'Look, baby, you're getting something out of this, I'm getting something out of this, so why push it, blah, blah, blah.'" The SOS Band made a living out of putting women's pursuits of intimacy with intransigent, one-up men to a good beat and haunting melody.

In this context it's exceedingly difficult for men and women to form personal attachments that are not tainted by the lash of the market. Engels was right: healthy and honest attachments are scarcely possible under patriarchal capitalism. The fact is that we have no idea about what a family form worth valuing would be for our society and can't until we overcome gender inequality. To that extent, whatever works for individuals freely choosing is what's right.

# —We Were Framed

I tried sedulously to ignore O. J. He's been my prime suspect in the killings since the disclosure of his history as a batterer, but I argued that this trial shouldn't be seen as a metaphor for race relations or even spousal abuse. If anything, it was a lurid melodrama of celebrity justice—just another instance of the American version of Weimar decadence, in which trash TV provides the basis and frame for collective social experience.

Well, that view didn't have a chance in an environment saturated by the mass media's tabloid tropes—morbid curiosity, Schadenfreude, and prurient moralism. Yeah, yeah, I know the defense: "Of course the public would be interested; O. J. and Nicole were beautiful people, and he was a major celebrity. . . . And maybe the back-drop of interracial sexuality added titillation." Bullshit. A simple supply-side explanation is all we need to make sense of public fixation on this case. Of course people focused on it; we were carpet-bombed with it. Most of what I saw of the trial was in my futile attempts to escape through ESPN's *SportsCenter*, which covered it daily, complete with play-by-play, color commentary, and expert analysis. People "wanted" to follow the trial in the same way that they "want" to keep up with "All My Children" or "Melrose Place" or the Yankees' club-house politics—because it's what's there to attend to in the public domain. Does anyone imagine that Americans have an autonomous, collective yearning to see Heather Locklear on television?

The mass media gave the case its primary frames. *The New York Times*'s Don Terry has protested the media's invention of O. J. as a "black icon," noting that black people didn't even rent his movies on video. At least through the early phases of the trial there was little evidence in everyday life of sharp racial or even gender fault lines in opinions about the case. Remember the white-guy bystanders— what struck me as the batterers' lobby—cheering "Go, Juice, go" as part of the chorus for the low-speed Bronco chase? I also heard any number of black people remark on the stark contrast with the LAPD's pursuit of Rodney King, thus hardly embracing O. J. as Everyblackman.

Intimations of America's long-running racial morality play were always there, to be sure. Black female pundits turned themselves inside out trying to defend racial and gender interests perceived to be in conflict, and there was always a view that O. J. didn't deserve black support because he'd cut himself off from the race. But I was hardly alone in balking at the idea that we should be obliged to feed any particular affinity with O. J., insisting that the trial was a simple murder case, and that Simpson's guilt or innocence should carry no implications for other black Americans. Alas, that was spitting into a high, foul wind.

*Newsweek* diagnosed him as a victim of "double consciousness," a putatively racial condition made trendy in recent years by English professors, and comparisons to Othello began popping up. Johnnie Cochran joined the defense team. Gil Garcetti and Marcia Clark announced gratuitously and disingenuously that Chris Darden was fully competent to join them on the prosecution. Then came Mark Fuhrman; the game was on.

The mainstream media's initial reports of the allegations against Fuhrman had that "there-they-go-again-finding-racism-everywhere" quality. The Rodney King comparison now became the property of a racialized white skepticism: O. J. wasn't run down and beaten on the roadside, after all; the star-struck cops treated him with kid gloves.

Clark indignantly vouched for Fuhrman's decency, and white pundits, who never uttered a peep about Barry Slotnick's courtroom appeals to the basest racial stereotypes in the Bernhard Goetz trial, joined the prosecution in deploring the defense's resort to "playing the race card," itself originally a euphemism for the Republican right's luridly racist rhetoric. When the depth and intensity of Fuhrman's racism became known, the story line shifted to focus on whether "race"—that is, black people's concerns about police racism—would affect the outcome of the trial, and then to the standard "blacks and whites see things differently" frame.

This then became the lens through which black and white Americans perceived the spectacle, and they gravitated toward their scripted parts. Public opinion polls appeared to validate the frame, though to a significant degree they just measured its successful propagation. And that may be an overstatement; it's not clear that the white O. J. fans have entirely vanished, though many of them have at least temporarily traded patriarchal solidarity for what Victorians called "racial group idealism."

I hoped for a guilty judgment, both because I am convinced that Simpson is the murderer and because I wanted to avoid precisely the kind of vapid yet hideous discourse now shaping public consciousness. Black celebration of the verdict reflects the desperation and lack of credible options that currently define black politics. This is a pathetic travesty of racial independence and autonomy, betraying the celebrants' naive blindness to the fact that they, far more than O. J., have been set up to act out a part that at best mistakes empty symbolism for political victory and at worst is a pretext for declaring black people unworthy as citizens. Relentless proclamation that the trial was a racial fault line helped to create a powerful strain of black investment in acquittal, which then became the basis for white hand-wringing and moralizing. The media's simultaneous elevation of Farrakhan's Million Man March only highlights the cynicism underlying this cycle.

White disparagement of the verdict has come frighteningly close to resuscitating nineteenth-century demands to prohibit blacks from jury service, reflecting the racist presumption that whites alone are capable of impartiality. This reaction also drew attention away from the question of whose bad faith actually let O. J. off the hook. In essays in *The New York Times* and *Chicago Tribune*, Scott Turow, author and former federal prosecutor, and Philip Corboy, former president of the Chicago Bar Association and the Illinois Trial Lawyers Association, pointed out that the prosecution undermined its credibility by accepting substantial police misconduct. The warrantless search at Simpson's house violated the Fourth Amendment, and the LAPD's exculpatory claim that they went only to inform O. J. of the murders and out of concern for his safety was transparently bogus. Serious breaches in collecting and maintaining evidence provided a legitimate basis for charges of contamination, if not actual tampering. The LAPD very well may have attempted to railroad a guilty man. The district attorney's office, as well as the judges who presided at the preliminary hearing and trial, colluded in the LAPD's disreputable practices and paid the price. In arrogant disregard for constitutional protections they created the basis for reasonable doubt, and in a repugnant but all too familiar way shifted responsibility for their failure to the jury.

As Corboy notes, a case built on circumstantial evidence requires confidence in the credibility of those who present it. I don't propose that this jury emerged from the pages of a civics text to render a heroic judgment. At least one member has expressed views denying the relation between spousal abuse and homicide that reveal either woeful ignorance or denial. However, even a reluctant spectator could see Garcetti's and Clark's racial bad faith in the condescending way they pushed Darden out as their black attack dog, their outrage at any suggestion that the LAPD might be capable of racist misconduct, and in Clark's convictionless dismissal of the horror of Fuhrman in her summation. After the verdict, Garcetti immediately reached for one of the oldest racist canards, charging that jurors acted from emotion rather than reason. (Clark went still further: "Liberals don't want to admit it, but a majority black jury just won't convict in a case like this. They won't bring justice.") Can we really think that the jurors couldn't detect this bigoted contempt? This is the opening the defense exploited. Unappealing as the tandem of Cochran, Bailey, Dershowitz, Shapiro, et al., are, they were only doing their job.

# —What Color Is Anti-Semitism?

I long ago stopped reading Nat Hentoff, even though we've been columnists simultaneously for the *Village Voice* and the *Progressive*. Although I respect his resolute opposition to capital punishment, his fetus fetish, among other things, has just been too much to bear. A fetus is not a human being; it's an organism growing inside a woman's body, albeit an organism with the potential to become a human being. And it doesn't have a higher claim on our regard than its sentient host, who is already a member of the polity. When you boil off his floridly civil libertarian moralism, Hentoff's brand of fetal fetishism rests, like everyone else's, on trivializing women's citizenship. (Sorry about the digression. I've been storing that up.)

But Hentoff's tirade about Sharod Baker, the anti-Semitic black Columbia student, has given me a prod to make a point I've wanted to make for some time: There's no such thing as *black* anti-Semitism.

Obviously, I don't mean that there are no black people who are anti-Semites. Young Sharod Baker quite plainly appears to qualify as one. Khallid Muhammad certainly deserves the label, though perhaps as a subset of the classification "dangerous psychopath." Louis Farrakhan, Steve Cokely, and Len Jeffries also have earned it, as have many other, anonymous black Americans. Nor do I mean to suggest that anti-Semitism among black people doesn't count because: (a) they got it from white Christians or (b) they don't have the power to enforce it. Those arguments are just immoral sophistry. Is Dinesh D'Souza not really a racist because his views come via his Anglo-American tutors? Did David Duke only become one officially when he won a seat in the Louisiana legislature? Anti-Semitism is a form of racism, and it is indefensible and dangerous wherever it occurs.

What doesn't exist is Blackantisemitism, the equivalent of a German compound word, a particular—and particularly virulent—strain of anti-Semitism. Black anti-Semites are no better or worse than white or other anti-Semites, and they are neither more nor less representative of the "black community" or "black America" than Pat Buchanan, Pat Robertson, Tom Metzger—or your coworker or roommate who whispers about "their" pushiness and clannish-ness—are of white American gentiles.

Blackantisemitism is a species of the same genus as "African-ized" killer bees, crack babies, and now the rising generation of hardened ten-year-olds soon to be career criminals. It is a racialized fantasy, a projection of white anxieties about dark horrors lurking just beyond the horizon.

Yet there's more at work here than arbitrary, irrational scape-goating, which doesn't explain how black people become the repositories of those anxieties. As Stephen Steinberg argues force-fully in *Turning Back: The Retreat from Racial Justice in American Thought and Policy*, reducing racism to its generically psychologi-cal dimension obscures its roots in structured inequality. American racism, as is the nature of ideologies, is a complex dialectic of atti-tudes and material relations, but psychological scapegoating is ulti-mately more its effect than its cause. (I'm reminded here of a quip, attributed to Bob Fitch, that 90 percent of what goes on in the world can be explained adequately with vulgar Marxism.) After all, the social categories "white" and "black," and "race" itself, only arise historically from a concern to formalize a system of hierarchy and define its boundaries. These boundaries—expressed as law, en-forced custom, and structures of feeling—create the populations that enact them, so that, for example, in W. E. B. Du Bois's won-derful definition, "the black man is a person who must ride 'Jim Crow' in Georgia." Racial stereotypes are a feature of oppression, not its source.

Black anti-Semitism's specific resonance stems from its man-bites-dog quality. Black Americans are associated in the public realm with opposition to racial prejudice, so the appearance of big-otry among them seems newsworthy. But that newsworthiness also depends on a particular kind of racial stereotyping, the notion that, on some level, all black people think with one mind. Ralph Ellison complained most eloquently about white Americans' general re-fusal to recognize black individuality. Charles Rangel put the prob-lem succinctly: When approached to declare himself on Khallid

Muhammad, he complained that he was tired of being called on to denounce people he'd never even heard of. Any black anti-Semite is seen not as an individual but as a barometer of the black collective mind; belief in Blackantisemitism, therefore, is itself a form of racialist thinking.

In an overheated moment a couple of years ago, during Khallid's elevation to cause célèbre and the concurrent wave of ritual demands on black political leaders to denounce him and Farrakhan, *The New York Times* exposed this notion's repugnant face. In response to protests like Rangel's, the *Times* editorialized that indeed all black leaders (whoever that group includes) must "renounce root and branch Mr. Farrakhan's . . . message" and that *"in return,* black organizations and leaders have a right to ask for heightened white sensitivity to the commonplace discrimination of everyday life and to the increasing tolerance for parlor—and campus—prejudice against blacks" [my italics]. So black people must prove, by passing a litmus test for moral and ideological responsibility, that they deserve basic protections accorded automatically to all other citizens; unlike everyone else (at least at the moment), black Americans' claims to equal rights depend on their demonstration of moral rectitude. If this isn't racism, the term has no meaning.

But Blackantisemitism appeals to more actively malicious sentiments as well. The patient-suffering, slow-to-anger, morally superior imagery on which the civil rights movement traded was always at bottom a homegrown representation of the Noble Savage. As such, it's set up for the Nasty Savage response. And that's what Blackantisemitism is. Here's how it works. First, posit the single racial mind, so that whatever any black person does speaks for— and reflects on—all others. Then comes the syllogism: Blacks deserve equal rights to the extent that they are morally exemplary. Blackantisemitism shows that blacks aren't morally exemplary. Therefore, black demands for equal citizenship are tainted, and need not be taken seriously.

That partly explains why black anti-Semites ruffle public feathers—even among Jewish interest group elites—in a way that

more powerfully connected, and therefore more potentially dangerous, white anti-Semites don't. Sure, a kind of biting-the-hand-that-
feeds-you, after-all-we've-done-for-you, you-always-hurt-the-one-
you-love paternalistic thing is going on, based on the peculiar
tensions of the "special relationship" between blacks and Jews. But,
generally speaking, Blackantisemitism is a rationale, an excuse for
whites who either want to demand that blacks be uniformly decent
and admirably fair in ways that apply to no other group of Americans, or are simply looking to justify their dissent from a racially
egalitarian social and political agenda. That's the beauty of the one-
mind view: What any lone black person does can be a pretext for
joining the racist opposition. Remember all those outraged white
people who announced that the O. J. Simpson verdict ended their
support for affirmative action, social spending, and the Reconstruction Amendments?

# —The Rise of Louis Farrakhan

L ouis Farrakhan was all over America as the 1990s took shape. He has been the subject of widely publicized, feature-length interviews in *The Washington Post* and *The Washington Times*, and in other non-black publications as well. He tore up the campaign trail on behalf of local and Congressional candidates in the Nation of Islam's first direct foray into electoral politics. He was prominent at rallies and demonstrations in support of embattled former Washington Mayor Marion Barry, despite having denounced him only a few months earlier as a drug fiend and philanderer. Farrakhan was even a featured solo guest on "Donahue." He has kept up a torrid pace of speaking engagements and began to stake out a position critical of U.S. intervention in the Persian Gulf.

Recognition of Farrakhan as a public figure has been growing since his involvement in Jesse Jackson's first campaign for the Democratic presidential nomination in 1984. But understanding what his rise means in American life requires going back much further than that.

Louis Farrakhan, born in 1933, has been around a long time. Like Otis Redding, Aretha Franklin, and hip-hop, he had considerable visibility among blacks before whites discovered him. For well over thirty years he has propagated a vision of political separatism and a program of moral rearmament, "self-help" business development, and an idiosyncratic brand of Islamic religion. That vision and program, as well as his personal stature, grew from the soil of black nationalist politics in the civil rights/black power era. To make sense of Farrakhan requires situating him within the organizational and ideological contexts from which he emerged. Doing so, moreover, indicates that his anti-Semitism and whatever he might think of whites in general are ephemeral in comparison with the truly dangerous tendencies he represents.

In the early 1960s, as Louis X, Farrakhan was minister of the Nation of Islam's important Boston mosque and a kind of understudy to Malcolm X. He sided conspicuously with Elijah Muhammad, founder and "Messenger" of the Nation, against Malcolm in the bitter 1963–65 conflict that ended with the latter's murder. Farrakhan replaced Malcolm as minister of the Harlem mosque and later became Muhammad's National Representative.

The Messenger's core teachings include claims that blacks were the world's "original" race, from which all others derived; that black Americans are descended from an ancient, "lost" Asian tribe; that the white race originated from a demonic laboratory experiment and that Elijah Muhammad was divinely inspired. Following nationalist convention, the Muslims advocate the subordination of women, drawing on a rhetoric of domesticity, moral purity, and male responsibility; predictably, they denounce feminism and gay rights as white decadence and as strategies to undermine black unity and moral fiber.

The Nation's secular program has always focused on "nation building," which in practice has meant business development and the creation of separate schools and other institutions. Those activities have been harnessed to the ultimate goal of political separation and the formation of an independent state. Under Muhammad that goal remained inchoate, appearing mainly as a millenarian dream, but for Farrakhan it figures more directly into programmatic rhetoric. Discussion of the proposed state's citizenry characteristically elides the distinction between the membership of the Nation of Islam and black Americans in general, but Farrakhan has indicated that one possible model entails putting the former in charge of the latter. The nation-building agenda also reinforces the organization's natalist ideology and long-standing opposition to abortion, which both Muhammad and Farrakhan have denounced as genocidal as well as immoral.

Farrakhan rose to prominence during the late 1960s and early 1970s, when Muhammad's Nation was trying to become more visible in public life and to establish a greater presence in the black activist arena. As Muhammad's representative, he participated in national black political forums, addressed the 1970 Pan-African Congress of nationalist activists (as did first-time black Mayors Richard Hatcher of Gary, Indiana, and Kenneth Gibson of Newark; Ralph Abernathy; National Urban League director Whitney Young, Jr.; Jesse Jackson and others) and frequently spoke on black college campuses. During that period the Nation also expanded its business development agenda, which until then had centered mainly on mom-and-pop restaurants, takeout sandwich and baked goods shops, cut-and-sew operations catering to the organization's members (to satisfy the Muslim dress code) and the newspaper *Muhammad Speaks*. The Nation unveiled a set of ambitious goals, including establishment of agribusiness in the South, a medical complex in Chicago and large-scale international commerce anchored by fish imports from Peru. There was even talk that Muhammad would take advantage of Richard Nixon's definition of "black power" as "black capitalism" and apply for funds from minority economic development programs in the Office of Economic Opportunity or the Small Business Administration.

Two personal encounters I had with Farrakhan in late 1970 and early 1971 neatly reflect the discordant aspects of the Nation of Islam's thrust then and his place in it. One was a speech he gave at the predominantly black Fayetteville State University in North Carolina, where he excoriated mainstream civil rights spokespersons for their spinelessness and lack of vision. Of Ralph Abernathy's pledge to pursue King's "dream" as his successor at the Southern Christian Leadership Conference, Farrakhan quipped, "Talking about dreaming somebody else's dream! Don't you know that when you're dreaming, you're *asleep? Wake up,* black man!" And he chastised his mainly student audience for putative moral weakness. "Just as a bootmaker molds a boot, so the teacher molds the hearts and minds of the youth of our nation," he said, playing on the institution's history as a teachers' college. "And what are you going to teach them, *drunkard?* What are you going to teach them, *dope fiend?* What are you going to teach them, *foul, frivolous woman* who will lie down with a teacher to get a passing grade?" (Note that the woman, not the teacher, is his target.) With striking theatricality and stage presence, he punctuated each charge by pointing to a different section of the auditorium, as if exposing particular culprits.

The second encounter came soon thereafter. Along with other field-staff members of the North Carolina-based Foundation for Community Development, I was called in to Durham to attend a meeting with Farrakhan. He had come to the area as Muhammad's delegate, mainly to pursue contacts with officials of a well-established black bank and the North Carolina Mutual Life Insurance Company, then one of the largest black-owned businesses in the United States. He also wanted to examine the operations of the community development corporation that our agency had helped the local poor-people's organization create. At the meeting his demeanor was reserved, almost stilted, and he seemed (or tried to seem) in thrall to an image of black Durham as a center for business enterprise. (He had attended college in Winston-Salem during the early 1950s and quite likely imbibed that image then.) Although he made perfunctory gestures of appreciation for our reputation for grass-roots activism and black-power radicalism, he expressed only polite interest in the participatory and cooperative aspects of our community development approach. He was not much moved by the idea of organizing poor people to act on their own behalf.

While the Nation seemed to be growing and consolidating itself as a corporate enterprise, many of us in movement circles who watched from the outside wondered then how it would resolve the evident tension between its flamboyant rhetorical posture, so clear that night at Fayetteville State, and its very conventional business aspirations. Central in our minds was anticipation of the succession crisis likely to occur when Muhammad, who in 1970 was already a feeble septuagenarian, died or stepped down. For not only could Muslim operatives be seen hanging out with denizens of the underworld, but sectarian zealotry often condoned a strong-arm style.

The Uhuru Kitabu bookstore in Philadelphia, for example, was firebombed in 1970 when its proprietors—former Student Non-Violent Coordinating Committee workers—refused to remove a Malcolm X poster from the store's window after threats from local Muslims. In Atlanta in 1971 a dispute between Muslims and Black Panthers over turf rights for streetcorner newspaper hawking erupted into a hundred-person brawl. In 1972 strife within New York's Temple Number 7 culminated in a three-hour fight and shootout that began in the mosque and spilled outside. A purge of remaining Malcolm X loyalists followed in New York and elsewhere, and factions within the Nation were implicated in assassinations of outspoken followers of Malcolm in Boston and in Newark where the presiding minister of the mosque was gunned down.

Most chilling, in January 1973 a simmering theological dispute with members of the Hanafi Islamic sect in Washington ignited into an attack of which only zealots or hardened killers are capable. Seven Hanafis were murdered in their Sixteenth Street residence, owned by Kareem Abdul-Jabbar; five of the victims were children, including babies who were drowned in the bathtub. (The Hanafis held the Nation responsible and four years later occupied a government building and B'nai B'rith center and took hostages to press their demands for retribution.)

In that climate it was reasonable to worry, upon Elijah Muhammad's death in 1975, that the friction might lead to open warfare among the organization's contending factions, particularly between those identified with Farrakhan, who stood for a primacy of ideology, and the Messenger's son Wallace (Warith) Deen Muhammad, who had been linked much more with the Nation's business operations than with its ideological mission. Consequences of that sort did not materialize, and W. D. succeeded his father without apparent conflict, or at least with no immediate, publicly noticeable disruption.

The tension between the two agendas inevitably came to a head, however. Since the early 1970s the Nation had sought explicitly to recruit a middle-class membership as part of its drive for economic development. College students and professionals who joined were likely to be rewarded with responsible positions in the administrative hierarchy, but the Nation had only limited success in gaining petit-bourgeois adherents. It was, after all, a bit much to expect a college-educated constituency to accept as religious principle that the pig is a hybrid of the dog, the cat, and the rat or that whites derive from an evil wizard's botched experiment on subhuman creatures.

At the same time, instability grew in the Muslim business operations. For whatever reasons—probably among them was a reluctance to open records to outside scrutiny—the organization retreated from its ambivalent interest in pursuing federal economic-development support. Yet the projects on the board required both considerable specialized expertise and capitalization surpassing the Nation's liquidity. A $3 million "loan" from the Libyan government in 1972 was a stopgap. Despite its ideological boost as a statement of Islamic solidarity, however, the Libyan deal was also a signal that the Messenger Muhammad could not finance his bold schemes internally and was unwilling to do so through regular outside sources.

The desire to broaden the Nation's class base rested on more than a need for expertise. The early newspaper and the bean pie, restaurant, and fish ventures relied on the super-exploitation of members' labor. The religio-racial ideology — much like family ideology in a mom-and-pop store — could impose on members, at least in the short run, jobs offering low wages, no benefits, and sometimes even no wages. But while it might help keep a newspaper solvent or finance a new restaurant, that ideologically driven accumulation strategy could not begin to support hospital construction or complex international commerce. Tithes or direct investment by a more affluent membership might better help meet capital needs.

Thus, when W. D. Muhammad inherited the Nation of Islam, it was stymied by a fundamental contradiction: The motors of its success — the religio-racial ideology, hermetic separatism, and primitive strategy of capital accumulation — had become impediments to realizing the objectives that success had spawned. Negotiating the contradiction was constrained, moreover, by Farrakhan, who constituted himself on the right flank as guardian of the Messenger's orthodoxy, ready to challenge deviations.

Those contrary tendencies coexisted no more than three years. Before the split became public knowledge Muhammad had introduced sweeping changes. He repudiated his father's idiosyncratic doctrines — no more Yacub, the evil wizard — in favor of conventional Islamic beliefs. He changed the sect's name to the World Community of Islam in the West to reflect a move toward traditional Islam. He rejected the Messenger's insistence on abstaining from secular politics; instead, he actively urged political participation. In 1976 Muhammad gave up on the goal of economic independence, dismantled the group's holdings and considered seeking Small Business Administration assistance for member-entrepreneurs. (Rumor has it that titles to all the Nation's assets were held not by the organization but by the Messenger himself, who died intestate. Supposedly, W. D. hastened to sell off everything and divided the proceeds equally among all his father's legitimate and illegitimate offspring.)

W. D. had been a very close ally of Malcolm X, reputedly even through the break with his own father, and within his first year as leader of the organization he renamed the Harlem mosque in Malcolm's honor. To Farrakhan's partisans, who often pointed to W. D.'s support for Malcolm as evidence of filial impiety, that gesture must have affirmed suspicions of his blasphemous inclinations. More strain must have developed from W. D.'s proclamation in 1975 that whites thenceforth would be welcome as members of the sect. In 1978 Farrakhan announced his departure and the formation of a new Nation of Islam on the basis of the Messenger's original teachings. In 1985 the World Community of Islam in the West officially disbanded, leaving Farrakhan's group as Elijah Muhammad's sole organizational legacy.

Through the early 1980s Farrakhan maintained a relatively low profile as he built his organization by replicating the old Nation's forms and cultivating a membership drawn from its main social base on the margins of black working-class life. He re-established the Fruit of Islam, the paramilitary security force, and he restored the old ideology, Yacub and all. He even concocted a version of the old bean-pie-and-fish economic development formula via Power Products, a line of household and personal items. (To date, the line has not done well, and Farrakhan seems not to have given it much attention.) As if to underscore his loyalty to the elder Muhammad's vision, Farrakhan resumed his old title, National Representative of the Honorable Elijah Muhammad and the Nation of Islam. The chief public signal of the Nation of Islam's return was the appearance of young men on inner-city streets wearing the group's distinctive suit and bow tie and aggressively selling the *Final Call* newspaper, which, but for the different title, follows the format of the old *Muhammad Speaks*.

The original Nation of Islam had grown in prominence in the years after the Supreme Court's 1954 *Brown v. Board of Education* decision because the organization, primarily through Malcolm, chose to operate within the discursive realm created by the developing activist movement. Debate about politics and racial strategy—at widely varying levels of sophistication—was extensive, and the rising tide of activism lifted all ideological and organizational boats.

In the early 1980s, though, there was no hint of a popular movement, and black political discourse had withered to fit entirely within the frame of elite-centered agendas for race-relations engineering. The cutting edge of racial advocacy, for example, was what political scientist Earl Picard described astutely at the time as the "corporate intervention strategy," pioneered by Jesse Jackson at Operation PUSH and adopted with less rhetorical flair by the National Urban League and the N.A.A.C.P. This strategy consisted in using the threat of consumer boycott to induce corporations to enter into "covenants" binding them to hire black managers, contract with black vendors, deposit in black banks, and recruit black franchisees. (For a while, the N.A.A.C.P. concentrated on Hollywood, identifying the fate of the race with its representation in the film industry.) At the same time Ronald Reagan was pressing ahead with a rhetoric and battle plan steeped in racial revanchism, and official black opposition ranged from feeble to incoherent. In that context, the Fruit of Islam selling newspapers outside the supermarket looked for all the world like living anachronisms.

In the race for the 1984 Democratic presidential nomination, however, Farrakhan demonstrated the new Nation of Islam's political departure from the old. Unlike Elijah Muhammad, Farrakhan did not remain publicly aloof from electoral politics. He openly supported Jackson's candidacy and even provided him with a Fruit of Islam security force. Because of Farrakhan's and the Nation's long association with anti-Semitic rhetoric, his closeness to Jackson was thrown into relief in the wake of the "Hymietown" controversy.

Milton Coleman, the *Washington Post* reporter who disclosed Jackson's remarks, was condemned widely as a race traitor, but Farrakhan raised the ante: "We're going to make an example of Milton Coleman. One day soon, we will punish you by death, because you are interfering with the future of our babies—for white people and against the good of yourself and your own people. This is a fitting punishment for such dogs." (Farrakhan has always denied he made these remarks.)

That inflamed rhetoric, along with Farrakhan's reference to Judaism as a "gutter religion," prodded a temporizing Jackson to distance himself publicly from Farrakhan, and the incident made sensationalistic copy throughout the information industry. For those with memories Farrakhan's attack on Coleman was a chilling reminder of the thuggish currents of the past. Indeed, his theretofore most notoriously threatening pronouncement—against Malcolm X—had set a frightening precedent. In December 1964 he wrote in *Muhammad Speaks*

> Only those who wish to be led to hell, or to their doom, will follow Malcolm. The die is set and Malcolm shall not escape, especially after such foolish talk about his benefactor in trying to rob him of the divine glory which Allah has bestowed upon him. Such a man as Malcolm is worthy of death—and would have met with death if it had not been for Muhammad's confidence in Allah for victory over the enemies.

Two months later Malcolm was assassinated.

In retrospect, the significance of the Milton Coleman incident lay in how it propelled Farrakhan into the new, mass-mediated space in Afro-American politics first carved out by Jesse Jackson. Jackson's 1984 campaign oscillated between simplistic racial appeals ("It's our turn now!") and claims to represent some larger "moral force." As I have argued in *The Jesse Jackson Phenomenon*, that oscillation was rooted in a contradiction between the campaign's public posture as the crest of a broadly based social movement and the reality that it could rely on black votes only. The pressure to increase the black vote justified a mobilization strategy that often approached pure demagogy. In an August 1984 interview with *Ebony*, Jackson described himself as the carrier of "the emotions and self-respect and inner security of the whole race." The messianism implicit in that perception of his racial role appeared more clearly in his insinuation in that same interview that a Virginia supporter's terminal cancer was cured by going to a Jackson rally. In the midst of the Reagan counterrevolution and black elites' typically uninspired and ineffectual responses, that sort of demagogic appeal found a popular audience. With no more promising agenda available, racial cheerleading at least offered a soothing catharsis. The promise of deliverance by proxy, of racial absorption into Jackson's persona, consoled some with simple explanations and apparently easy remedies ("If all black people could just get together behind Jesse . . .").

But between 1984 and 1988 Jackson moved to consolidate his position as a racial broker in mainstream national politics and to expand his domain to include putative representation of all the "locked out." That shift required soft-pedaling the race line, and instead of making sharp denunciations of the nasty grass-roots racism expressed in Howard Beach and Forsyth County, Georgia, he attempted to invoke the common interests of poor whites and poor blacks. Jackson's transition from the posture of militant insurgent to a more subdued insider's style left vacant the specific racial space that he had created and that had proved to be marketable. Louis Franklin's emergence as a national political figure is largely the story of his efforts to replace Jackson as central embodiment and broker of the black race–nationalist political persona. Those efforts began, at least symbolically, with Jackson's grudging acquiescence to white pressure to criticize Farrakhan after the "Hymietown" incident.

The notoriety acquired in that incident fueled Farrakhan's rise in two ways. First, it simply increased his name recognition, especially among a younger generation with no recollection of the old Nation of Islam and his role therein. Second, the heavy barrage of sensationalistic coverage and the sanctimonious white response to the affair afforded an image of Farrakhan and Jackson joined in racial martyrdom. Repudiation of Farrakhan has become a litmus test imposed by white opinion makers for black participation in mainstream politics, and many blacks perceive the test as a humiliating power play. Farrakhan's messianic pretensions, moreover, give him a style something like a counterpunching boxer, and he deftly turned the assault on him into evidence of his authenticity as a race leader. Whites and their agents, the argument goes, expend so much energy on discrediting him because he is a genuine advocate of black interests and thus a threat to white racial domination. In that view, the more he is attacked, the greater his authenticity and the more emphatically he must be defended.

Farrakhan hardly invented this style. Jackson and his black supporters have routinely dismissed criticism by accusing critics of either racism or race treason. Marion Barry, Gus Savage, and legions of less prominent malefactors have wrapped themselves in red, black, and green rhetoric to conceal abuses of public trust or other failings. Nor is the practice an "African survival." Jimmy Swaggart, Billy James Hargis, Richard Nixon, and Oliver North all claim to have been beleaguered by a comparable conspiracy of liberal-communists. Farrakhan stands out because he has been cast in our public theater—like Qaddafi and Noriega, both of whom he has defended—as a figure of almost cartoonishly demonic proportions. He has become uniquely notorious because his inflammatory nationalist persona has helped to center public discussion of Afro-American politics on the only issue (except affirmative action, of course) about which most whites ever show much concern: What do blacks think of whites?

FALSE PROPHET—II

*All For One and None For All*

The hypocrisy in the white reaction to Louis Farrakhan's "hate mongering" is transparent. And beneath the platitudes and fatuities about Martin Luther King, Jr.'s dream, black Americans are aware of the dual standard governing public outcry. David Duke's racism and anti-Semitism have been more direct and vitriolic than Farrakhan's, but Duke has not provoked comparable public anxiety and denunciation—despite the fact that the ex-Nazi/Klansman has won a seat as a Louisiana State Representative, has run "legitimate" candidacies for the U.S. Senate and for Governor. The heavy-metal group Guns n' Roses maintains a repertoire that is unremittingly and unapologetically misogynistic, homophobic, racist, and xenophobic, yet the group has escaped the outrage and public censure heaped upon the no more (nor less, certainly) racist and misogynistic Public Enemy. The scurrilous Andrew Dice Clay is granted television specials and a film contract; the no more repugnant 2 Live Crew is censored for obscenity. Recognition of this hypocritical Jim Crow standard for targeting public scorn naturally breeds resentment and racial defensiveness. The retrograde racial climate fostered by Reaganism particularly stimulated that defensive tendency. It is also reinforced and cultivated by black elites of all sorts—from the national civil rights advocacy organizations, the Congressional Black Caucus, and Jesse Jackson, to small-town politicians, journalists, and academics, who opportunistically reproduce a political discourse among black citizens that takes race as its only significant category of critical analysis.

The Marion Barry case exemplifies the debilitating limitations of that discourse. With very few honest exceptions, black spokespersons failed to take a principled stand denouncing both the Bush Administration's disingenuous, irresponsible (and, yes, racist) use of public power in pursuit of Barry *and* the Mayor's culpability—not simply for his tawdry personal life but, much more seriously, for the contempt and neglect that his entire pattern of governance has directed toward his poor black constituents. One source of the reticence is the mutual protectiveness that operates within all elite networks; it is intensified no doubt by being a beleaguered community. But it also reflects the absence of explicit norms of civic life and ideals of political economy other than those connected to principles of equity among racial groups. Without such norms and ideals, race stands out as the sole unequivocal criterion of good and bad, right and wrong, truth and falsity. That context nurtures a variety of demagogues, hustlers and charlatans; in addition, it underlies an important characteristic of Farrakhan's black support.

Farrakhan has been attacked so vigorously and singularly *in part* because he is black. He is seen by whites as a symbol embodying, and therefore justifying, their fears of a black peril. Blacks have come to his defense *mainly* because he is black and perceived to be a victim of racially inspired defamation; he gets points in principle for saying things that antagonize whites. Few who rally to vindicate him know or have anything substantive to say about his program; most defend him as a strong black voice that whites want to silence. Farrakhan's wager is that he can build a personal following by asserting his apparent victimization as de facto evidence of political legitimacy.

Can he succeed? To what extent has he already succeeded? What difference does it make whether or not he ensconces himself as a major force in national Afro-American politics? The first two questions, commonly asked, express clear, immediate concerns but can be answered only contingently. The third is almost never asked, but it goes to the heart of the most disturbing qualities of the Farrakhan controversy and what it says about the state of black politics.

If mass conversion to the Nation of Islam is the measure of success, then Farrakhan does not seem to have got very far. Nor is it likely that he will. The organization's strict dietary code and other behavioral disciplines—not to mention its bizarre and non-Christian theology—greatly limit his membership pool, as they did Elijah Muhammad's. There is, however, an intermediate zone between adhering to the Nation's doctrines and *pro forma* support, and I suspect that is the terrain on which Farrakhan has staked his aspirations.

He seems to have made some headway, at least within the college-age population, in propagating an image of himself as the quintessential representative of black assertiveness. Black student groups now almost routinely make headlines and raise hackles by paying top-shelf lecture fees (reportedly $17,000 for speaker and entourage at the University of Massachusetts, Amherst) to hear Farrakhan's message. And those in both college and noncollege networks drop his name as a signifier of being conversant with the state of chic in race militancy, just as semireverent, faux intimate invocations of Michael Jordan or Teddy Riley (or some other pop cultural flavor-of-the-moment) conveyed being *au courant* in other contexts.

Embracing Farrakhan's image—like wearing an Africa medallion—is an act of vicarious empowerment. More clearly on the campuses but probably outside student life as well, it is a totemic act of the sort distinctive to mass-consumption culture : highly salient but without clear meaning, effortlessly accessible but somehow bestowing in-group status. For college students, inviting Farrakhan forges identity with a power that counterattacks racism and isolation and soothes the anxieties around upward mobility or class maintenance. For nonstudents, invoking his name forges identity with a power that consoles fleetingly in the face of a marginalized life showing little hope for improvement. Each domain seems preponderantly male. On the one hand, Farrakhan's stridency and martial style have a distinctly macho appeal. On the other, women of any stratum are not likely to respond enthusiastically to his philosophy, which assigns them subordinate status in a patriarchal family, stresses child-bearing and child raising as their main functions, and ties them to the domestic realm in a state of modified purdah.

How far that kind of ephemeral constituency can go is an open question. Some slender cohort will enter the Nation of Islam from the student and nonstudent populations, and Farrakhan's decision to have the Nation operate in electoral politics will probably help campus recruitment by providing a visible public career path, though that tactic has yet to produce any substantive victories. The vast majority will either retain a mainly symbolic identification by recycling signature catch phrases, lose interest entirely, or move back and forth between those two positions according to the vagaries of biography.

The impetus to invite Farrakhan to speak on campuses is driven by a combination of localized *cri de coeur* and protest, competition and solidarity with black students at other institutions, faddishness and racially mediated adolescent rebelliousness and anxiety. But what happens when he comes? What message does he deliver? What do students hear and how do they receive it? What can that tell us about the depth and meaning of his support?

For many the act of consuming the event is the principal gratification. In that sense going to a Farrakhan speech is identical to going to a hip-hop concert; it is the happening place to be at the moment. Farrakhan is a masterful performer and spellbinding orator. He offers his audience a safely contained catharsis: visceral rebellion without dangerous consequences, an instant, painless inversion of power and status relations. As a talented demagogue, Farrakhan mingles banalities, half-truths, distortions, and falsehoods to buttress simplistic and wacky theories. The result is a narrative in which he takes on the role of racial conscience and, in

Malcolm's old phrase, "tells it like it is." He cajoles, berates, exhorts, instructs, and consoles—all reassuringly, without upsetting the framework of conservative petit-bourgeois convention.

Indeed, Farrakhan has reproduced the contradiction within the old Nation of Islam, the tension between militant posture and conservative program. But that contradiction fits the ambivalent position of the student audience. Their racial militancy often rests atop basically conventional, if not conservative, aspirations: for example, the desire to penetrate—or create black-controlled alternatives to—the "glass ceiling" barring access to the upper reaches of corporate wealth and power. Radical rhetoric is attractive when it speaks to their frustrations as members of a minority, as long as it does not conflict with their hopes for corporate success and belief in their own superiority to a benighted black "underclass."

The combination of cathartic, feel-good militancy and conservative substance is the source as well of whatever comparable following Farrakhan may have generated among the older population. It is also what makes him a potentially dangerous force in American life—quite apart from what he thinks of whites in general or Jews in particular. He weds a radical, oppositional style to a program that proposes private and individual responses to social problems; he endorses moral repressiveness; he asserts racial essentialism; he affirms male authority; and he lauds bootstrap capitalism. In defining his and the Nation's role as bringing the holy word to a homogeneous but defective population, moreover, he has little truck for cultivation of democratic debate among Afro-Americans, and he is quick to castigate black critics with the threatening language of race treason.

Reports of Farrakhan's growing presence typically note that the crowds drawn to his speaking tours include many older, apparently well-off people who indicate that they appreciate his message of race pride and self-help community development. Observers from Benjamin Hooks to Phil Donahue have anointed his antidrug and bootstrap rhetorics as level-headed and unobjectionable, the stuff of an appropriate and reasonable approach to the problems of black inner cities. But his focus on self-help and moral revitalization is profoundly reactionary and meshes perfectly with the victim-blaming orthodoxy of the Reagan/Bush era.

To Farrakhan, the most pressing problems confronting the poor and working-class Afro-American population are not poverty and dispossession themselves but their putative behavioral and attitudinal by-products: drugs, crime, social "pathology." In an interview in *Emerge* he declared that to improve black Americans' condition it is necessary first to "recognize that we as a people are sick." In his March 13, 1990, "Donahue" appearance he maintained that blacks suffer from a dependent, welfare mentality inculcated in slavery; there and elsewhere (in a March 1, 1990, *Washington Post* interview, for example) he has implicitly trivialized and challenged the propriety of the Thirteenth Amendment, alleging that at Emancipation the infantilized blacks "didn't have the mentality of a free people to go and do for ourselves." (In this view Farrakhan echoes not only Daniel Patrick Moynihan's notorious 1965 report on the black family but also much older racist representations: the common belief in the early twentieth century that emancipated blacks would die out because of their incompetence at independent life in civilized society and the antebellum view that justified slavery as a humanitarian service for childlike savages who could not exist independently.)

Farrakhan romanticizes the segregation era as a time of black business success and laments that "throughout the South the economic advancement that we gained under Jim Crow is literally dead." He suggested in *Emerge* that civil rights legislation has done black citizens general harm because "women, gays, lesbians, and Jews have taken advantage of civil rights laws, antidiscrimination laws, housing laws, and they have marched on to a better life while the people who made it happen are going farther and farther behind economically." He proposed the "real solution" in a very sympathetic July 23, 1990, interview in *The Spotlight*, organ of the ultra-reactionary Liberty Lobby:

> If I am sick and I'm a member of your household and I have a communicable disease, what you do (so that the disease does not affect the whole family) you remove me from the house and you put me in a place which is separate to allow me to come back to health. Then I can return to my family. Here, when people have been under oppression for 400 years, it produces an ill effect. . . . You have . . . millions of [black] people

who are out of it in terms of our ability to take advantage of even the laws that are on the books right now. We are not creating jobs for ourselves. We are sitting in a dependent posture waiting for white people to create a job for us. And if you don't create a job for us we threaten to picket or wait on welfare to come.

Farrakhan's views of politics and government also share significant features with the Reaganite right. The flip side of his self-help notion is rejection of government responsibility for the welfare of the citizenry. The highly touted Muslim "Dope-busters" drug program in Washington's Mayfair Mansions (where I lived as a child, incidentally) is, after all, advertised as a case of successful privatization. Predictably, Farrakhan shows little regard for the state's integrity as a secular institution. In announcing the Nation's foray into running candidates for public office (for the Washington school board and two Congressional seats, one of them contested by Dr. Abdul Alim Muhammad of Dope-busters fame), he maintained in the Nation's organ, *The Final Call*, that politics needs "somebody trained in divine law, then trained in the law of the land" and announced that the Nation of Islam has been "given by Allah the right guidance for our people and the right guidance for our nation." Like Reagan, he assumes the classic demagogic tack of an antipolitical politics, presenting himself and his subalterns as redeemers coming from outside the political realm and untainted by its corruptions. Their mission is to bring moral order.

Clearly, this is a very disturbing, regressive social vision, and it is instructive that Farrakhan has received the Liberty Lobby's enthusiastic stamp of approval. The good news is that his vision is most unlikely to win mass Afro-American adherence; the bad news is that doing so is not a necessary condition for Farrakhan's becoming a central race spokesperson. Instead, he seems to be following the route that Jesse Jackson pioneered.

With his 1983 speaking tour Jackson gained acclamation as a paramount figure in Afro-American politics by parlaying media images of enthusiastic audiences into a claim to represent a mass constituency. He succeeded without having articulated a program or coherent vision for those supposed constituents to accept or reject. In claiming to embody their aspirations simply in his being, he also sought to merge collective racial fortunes into his own, a strategy that entailed defining support of Jackson as an act of race loyalty.

Jackson's strategy exploited longstanding and hegemonic presumptions in American society that black people naturally speak with a single voice as a racial group, that the "leaders" who express the collective racial interest emerge organically from the population, and that the objectives and interests of those organic leaders are identical with those of the general racial constituency. Those presumptions eliminate the need to attend to potentially troublesome issues of accountability, legitimacy, and democratic process among Afro-Americans, and they give whites easy, uncomplicated access to a version of black thinking by condensing the entire race into a few designated spokespersons. They also simplify the management of racial subordination by allowing white elites to pick and choose among pretenders to race leadership and, at their own discretion, to confer "authenticity." Thus Jackson generated the dynamic of personalistic legitimation that created his national status almost as self-fulfilling prophecy, without regard to the specific character of his popular support. Jackson has shown that it is possible to penetrate the innermost circles of the national race-relations management elite without coming from a clearly denominated organizational, electoral or institutional base. Farrakhan could follow that same path, though he might be constrained as well as aided by the fact that he does have an organizational base, and by that base's particular nature.

Operation PUSH under Jackson was purely an extension of his person, and it cohered around opportunism as a raison d'être. The National Rainbow Coalition, Inc., is an organizational fiction. Both have therefore been well suited to the protean style that Jackson employed to establish himself first as embodiment of insurgent mass racial aspirations and then as generic "moral force" in elite national political circles. While the Nation of Islam is an extension of Farrakhan's objectives, it also has a governing ideology and world view. He may be limited — in the same way that he hampered Wallace Muhammad — in his ability to bend that orthodoxy to suit his immediate political purposes.

Farrakhan may differ from Jackson in yet another consequential way. Where Jackson's history has been marked by self-promotion more than propagation of a durable set of beliefs, Farrakhan — though obviously opportunistic — has built his career and organization around a clear, aggressive ideology. His ambitions appear to be in a way narrower, in a way broader than Jackson's. Farrakhan is more likely to be content with a status defined in purely racial terms and has been less inclined to moderate his race line in exchange for access to privileged insider status. On his own and through the Nation he has been sharply censorious and disparaging of what he construes as Jackson's knuckling under to white criticism. In part, I suspect, that difference reflects the fact that Farrakhan has an organizational apparatus that permits him to maximize the returns of a purely racial focus by engineering symbols of legitimacy and continual mobilization (rallies, conferences, community visibility). The difference also underscores the fact that Farrakhan's ideology decrees an explicit racial mission — purification (by the Nation's standards) of Afro-American life. Unlike Jackson, who has capitalized on the image of control of the black American population, Farrakhan wants real control.

His suggestion that some 600,000 incarcerated blacks be released to his authority in Africa is more than a publicity stunt. It expresses a belief that in the best-case scenario he should be put in charge of black Americans. His request in the *Washington Post* interview to be "allowed the freedom to teach black people unhindered" sounds mild enough, but only because it leaves ambiguous what he considers improper hindrances. Opposition of any sort falls into that category, and his 1984 threat to Milton Coleman for race treason in the "Hymietown" affair reveals the place of dissent in the society he would make. Of the model of racial authority he would assert, he makes a revealing comparison in the *Emerge* interview: "I am to black people as the Pope is to white people." That enlarged self-image can approach a lunatic megalomania. He alleges in *Emerge* that the revival of interest in Malcolm X is the work of a conspiracy aimed at undermining his mission; to *The Washington Post* he traced the spread of crack in inner cities to a similar conspiracy against him, and he claimed to have been transported in

1985 into a spaceship where Elijah Muhammad gave him general instructions and prophesied Reagan's attack on Libya.

How can it be that Farrakhan's actual vision of and for black America has been so noncontroversial? Why have the civil rights establishment and other liberal black opinion leaders not publicly expressed more vocal concerns about its protofascist nature and substance? Some of the reticence may derive from fear of being attacked for race disloyalty, but the black petit-bourgeois chorus of praise for the Nation's rhetoric of self-help and moral rearmament reveals a deeper reason for the absence of criticism. The same repugnant, essentially Victorian view of the inner-city black poor as incompetent and morally defective that undergirds Farrakhan's agenda suffuses the political discourse of the black petite bourgeoisie. That view informs the common sense, moreover, even of many of those identified with the left. Of course, not many would admit to the level of contempt that Farrakhan has expressed publicly:

> Not one of you [*Spotlight* editorial staff] would mind, maybe, my living next door to you, because I'm a man of a degree of intelligence, of moral character. I'm not a wild, partying fellow. I'm not a noisemaker. I keep my home very clean and my lawn very nice. . . . With some of us who have learned how to act at home and abroad, you might not have problems. . . . Drive through the ghettos, and see our people. See how we live. Tell me that you want your son or daughter to marry one of these. No, you won't.

Some, like Harvard sociologist Orlando Patterson, share Farrakhan's contention that the black poor's pathology is a product of the slavery experience. Others, like the Carter Administration's Equal Employment Opportunity Commission director and Washington Congressional delegate Eleanor Holmes Norton or sociologist William Julius Wilson, maintain that this pathology is a phenomenon of the post-World War II or even postsegregation era. Still others, like Roger Wilkins, have embraced both narratives of origin. There is, however, nearly unanimous agreement with Farrakhan's belief that defective behavior and attitudes are rampant among the poor. In an article in *Dissent*, Patterson points to an underclass bent on "violence and destruction." Norton, calling for "Restoring the Traditional Black Family" in *The New York Times*

*Magazine* (June 2, 1985), sees a "self-perpetuating culture of the ghetto," a "destructive ethos" that forms a "complicated, predatory ghetto subculture." Wilson frets over the "sharp increase in social pathologies in ghetto communities" in his opus on urban poverty, *The Truly Disadvantaged* (1987); Wilkins cited in *The New York Times* the authority of Samuel Proctor—then a retired Rutgers professor; also a civil rights veteran and minister emeritus of Harlem's Abyssinian Baptist Church—who fears that the "uneducated, illiterate, impoverished, violent underclass" will "grow like a cancer," producing "losers who are destroying our schools . . . who are unparented and whose communities are morally bankrupt." Being associated with the more radical left does not imply immunity from the rhetoric of spreading pathology among the black poor. In *The Progressive* Manning Marable reproduces uncritically the mirage of "growing numbers of juvenile pregnancies" among his litany of "intractable social problems proliferating" in black inner cities despite his observation that such problems have structural causes and his call for good social-democratic solutions. Cornel West in *Prophetic Fragments* sounds the alarm about the cities' "cultural decay and moral disintegration."

This often lurid imagery of pathology naturally points toward a need for behavioral modification, moral regeneration and special tutelage by black betters; black middle-class paternalism is as shameless and self-serving now as at the turn of the previous century. Patterson, Norton, Wilson, and Wilkins announce the middle class's special role in making certain that the poor are fit into properly two-parent, male-headed families. Proctor, presumably giving up on adults, proposed the use of military discipline to insure that children have "breakfasts with others at a table." West would send them into churches for moral rehabilitation. And the Committee on Policy for Racial Justice of the Joint Center for Political Studies (whose members include Norton, Wilkins, and Wilson) lauds self-help in its manifesto, *Black Initiative and Governmental Responsibility*, and calls on black "religious institutions, civic and social organizations, media, entertainers, educators, athletes, public officials, and other community leaders" to "emphasize . . . values."

It was a master stroke of Reagan's second-term spin doctors to sugarcoat the offensive on the black poor with claptrap about special black middle-class responsibility for "their" poor and the challenge of self-help. The black leadership elite fell right into line and quickly institutionalized a cooing patter of noblesse oblige.

From that hegemonic class standpoint there is little room and less desire to criticize Farrakhan's contemptuous, authoritarian diagnosis and remedy. As he instructed *The Spotlight*:

> We must be allowed the freedom first to teach our people and put them in a state of readiness to receive justice. . . . Blacks in America have to be concentrated upon, to lift us up in a way that we will become self-respecting so that the communities of the world will not mind accepting us as an equal member among the community of family of nations. . . . But when we [the Nation of Islam] get finished with these people, we produce dignified intelligent people. The American system can't produce that. We can.

In sum, Louis Farrakhan has become prominent in the public eye because he appeals symbolically both to black frustration and alienation in this retrograde era and to white racism, disingenuousness, and naïveté. He also responds to the status anxiety, paternalistic class prejudice, and ideological conservatism embedded within black petit-bourgeois race militancy. His antiwhite or anti-Semitic views are neither the most important issue surrounding Farrakhan nor the greatest reason for concern about his prospects for growing influence. After all, he will never be able to impose his beliefs—no matter how obnoxious or heinous—on any group of white Americans. More significant, and more insidious, is the fact that racial units are his essential categories for defining and comprehending political life. That fact obviously establishes him on common conceptual ground with all manner of racists. (*The Spotlight* was happily curious about whether he and David Duke actually would disagree on anything in a debate rumored to be in the works.)

His racial essentialism has an appeal for many blacks in a purely demagogic way. It also gives him an outlook that seems disarmingly sensible to whites—at least those who can overlook his fiery pro-black sentiments and devil theories—because it fits into the hoary "What do your people want?" framework for discussing black

Americans. That essentialist outlook also underlies his self-help rhetoric, which appeals to both whites and middle-class blacks. Whites like it because it implies that blacks should pull themselves up by their bootstraps and not make demands on government. Middle-class blacks like it because it legitimizes a "special role" for the black petite bourgeoisie over the benighted remainder of the race. In both views, "self-help" with respect to ordinary black Americans replaces a standard expectation of democratic citizenship—a direct, unmediated relation to the institutions and processes of public authority. Self-help ideology is a form of privatization and therefore implies cession of the principle that government is responsible for improving the lives of the citizenry and advancing egalitarian interests; it also rests on a premise that black Americans cannot effectively make demands on the state directly as citizens but must go through intermediaries constituted as guardians of collective racial self-interest. Ironically, "self-help" requires dissolution of the autonomous civic selves of Afro-Americans.

The link between self-help rhetoric and racial custodianship is as old as Booker T. Washington, the model of the organic racial leadership Farrakhan articulates. The idea that black racial interests can be embodied in a single individual has always been attractively economical for white elites. Giving Washington a railroad car for his own use to avoid Jim Crow was a lot cheaper for white elites and less disruptive than socioeconomic democratization and preservation of citizenship rights. Jesse Jackson updated the claim to organic racial leadership and brokerage by enlisting mass media technology to legitimize it, and Farrakhan is following in Jackson's steps. Because of his organization and ideology, however, Farrakhan more than his predecessors throws into relief the potentially fascistic presumptions inscribed at the foundation of that model. That—underscored by the brownshirt character of the Fruit of Islam and the history of the old Nation during Farrakhan's ascent—is what makes him uniquely troubling. But demonizing him misses the point; it is the idea of organic representation of the racial collectivity that makes him possible.

It is the idea, whether expressed flamboyantly by Farrakhan or in the more conventional petit-bourgeois synecdoche that folds all black interests into a narrow class agenda, that most needs to be repudiated. Its polluting and demobilizing effects on Afro-American political life have never been more visible, thanks to promotion by the mass media's special combination of racist cynicism and gullibility. Cheap hustlers and charlatans, corrupt and irresponsible public officials and perpetrators of any sort of fraud can manipulate the generic defensiveness decreed by a politics of organic racial representation to support their scams or sidestep their guilt—all too often for offenses against black constituents. A straight line connects Washington's Tuskegee Machine, which sought to control access to philanthropic support for racial agendas, to Jackson's insinuation that "respect" for him is respect for all black Americans, to Farrakhan's death threat against Milton Coleman, to the pathetic specter of the rogues' gallery of Farrakhan, Illinois Representative Gus Savage, the Reverend Al Sharpton, the Reverend George Stallings, and Tawana Brawley sharing the stage with Marion Barry at a rally to defend the corrupt Mayor's honor. That image captures the depth of crisis of political vision that racial organicism has wrought.

# —Triumph of the Tuskegee Will

I never thought I'd be thankful for Louis Farrakhan's abominable anti-Semitism, but right now that's all that's slowing down his coronation as the new Booker T. Washington. My fears are that he and Abraham Foxman of the Anti-Defamation League will strike some kind of accord, or that the corporate elite will just decide that this is too good to let pass and tell the Jewish interest groups to shut up, or that the *Commentary* crowd will figure out that Farrakhan is the best way to get rid of their Negro Problem—and the best way to pry liberal Jews away from a progressive social agenda.

A week or so before the Million Man March, mainstream media fastened onto it, and coverage was—Farrakhan's complaints notwithstanding—decidedly positive, virtually part of the promotional campaign. Why? Because, as a friend quipped, this was the first protest in history in which people gathered to protest themselves. Farrakhan's conventionally black nationalist "do-for-self, can't-look-to-government, develop-our-own-communities" line meshes perfectly with the bipartisan right-wing consensus about social policy and civil rights enforcement—just as Booker T.'s version of the same line legitimized the bipartisan consensus to restore white supremacy in the South. And Farrakhan's victim-blaming rhetoric echoes Washington's in a more vicious tone.

The viciousness is not happenstance. Farrakhan is a fascist, and he would be if there were no white people on the planet. His vision for black Americans is authoritarian, theocratic, homophobic, and like nationalisms everywhere, saturated in patriarchal ideology. Like his antecedents Washington and Marcus Garvey, Farrakhan is militantly procapitalist (he reportedly indicated that black trade union leaders were not welcome on the dais) and antidemocratic.

Washington wanted to control all race-uplift activity and enforce the gospel of submissiveness—while patrolling black politics to root our radicals. Farrakhan also wants to establish a regime of ruthless moral regeneration according to his standards. That's why the sycophantic performances of academic wannabe racemen Michael Dyson and Cornel West are so contemptible. West has gone to the limit of his capacity for double-talk to rationalize association with Farrakhan's agenda; Dyson played Goebbels on "Nightline," declaring the march to be *against* sexism and homophobia. They have nice, secure jobs and lives outside the Bantustan; they'll never have to worry about the Fruit of Islam kicking down their door to beat them for stopping at the liquor store after work or for eating a pig foot or because their wives wore short skirts. Think that vision is paranoid? Consider three things: (1) Farrakhan already has a paramilitary apparatus in the Fruit of Islam and the Unity Nation, his skinhead *Jungvolk*; (2) the Nation's contract "security" forces have a history of beating and brutalizing supposed criminals — a record, NBC news noted almost gleefully, that would prompt legal action if it belonged to the police; (3) Malcolm X.

Because I spent most of the week before the march fending off media requests, I saw clearly how journalists wanted to frame it. Only conservative black opposition was newsworthy; it shared the march's premises while objecting only to Farrakhan's anti-Semitism and racism. The "woman question" was reduced to a simple inclusion-exclusion debate that accepted the patriarchal assumptions fundamental to the event. The condescending spectacle of black men sharing their pain in public and stepping up to take their rightful place was just — as befits Ben Chavis and the reborn Marion Barry — the Hugh Hefner-Robert Bly-Steven Seagal sensitive man in blackface. The focus on "responsibility" provided a backhanded assertion of male priority in families and communities. Beneath the patronizing acknowledgment that black women have played important roles in community life lay the punch line — that the brothers are here to take care of business now, so you honeys can go cook something and watch the kids.

The idea of gathering to accept responsibility also rests on two intertwined but quite different objectives. One is for the marchers to counter the stereotyping and stigmatizing of black men. (But for whom anyway?) The second, which overlaps "atonement," is to exhort miscreant brothers to mend their ways. These objectives are contradictory; one admits what the other challenges. What appears to resolve the contradiction is the slippage between "I" and "we" that is greased by nationalist notions of a uniform black male collectivity. A bunch of "I"s gathered to pat themselves on the back for being "responsible" and to provide a model for those benighted bloods—the "we" who are really "they"—who need moral tutelage.

The call to atone presumes—as Farrakhan and his ilk always have—Daniel Moynihan's and Dinesh D'Souza's views of black American life. The god-drenched rally was to that extent a sort of baptism, cleansing the congregants of the racial original sin identified in the 1965 Book of Daniel, Moynihan's scurrilously racist and misogynist *Report on the Negro Family*. Unsurprisingly, therefore, the responsibility-atonement paradigm also shifts discussion of inequality away from public policy to victim-blaming underclass ideology. This is the wet dream of all those who would like to be rid of the "race problem"; liberals would be off the hook for those messy civil liberties and civil rights issues, because black people would administer themselves in line with "their" special needs, etc. No need to link black dispossession to capitalists' global restructuring and corporate downsizing. Nor to the reactionary assaults on public responsibility for civic welfare and on mechanisms for countering discrimination. Let them eat bean pies!

In the political desperation of the moment, and given the bankruptcy of the manifest options in black politics, many decent, honest progressives attended the march, trying to distance themselves from its official message of black male atonement, trying to shout their own agendas over the din of the dominant chorus whose "(those other) niggers ain't shit" melody was softened by the psychobabble of pop spiritualism and religiosity. The ploy won't work now, just as it didn't work in the '70s when black progressives tried to ride on the coattails of the rising stratum of black public officials or in the '80s when they tried it with Jesse Jackson. The weakness that makes us seek to join also means that we can have no influence on the motion. The stakes are greater now than before; remember what happened to the German left.

# —Martyrs and False Populists

In desperate times we strain to find something to celebrate. There is an understandable tendency to romanticize the oppressed, and to grasp at anything that looks like alternative politics.

Hence the recent, disturbingly knee-jerk reactions within the left to such disparate phenomena as the militia movement and the Mumia Abu-Jamal case.

I was surprised by the letters in *The Nation* and *The Progressive* from readers who were affronted by negative coverage of the militias in each magazine. I've heard the same kind of position taken in conversations with people I know personally who identify with the left. The substance of this ostensibly progressive defense of the militia movement goes something like this: the militia supporters are by and large working class; they often are recruited from especially depressed local economies; their membership expresses their alienation from politics-as-usual; therefore, we shouldn't dismiss their populist frustrations.

It is true that militia members want to curtail the repressive power of the state and complain about the predatory power of large corporations. They oppose NAFTA and want to assert popular, community control of government. But defending them on these grounds is naïve and short-sighted, and reflects a broader, perhaps more insidious tendency—including a kind of accentuate-the-positive bias toward whatever looks like autonomous, populist action. This is the same tendency that willfully inflates any sort of apparently group-conscious activity—for instance, youth fads—into the status of political movements.

On the militia issue, the first problem is that class origin, or for that matter class identity, isn't an adequate criterion for making judgments about political positions. The principle that if it comes from the oppressed, there must be something OK about it, is not only simplistic; it can have truly reactionary implications. This kind of thinking has too often led down the road to complete accommodation to the worst strains arising from working classes. In fact, it's almost routine now that calls for sympathetic understanding of working-class history—"We need to recognize the genuine fear of loss of control of the family, traditional values, close-knit neighborhood, jobs, way of life, etc."—are the first steps down the road to full-scale retreat from commitment to equality and social justice. Think about the Democratic Leadership Council.

There is a long history of rationalizing working-class nativism and racism. It helped sanitize the regime of terror that was the Southern Redemption, restoring unadulterated white-supremacist rule after Reconstruction. The architects of that restoration's ideology characterized the racist putsch in the South as a revolt of the common people against a corrupt elite that cynically used blacks to further unpopular aims.

The same mindset counseled sympathetic understanding for labor's rabid anti-Asian racism in the West in the nineteenth century, and tolerated the New York draft riot of 1863, anti-feminist and anti-abortion activism, and whites' anti-busing riots. One version even sympathized with official resistance in Yonkers, New York, to court-ordered remediation of a lengthy, nefarious history of racial discrimination. Yonkers, the line went, was being penalized as a working-class/lower-middle-class suburb that can't afford to use exclusionary zoning to keep blacks and Hispanics out.

Of course, most leftists who have a warm spot for the militia movement would not support these positions. But the differences are more of degree than of kind. Today, we hear arguments that we should focus on common class interests like living-wage jobs for all rather than affirmative action, and "universalistic" rather than "race-based" social policy. In his book, *Turning Back: The Retreat from Racial Justice in American Thought and Policy*, Stephen Steinberg discusses how this ostensibly farther-reaching alternative often masks a retreat from the struggle for equality within the working class. Sometimes, he notes, it yields a racial trickle-down argument that the best way to fight racism or sexism is to direct benefits to whites and men.

Racist and fascist movements always have some popular, working-class base. Mussolini came out of the Italian Socialist party, and National Socialism sought actively to compete for the hearts and minds of politically unsophisticated German workers disposed to authoritarian, conspiratorial, and scapegoating theories. In both cases, the movement drew energy from the same kind of superficially anti-capitalist rhetoric that the militias project— complete with their versions of "black helicopter" fantasies. The Nazis also pioneered, in their conspiratorial mythology about German defeat in World War I, the "stab in the back" theory that underlies the POW/MIA lunacy running through the ideological pools in which the militia movement swims. And, as with their precursors who imposed the segregationist regime in the American South, their appeal to a bigoted and politically unsophisticated popular base was combined with ruthless suppression of populist and working class forces that presented more substantial progressive, egalitarian alternatives.

And, besides, their anti-statism really isn't the same as ours, or it shouldn't be anyway.

But confusion on this score points up another problem in the left. We often aren't clear enough about distinguishing opposition to the actions of particular governments and regimes from hostility to the actions of government in principle. As a result, we sometimes overvalue anything that looks like an insurgency against concentrated power.

It's easy, for instance, to paint ordinary Not In My Back Yard politics at the local level as something grander and more progressive. Mobilization by residents of a threatened neighborhood to stop a corporate development project can be a very good thing. But the visions that support such mobilizing aren't necessarily progressive; they can rest on the same kind of parochial territorialism that prompts demonstrations against housing desegregation. In fact, opponents of open housing routinely see themselves as the victims of oppressive government and evil realtors. Even the slow-growth movement in local politics isn't unambiguously democratic or anticorporate. Often enough it simply represents the efforts of those who arrived last week to keep anyone else from arriving next week. We have to recognize such struggles' ambiguity if we are to realize their best tendencies.

We have to recognize that not every popular mobilization is progressive just because it arises from the grassroots. Having experienced the underside of populist rhetoric in segregationism and opposition to civil rights, I'm perhaps especially sensitive to the fact that a lot of nastiness can lie under labels like "the people." Lynch mobs were, after all, a form of popular, direct action.

No matter what Alexander Cockburn says, I haven't seen anything to suggest that I shouldn't judge the militiamen by the company they keep politically. Nor have I seen any signs among them of a substantive vision for political and economic reorganization that would allay my fears.

I confess, as well, to being toward the statist end of the left, at least among those of us whose politics were formed in the 1960s and after. I'm always uneasy when we get fuzzy about the distinction between our objections to actions taken by those who control the American state and a more general objection to the State as an abstraction. Yes, government is ultimately a means of coercion. Therefore, it needs to be accountable to the citizenry. At the same time, government needs to be insulated from the whims of fleeting, potentially tyrannical majorities.

The experience of being black in the United States highlights the dangers of a simplistically majoritarian notion of democracy. Decentralization of public authority in the name of popular democracy—from "states' rights" to the "new (and newer) federalism"—has been a rallying cry of opponents of black civil rights for more than a century and a half.

The state is the only vehicle that can protect ordinary citizens against the machinations of concentrated private power. Even though it does function as an executive committee of the ruling class, the national state is the guarantor of whatever victories working people, minorities, gays, women, the elderly, and other constituencies we embrace have been able to win—often enough against the state itself. And this applies both to formalizing those victories as rights and using public policy to redistribute resources that make them practical reality.

The public sector is the area of the economy most responsive to equal-opportunity employment. And the national state—ours as well as others—is the only entity powerful enough to control the activities of piratical multinational corporations. That's what the fights against NAFTA and GATT (and now WTO) are all about—preserving the state's capacity to enforce social, economic, and environmental standards within its own territory.

And that's just the defensive side of the struggle. We need to press for a more active use of the state in international economic and foreign policy to combat the multinationals' depredations across the globe.

It always seemed to me that our struggle, to rehearse a long-outdated slogan, wasn't really to smash the state, but to seize it and direct it to democratic and egalitarian purposes.

I don't get a sense of anything compatible with this perspective from the militia movement. Empty clichés such as, "The government is the child of the people and has to be spanked when it gets out of line," don't inspire confidence. Who do the militiamen have in mind when they evoke the image of "the people"? What do they consider appropriate uses of public authority?

As Chip Berlet and others pointed out in *The Progressive*, there's not much reason to think that the militia movement's politics are anything other than paranoid proto-fascist. To say that they're not all racist, sexist, or xenophobic is both bizarre and beside the point. Organizationally and ideologically they're plugged into the most vicious, lunatic, and dangerous elements of the right. No matter that some individuals may think, or want to think, or want gullible journalists to think that they're just out playing a more strenuous version of Dungeons and Dragons.

So what if this puts me on the same side as the Justice Department? We're also on the same side when we demand enforcement of voting rights or redress from Ku Klux Klan violence or prosecution of corporate criminals. And, even if I weren't a former object of COINTELPRO-era surveillance and harassment, I would have no illusions about the really existing law-enforcement authorities—at whatever level of the federal system—being dependable allies. I grew up in inner cities where municipal police were clearly an occupying force. I lived through the civil-rights movement when the

state police and FBI worked hand-in-hand with the Klan. Nevertheless, it's important for us to recognize that in principle at least the
state belongs to us as much as to any other interests in the society,
and part of our fight must be to make it responsive to us.

The issue of our relation to the criminal-justice system highlights
another problematic tendency in the left, one that appears most
topically in the Mumia Abu-Jamal support movement. We often
have trouble keeping straight that being a victim of injustice has no
necessary relation to the quality of one's politics or character. A
friend in Atlanta, in the aftermath of Wayne Williams's conviction in
the city's missing-and-murdered-children case that drew national
attention in the early 1980s, observed that the state probably had
just railroaded a guilty man. We have to recognize that that is always
a possibility in the messy world of social experience.

This is true of organizations as well as individuals. Members of
the MOVE cult in Philadelphia certainly should not have been
bombed by the city, but it was reasonable to evict them after years
of their neighbors' complaints of harassment and public-health
violations.

I don't presume to pronounce on Abu-Jamal's guilt or innocence. At this moment only three issues should concern us: that
there are very persuasive reasons to believe that he didn't receive a
fair trial, quite likely for political reasons; that his freedom of speech
had been violated; and that he is an atypically visible victim of the
barbarity of capital punishment. We must avoid the temptation to
exalt him as a symbol of progressive politics. All that most of us
know about his politics, apart from his speaking out against police
brutality, is that he has some connection to MOVE—a group with
pretty wacky ideas. Certainly he is an activist, but there are a lot of
activists, some of whom have bad politics. Being victimized by the
state should not in itself confer political stature.

First of all, the evidence to which we have access leaves open a
possibility that Abu-Jamal could actually be guilty of the crime with
which he is charged. Second, whether he's guilty or innocent, his
ordeal doesn't indicate anything about the substance of his politics.
It's certainly right and important to rally and organize to support his

case. But we must take care neither to rush to make him a hero nor to let his appeal as an individual divert us from broader, more complex concerns.

Norma McCorvey (Jane Roe of *Roe v. Wade*), in her conversion to Operation Rescue's brand of holy rolling, should give us pause about loading too much significance onto individuals whose personal circumstances momentarily embody larger political concerns.

Some of us can recall as well the case of Joanne Little in the 1970s. Little's was an especially tragic story of an impoverished young woman from a small North Carolina town. While incarcerated on a breaking-and-entering charge, she escaped from jail after killing a white jailer who allegedly attempted to rape her in her cell. The state declared her an outlaw, which amounted to a shoot-on-sight order. Little became a cause célèbre for the women's movement in particular. But she was in far over her head as a celebrity. Her subsequent forays into petty criminality left the movement with egg on its face.

Even under the best of conditions a movement built around a single individual can go only so far. This approach trades on the imagery of martyrdom; yet its goal is to ensure that the putative martyrs are rescued. Rescued martyrs, however, are always a potential problem because they live on as fallible human beings.

The difference between James Meredith, who integrated the University of Mississippi and was later shot on a solitary march through the state, and Martin Luther King and Malcolm X is instructive. Unlike the others, Meredith survived and went on to follow the twists and turns of post-segregation politics in increasingly pathetic and perverse ways, bottoming out as an aide to Jesse Helms. Martyrs work best when they're dead.

The cause célèbre phenomenon, like fuzzy-mindedness about the militia movement, reflects a romantic, almost opportunistic tendency in the left. It is part of a soothing, "warm-bath" politics, a politics that is counterproductive because it imagines a specious, quick-fix alternative to the tedious, frustrating work that we most need: building support by organizing to create a base for a concrete, coherent political program.

# —Tokens of the White Left

For more than twenty years I refused on principle to use the phrase "the white left." I did not want to give any credence to the view, commonly expressed among black activists in the late 1960s and after, that the leftist critique of American society was somehow white people's property.

I maintained this resolve through SDS's 1969 proclamation of the Black Panther Party as the "vanguard of the black revolution"—based only on the Panthers' willingness to align with whites—and subsequent gushes of Pantherphile exoticism. I kept it through the "separate black movement divides the working class" line, which was one crude "Marxist" alternative to examining black politics. And I held on through similarly evasive Procrustean analyses, for example, casting the civil-rights movement as a "bourgeois democratic revolution." My resolve was unshaken through endless reification of the "black community" as a collective subject.

Even when Frederic Jameson, editor of *Social Text,* told me early in the Reagan era that he had published an article that he knew was drivel and didn't even conform to the bibliographical format of the rest of the journal because he "wanted to publish something by a black author and that's what there was," I remained true.

I stayed patiently silent as the Democratic Socialists of America anointed one star Black Voice after another throughout the 1980s, with never a hint of concern about the anointed's institutional links to any sort of autonomous black political activity. And I endured the total lack of curiosity about Jesse Jackson's new political fame and what his antics since 1984 have to do with tensions and cleavages among blacks.

I'm ready to toss in the towel. When all is said and done, it really is all too much the *white* left. In far too many quarters, identifying with progressive politics is perfectly compatible with reliance on racial shorthand and, therefore, with the disposition to view Afro-American life as simultaneously opaque to those outside it (thus the need for black interpreters and line-bearers) and smoothly organic (with exceptions made for the odd, inauthentic "sellout" leaders).

Perhaps I am finally giving in to this view because I'm old and tired. Perhaps it's the result of attrition. Mostly, though, it seems that the farther the memory — much less the actuality — of real political movements recedes on the horizon, the worse this problem has become. I confess that it is quite dispiriting. It also makes the issue of blacks' role in the left a matter for real concern; more and more that role seems to be in a line stretching back at least to Melville's Queequeg, that is, to put whites in touch with their "deeper humanity."

This complaint has absolutely nothing to do with leadership, or even representation, in left institutions. It's about Jim Crow standards on the left: the suspension, when making judgments about black people and politics, of critical scrutiny, along with the tough-minded, Enlightenment skepticism that is the foundation of the left critique's unique power.

The key problem is that whites on the left don't want to confront complexity, tension, and ambivalence in black politics. In general, they simply do not see political differences among black people. They do not see that blacks are linked to social, political, and economic institutions in a variety of different ways, and that those different links, and the networks that flow from them, shape interests and ideological perception no less, and no less subtly, than among whites.

Because of racial stratification, black and white links differ. For instance, middle-class black people, largely because of housing segregation, are more likely than middle-class whites to live close to poor people. And black people, especially in the middle class, are more likely to be public employees, thanks to more nearly equal employment opportunities in the public sector.

Examining how the public-sector economy is woven into the logic of black politics should be a central project for the left. We need to take account of the fact that, more than ever, black individuals at all class levels are likely to have direct connections — themselves or through relatives, friends, and neighbors — with the operation of public institutions. And we need to assess what that means for shaping varying black political perceptions.

The fundamental principles of this sort of social structure, however, are the same for blacks and whites, and, therefore, they should not be incomprehensibly foreign to whites. It's astounding to see repeatedly in the left press the contrast between the subtlety and critical confidence with which writers dissect politics in Somalia, Bosnia, Indonesia, and Ukraine, and the total absence of those qualities in discussions of Afro-Americans.

As a result of this failing, attention to black politics on the left tends to revolve around thin and simplistic definitions of good guys and bad, "true" leaders and false. This distorts political judgment into a search for authenticity, hauntingly like white youth's quest in the 1960s for the most "authentic" blues — "pure" and untarnished by instrumentation, cultivated virtuosity, air-conditioned nightclubs, or indoor plumbing. (No Bobby Bland or Little Johnny Taylor need apply, just solitary old guys on porches of croppers' shacks in the Delta, playing acoustic guitars with neck bones.) It's also the exact meaning of exoticism and has horrible political consequences. The "pure" black experience is monadic and antithetical to complexity in either orchestral arrangements or politics.

Assigning authenticity requires "finding" the pulse of the community. (Actually, as with SDS and the Panthers, it requires *designating* the pulse — thus whites determine black legitimacy, as they have since Booker T. Washington's day at the turn of the century.) This places a premium on articulate black people who will talk to the left. Whites tend to presume their inability — or tend not to want to expend the effort — to make critical judgments that might second-guess their designated black voices of authenticity, and therefore do not attend closely to the latter's substantive arguments. The result is that these "authentic" voices are treated mainly as personalities — without much regard to the political implications of the stances they project.

In fact, it is apparently possible to maintain one's status as Bearer of the Left's Authentic Race Line while articulating arguments that scarcely resemble views we normally think of as leftist. So Cornel West can retain his star status in the white left as he blathers on conspicuously about rampant "nihilism in black America," spouting breezy, warmed-over versions of the stock conservative — and utterly false—narrative of the fall from some earlier organic community, claiming that black Americans suffer from a "collective clinical depression," calling for a "politics of conversion" and cultivation of a "black love ethic" (is this Robert Schuller meets Barry White, or what?), as well as embracing the black conservatives' self-help rhetoric.

That West's explicit embrace of victim-blaming, pathologizing rhetoric about inner-city poor black people has provoked no real controversy in the left underscores the fact that the "noble savage" face of exoticism inevitably is only the obverse face of the "nasty savage" coin. The premise of blacks' deeper humanity is at bottom an assumption of their essentially *different* humanity, and all it takes is a rude street encounter or a smashed car window to turn Martin Luther King, Jr., into Bigger Thomas as the avatar of the racial essence.

Ironically, this is the "othering" that the cultural-politics jockeys rattle on about from critique of one advertisement or Hottentot exhibit to the next. Yet they fail to grasp the dangers of their own breathless claims about the importance of race. Often, as with Michael Dyson's fawning endorsement of William Julius Wilson's line on black poverty, they also show an unexpected tolerance for talk about those "other," nasty savages.

This helps to explain why "underclass" imagery—properly spun with sanitizing allusions to ultimate sources in vaguely "structural" dynamics—has struck so many on the left as reasonable, as I've learned the hard way.

The simplistic, exoticizing approach to black politics is also susceptible to rhetoric about black people's intrinsic spirituality. This not only evokes hoary claims that blacks are closer to nature than whites, it also underwrites an increasingly troubling mystification of the church's role as the font of authenticity in black political life. After black Americans fought from the moment of Emancipation for the right to vote, then for two-thirds of the next century against Jim Crow disfranchisement, it's incredible to hear the left's black stars routinely and blithely dismiss the ability to elect leaders and participate in shaping public institutions as less genuine than religious expression as a form of black political engagement.

This view's currency reflects the fact that several of its propo-nents—like West and Dyson—are ministers and thus propagan-dists for the church. But it floats on whites' inclination to see black Americans as spiritual folk, huddled organically around the camp meeting, communing with the racial essence through faith in things unseen.

That might seem harsh, but what else would explain the appar-ent absence of concern about church/state separation when West, Dyson, and others rhapsodize about religion as the basis of genu-inely black political experience? Moreover, the effort to associate black legitimacy with the church is especially problematic now, when reactionary forces among black Americans are gaining steam precisely through church-based initiatives and jeremiads on the theme of moral crisis. These forces—in which church leaders are prominent—actively propagate moral and police repression as al-ternatives to humane social policy; calls for driving young people into churches, and jail if church fails, substitute for calls for job pro-grams and decent educational opportunity.

In Cleveland and elsewhere, multi-denominational groups of in-fluential black ministers have been agitating against gay-rights leg-islation, abortion, and gender equality. In many cities, black church-based groups are fighting sex education, contraceptives in the schools, and needle-exchange programs. And black church groups are becoming increasingly visible in the coalition of the Holy Roller Right.

Elevating church-based activity as most authentically black—besides overlooking the fact that *most* black people do not belong to any church—rationalizes the right's agenda of "privatization," and the ultimate dismantling of public functions. Encouraging church-based initiatives—which are inevitably inadequate responses to massive problems of state-supported dispossession—is part of the right's self-help program.

These are concerns that do not arise either in the patter of the left's black line-bearers or in response to them. They should be at a minimum, topics for strategic discussion, particularly in an other-wise rigorously secular left.

The prevailing take on black politics is part of a deep cynicism.

As we spin further and further away from mundane political struggles, there is ever less pressure on the star black voices to engage politics concretely. Instead of analysis of the way that black people and politics connect with the institutional exercise of power, we get either utterly predictable rehearsals of standard bromides and litanies — reminiscent of a Las Vegas act gone stale ("we need to build coalitions of the oppressed [here include a string of groups] that are multiracial but guard against racism, sexism, homophobia," et cetera, ad nauseam) — or the glib sophistries that fly under the "cultural-politics" flag.

Panegyrics on behalf of the intrinsic worth and significance of rap music, the repackaging of 1940s zoot suits and other youth fads as political opposition, incessant nattering about "positionality," representations in popular culture, and "voices" heard and silenced — these are by now formulaic exercises, as politically empty and wrong-headed as they are superficially clever. They replace in the left's public forum careful attention to the intricate social and institutional relations that shape black political resources and practice.

They also reduce to a discourse on how white people think about black people and how black people supposedly feel about it, buttressing a suspicion that this is all most whites care much about anyway, when it comes to deciphering what's up with black Americans.

So what can be done? Is there any useful way out of this situation I've described? The reflex is to lay out a detailed way of thinking about black people and politics. Until recently, I'd certainly have acted on that reflex. Now all it seems sensible to say is that the most important warrants are: (1) to insist on focusing discussion of black politics concretely, in relation to government, public policy, and political economy and (2) to presume that political dynamics operating among blacks are not totally alien, that is, they are understandable without the need for special native interpreters.

Beyond that we'll just have to wait and see what happens, won't we?

# —"What Are the Drums Saying, Booker?": The Curious Role of the Black Public Intellectual

In a typical episode of *Ramar of the Jungle*, an early television adventure series, the two heroes of the show spend most of their time on safari, attended to by a coterie of native bearers. Whenever they hear drums in the distance, the whites summon their head bearer. "Willie, what are the drums saying?" Willie, a Sancho Panza-like servant, steps forward. "Bwana, drums say simba come soon, much danger." On noticing a furtive sullenness among the bearers, the hero again inquires: "Willie, what's going on with the men?" Willie answers dutifully. "Men afraid. Say they don't want to go into Leopard Men territory, afraid of evil spirits."

In these vignettes, Willie was enacting the definitive role of the black public intellectual—interpreting the opaquely black heart of darkness for whites. Of course, this connection couldn't be observed at the time because the category "black public intellectual" didn't yet exist. It wasn't invented until nearly four decades later when several youngish black professors with ties to and visibility within the cultural studies/cultural politics precincts of the academic left began using it to refer to themselves and one another. This group includes most prominently Cornel West, Henry Louis Gates, Jr., Gloria Watkins (bell hooks), Michael Dyson, and Robin Kelley, though others in that world no doubt feel comfortable wearing the label. And people with varying professional and political affiliations—like Stanley Crouch, Stephen Carter, and Shelby Steele—increasingly turn up under the black public intellectual rubric, as the Warholian imperatives of fame send it rippling through the culture. But this identity is most clearly the product of the cultural wing of the left academy and its extramural offshoots.

In the last months of 1994 and early 1995, the notion gained greater currency. It has been addressed in successive articles by Michael Alan Bérubé in *The New Yorker* and Robert Boynton in *The Atlantic*, while Leon Wieseltier's right-for-the-wrong-reasons attack on Cornel West in *The New Republic* spawned commentary by James Ledbetter and Ellen Willis in the *Voice*. Although these white writers obviously didn't invent the black public intellectual identity, they certainly anointed it as a specific, notable status in upper-middle-brow American culture. Despite gestures in the direction of serious critical analysis, the Bérubé and Boynton essays are really press releases. Their explorations of their subjects' substantive output are thin and breezy. And I'm certain that not all of the individuals on Boynton's rather ecumenical list—the criterion for which seems to be "black people who write social commentary and are known to white elite institutions"—would embrace the black public intellectual label. But now that the concept has been formalized as a social type, it is useful to consider exactly what this phenomenon is, where it came from, and what it means.

The "public intellectual" notion emerged in 1987, when Russell Jacoby published *The Last Intellectuals*, which was in part a nostalgic exaltation of a previous cohort of politically engaged writers and critics. Jacoby contended that public intellectuals such as Dwight MacDonald, Irving Howe, Philip Rahv, and others were only marginally tied to the academy, and that their freedom from institutional constraint enabled them to fashion an autonomous, macroscopic view of American society and culture. The cohort of black people who call themselves black public intellectuals seem to suggest that they constitute a new social and political identity. But on closer examination, the role is all too familiar.

We might see today's black public intellectuals as lineal descendants of the authors of nineteenth-century slave narratives, if we understand those narratives as attempts to articulate a collective racial voice. The major difference is that slave narrators—with the partial exception of Frederick Douglass—did not attain celebrity as individuals. Rather, their public significance lay in embodying black people's collective capabilities.

The role of cellular representative reflected the prevailing view that a race's ideals are carried by its exceptional members. Personal attainment was less meaningful as a statement about the worth or prowess of the narrator than as a vindication of black humanity. Even the most accomplished authors or those whose odysseys had been most arduous or led to the greatest triumphs did not develop intensely *personal* followings. They remained primarily data points attesting to black possibility, and cogs in a larger abolitionist conversation.

The black public intellectual's more direct progenitor is Booker T. Washington, who turned the slave narrative into a saga of personal triumph befitting his era. In *Up From Slavery* (1901) Washington constructed a program and a rhetoric that promised group progress through acquiescence to white supremacy. He crafted it in the idiom of the gospel of personal enrichment then popular in both religious and secular (and often overlapping) forms. In presenting his tale of individual and group success through strength of character and perseverance, he simultaneously presented himself as a Horatio Alger figure and an Andrew Carnegie dipped in chocolate.

More than Douglass ever had been, Washington became the singular, trusted informant to communicate to whites what the Negro thought, felt, wanted, needed. Washington's stature derived from skill at soothing white liberals' *retreat* from the Reconstruction era's relatively progressive racial politics. He became the first purely freelance race spokesman; his status depended on designation by white elites rather than by any black electorate or social movement. To that extent he originated a new model of the generic Black Leader—the Racial Voice accountable to no clearly identifiable constituency among the spoken for.

What made this possible, and credible, was black Americans' expulsion from civic life. The role was unthinkable, even for a figure as prominent and respected as Douglass, during the first three decades after the Civil War because a culture of broad, democratic political participation flourished among black citizens. The obvious multiplicity of articulate black voices, from the local Union Leagues and Loyal Leagues to the United States Congress, would have immediately exposed as absurd the suggestion that any individual carried—or should carry—a blanket racial proxy. The idea of the free-floating race spokesman was a pathological effect of the disfranchisement specific to the segregation era, the condition to which Washington contributed.

Washington's paramountcy as bearer of the race's interests was always contested by other blacks, and no one claimed the mantle after him. In fact the fifty years between his death in 1915 and the final defeat of the Jim Crow regime were punctuated by periods of intense, politically engaged debate among black intellectuals. In addition to the famously vibrant discursive community of the 1920s, a lively current of engaged scholarship and commentary ran through the 1930s and 1940s, centered institutionally in the *Journal of Negro History*, the *Journal of Negro Education*, and Du Bois's *Phylon*. Participants in this community—which included humanists such as Sterling Brown, Jessie Fauset, Zora Neale Hurston, James Weldon Johnson, and John S. Lash, as well as such social scientists as Abram Harris, Charles S. Johnson, and Joseph Sandy Himes (novelist Chester's brother)—converged on such questions as the definition, status, and functions of black literature, the foundation of black identity, topical critiques of ideological programs and tendencies in social affairs, and the character and obligations of Afro-Americanist intellectual activity itself. Many, such as Ralph Bunche, E. Franklin Frazier, Doxey Wilkerson, and Oliver Cox, operated simultaneously in academic and activist domains. Others, like James Ford, A. Philip Randolph, and George Schuyler, functioned entirely outside the academy.

Cold War antiradicalism and the apparent successes of an atheoretical, desegregationist politics narrowed the scope and blunted the critical edge of black intellectual discourse in the 1950s, although Baldwin and Ellison pushed against the boundaries of convention. And civil rights activism soon created its own eddies of debate and commentary. From the mid 1960s to the late 1970s another wave of engaged political and cultural critique defined black intellectual life; this movement was sustained most visibly in the *Negro Digest* (later *Black World*) and *The Black Scholar*, but it was propelled as much through ephemeral, samizdat-like writing (for example, Amiri Baraka's paper, "Why I Changed My Ideology"). More directly tied to activist politics, this pattern of debate was more sharply contentious and aggressively oppositional (and perhaps less sophisticated) than that of the interwar years.

Each of these discursive moments, however, was haunted by the problem of speaking for the race—how to delineate the characteristics and warrants of black leadership, how to authenticate it, the difficulties associated with assuming the racial voice, the conundrum of undertaking social or cultural criticism without accepting the role of race spokesperson. Bunche and Cox tried to generate a rigorous critique of prevailing styles of political leadership. Baldwin and Ellison strained mightily to comment on topical issues in a racially conscious way while rejecting designation as black spokesmen. All these concerns are responses to the conventional presumption—Washington's unacknowledged legacy in the modern era—that any black individual's participation in public life always strives to express the will of the racial collectivity.

This presumption in turn reflects an important complication facing black intellectuals; they need to address both black and white audiences, and those different acts of communication proceed from objectives that are distinct and often incompatible. James Weldon Johnson identified this peculiar burden in a 1928 essay "The Dilemma of the Negro Author," noting that black writers face "more than a double audience; it is a divided audience made up of two elements with differing and often quite opposite and antagonistic points of view." Although Johnson focused primarily on creative writing, his observation that the white audience's biases dispose black authors toward a "defensive and exculpatory literature" applies more generally. Historian Lawrence D. Reddick and the philosopher William T. Fontaine in the '30s and '40s similarly complained of the "defense psychology" of black scholars, maintaining that it undermines examination of the black experience by grounding Afro-Americanist inquiry in the narrow, other-directed objective of demonstrating black people's equal humanity.

\*　　\*　　\*

Those who now describe themselves as black public intellectuals diverge significantly from the rich history of black commentary. Their differences speak to the character of our time and the changes in black intellectual life ensuing from the passage of the segregation era. The contemporary public intellectuals are unique in that they exhibit little sense of debate or controversy among themselves as a cohort. To the contrary, they seem rather to come together as a publicist's delight, a hyperbolically log-rolling lovefest. Watkins and West gush over each other's nonpareil brilliance; Gates proclaims West "the preeminent African-American intellectual of our generation"; and Gates, West, and Kelley lavish world-historical superlatives on Dyson, who, naturally enough, expresses comparable judgments about them. Their anthologies and conferences feature no sharp disagreements. Instead, they function as a kind of Tuskegee Machine by committee. Their political utterances exude pro forma moralism, not passion. Their critiques are only easy pronouncements against racism, sexism, homophobia, anti-Semitism or equally easy dissent from a lame Afrocentricity that has no adherents among their audience anyway.

The point is not that controversy by itself makes for purity or legitimacy but that in this instance at least, the absence of controversy betrays a lack of critical content and purpose. The stance of these black public intellectuals is by and large just that—not a stand but a posture. Can the reader familiar with their work recall without hesitation a specific critique, a concrete formulation—an extended argument that is neither airily abstract nor cozily compatible with what passes for common sense at the moment? I'd bet not, because in this arena prominence of author counts more than weight of utterance.

The posture of the black public intellectual is a claim to speak from the edges of convention, to infuse mainstream discourse with a particular "counterhegemonic" perspective at least implicitly linked to one's connectedness to identifiably black sensibilities or interests. It is also therefore, again at least implicitly, a claim to immersion in a strategic conversation among black Americans about politics, culture, and social affairs. The posture is flimflam that elides the dual audience problem.

To expand on Johnson's initial formulation, for the black audience the focus of critical intellectual activity is—or should be—on careful, tough-minded examination of the multifarious dynamics shaping black social life. To that extent, the black intellectual positions herself metaphorically at the boundary of the black experience and faces in, establishing enough distance to get a broad perspective but intent on contributing to a conversation that presumes not only intricate knowledge but also an interpretive orientation filtered through shared, racially inflected assumptions that inform strategic thinking. The racially and politically attentive black intellectual is in this sense engaged in a discourse of group self-examination.

In addressing the white audience, the task remains all too much explaining the mysteries of black America. For that project one still positions oneself on the metaphorical boundary of the Bantustan, but facing outward. This is why there isn't much attention to flux, differentiation, contingency, or even analysis of social process in our public intellectuals' accounts of black life; you don't see nuances with your back turned, and besides that sort of messy texture doesn't count for much because the white audience mainly just wants the executive summary anyway. Why do they act that way? How can I keep from gratuitously offending my coworkers or housekeeper? What do the drums say, Cornel?

The different objectives involved in addressing the two audiences become more important in the post–Jim Crow world. The demise of *Black World* and atrophy of *The Black Scholar* both fuel and reflect the shriveling of an autonomous domain for black debate. At the same time, the opening up of employment opportunities at elite academic institutions has increased the likelihood that black intellectuals operate in multiracial discursive networks and has greatly enhanced the visibility of a lucky few. Therefore, white forums, particularly those associated with the left, have become the primary arenas for elaboration of black commentary and critical public discourse, which makes a principled self-consciousness in negotiating the two audiences all the more essential. But the discursive space constructed by the black public intellectuals either conflates the audiences into an unhelpful least common denominator or undertakes a misdirection in combining an insider's "it's a black thang" posture with a superficial, other-directed analysis explaining or defending the Negro. The result is an all-purpose message, equally suitable for corporate boards, rarefied academic conferences, White House dinners, and common folk. And, unsurprisingly, the white audience overwhelms and sets the terms for the black, repeating an ironic pattern begun with Washington.

Traditionally, engaged black intellectuals have also addressed a third audience—a transracial community of progressive activists. This is a pattern that can be seen from the abolitionist Douglass through the middle-aged and elderly Du Bois, the young Bunche and others in his cohort, down to Lani Guinier, Julian Bond, and hosts of others less well known. They haven't functioned as interpreters of an esoteric black experience or bearers of a "black position" or as itinerant Moral Voices, but as participants in a common debate aimed at stimulating, directing, and taking political action.

Where Baldwin and Ellison bristled at the Black Voice designation, today's public intellectuals accept it gladly. And they have to, because maintaining credibility with their real, white audience requires that they be authentically black, that their reports on the heart of darkness ring with verisimilitude. ("Drums say nihilism, moral breakdown. Need politics of conversion, love ethic.") This underscores the extent to which—beneath all the over-heated academic trendiness—the black public intellectual stance merely updates Booker T. Washington's role, but without the institutional trappings and, for the moment at least, without the power.

As with Washington, the public intellectual's authenticity is conferred by white opinion makers. The typical trajectory of stardom is instructive. First, one becomes recognized as a Black Voice in the intellectual apparatus of the left, which—out of a combination of good intentions and bad faith—stands ever ready to confer prominence on any reasonable articulate black person willing to associate with it. To qualify, one need not even put forward a critique that seems leftist by usual standards: secular, rooted in political economy, focused on stimulating political mobilization. After all,

the "black community" is different, has different needs, etc. Reputation spreads, and eventually opportunities present themselves to
cross over from the left intellectual ghetto to the status of Black
Voice for the mainstream. All it takes is the courage to square off in
the white public sphere against black anti-Semitism on the Anti-
Defamation League's terms, or to join the chorus lamenting the putative social pathology of the inner city. Not to mention a knack for
packaging the center-right wisdom of the moment as well-
considered, yet bold and personally risky challenge to convention.
This is the path blazed so far by Gates and West, and Dyson, as
usual, is bringing his best Pigmeat-Markham-Meets-Baudrillard act
along behind.

The consummate irony of the puffery is that it is misdirected all the
way through. Jacoby's archetype is only weakly connected to the
bureaucratized intellectual life of the academy. His public intellectual figures in a critique of the politically corrosive effects of the left's
having settled into the university after the collapse of extramural
radicalism. But those now wearing the black public intellectual tag
as a red, black, and green badge of courage are not only deeply embedded in the higher reaches of the academic celebrity system, they
are also its unalloyed products. This brute fact is obscured by another flimflam—what we might call the Proudhon Scam. Marx
quipped that the anarchist Pierre-Joseph Proudhon represented
himself in Germany, where they didn't know much political
economy, as a political economist, and in France, where they didn't
know much philosophy, as a philosopher. West, Dyson, et al., use
the public intellectual pose to claim authority both as certified,
world-class elite academics and as links to an extra-academic
blackness, thus splitting the difference between being insiders and
outsiders. In the process, they are able to skirt the practical requirements of either role—to avoid both rigorous, careful intellectual
work *and* protracted, committed political action.

Gates is the most complicated, most intellectually probing, and
most consistent of the group. Unlike the others, he makes no pretense of being a conduit to some sort of grassroots black authenticity. He has publicly criticized the notion that there are leaders who

are singular representatives of the race. His position is perhaps most like that of Bayard Rustin, as a freelance advocate for black political centrism. Like Rustin, Gates has without equivocation chosen as the forum for his advocacy the largely white circles of elite opinion, most conspicuously as a staff writer for *The New Yorker*. A significant difference is that Rustin in his last years was primarily an arbiter of the boundaries of "responsible" black spokesmanship for the right wing of the Democratic Party coalition. Gates also sometimes functions as an arbiter of black political etiquette, but he is more actively concerned with articulating the voice of an autonomously black, self-consciously petit-bourgeois centrism.

West's program is less coherent and less concrete than Gates's. He has postured as a link to black activist authenticity, holding an honorary leadership position in the Democratic Socialists of America and referring frequently to associations with supposed grassroots leaders and organizations. At the same time, he has no particular history of concrete political practice or affiliation and has shown no reticence about operating as a freelance race relations consultant and Moral Voice for white elites. Most of all, the substance of his public commentary — when it descends from sonorous platitudes and well-hedged abstractions — is, to resuscitate an old slogan, "left in form, right in essence." As Stephen Steinberg has demonstrated in a thorough and powerful critique in the summer 1994 issue of *New Politics*, West's interpretation of contemporary social and political life derives directly and definitively from Daniel Patrick Moynihan's scurrilous arguments about black pathology.

Kelley's *Hammer and Hoe* (1990), about black communists in 1930s Alabama, is a credible piece of scholarship. But too often with Kelley, politics reduces to the academic pose, the combined stance of acting out flamboyantly crafted rituals of "blackness" in conventional settings and spinning narratives that ultimately demean concerted political action by claiming to find it everywhere. Dyson and Watkins/hooks are little more than hustlers, blending bombast, clichés, psychobabble, and lame guilt tripping in service to the "pay me" principle. Dyson, for instance, has managed to say absolutely nothing in a string of *New York Times* op-ed pieces.

"Public intellectual" is by and large an excuse, the marker of a sterile, hybrid variant of "bearing witness" that, when all is said and done, is a justification for an aversion to intellectual or political heavy lifting—a pretentious name for highfalutin babble about the movie you just saw or the rhyme you just heard on the radio. In its intimations of always being from and on the way to the other place, the label is an admission and exaltation of *dis*connectdness, a notion of the critical intellectual as Galahad or High Plains Drifter that is the opposite of rootedness in a discourse community. That is why this cohort's discussion of themselves and others seem so much like attempts to create all-star lineups—the greatest this, the most brilliant that, the preeminent other. They're more like the Super Friends than the Frankfurt School or the Howard University social scientists of the 1930s.

There's a lot about his charade that is distasteful, but one feature makes it especially hard to take. The dialectics of authentication trades on elaborate displays of what sociolinguists call code switching—in this case, going back and forth from rarefied theoreticism to slivers of one or another version of black vernacular expression. In academic lectures and scholarly writing, Kelley can "send a shout out" in the *Journal of American History* while dragging Gramsci to the root doctor and holy roller church. Dyson finds Michael Jackson's "postmodern spirituality" and in lectures lacks only for cork; West loads up on Continental theory to explain why the music he listened to in his undergraduate dorm is the apotheosis of black culture and why poor people need moral rearmament. When we consider that these performances are directed to white audiences, their minstrel quality stands out as especially distasteful because it masquerades as being in touch with the latest wrinkles of refined black hipness. This, admittedly, puts off those affronted by coon shows.

More significantly, the public intellectuals' style has baleful effects on the scholarly examination of black American life. In rejecting all considerations of standards of evidence and argument as expressions of naïve positivism, the cultural politicians get to make the story up as they go along. Graduate students can figure out that this gambit has two very attractive features: it drastically reduces the quantity of digging and thinking one has to do, and it clears the path to public visibility and academic recognition. Of course, it's not as if black public intellectuals were the only hustlers in an academic world largely defined by the politics of reputation; and all in all it's good that black people are getting paid, too. So why should anyone be concerned? The answer is that the public intellectuals cohere around a more or less deceptively conservative politics that is particularly dangerous at this moment in our history.

Political conservatism is fundamental to the Black Voice business now no less than in 1895, and Stanley Crouch and Shelby Steele have shown that it is sometimes the sole requirement. One can qualify for the job only by giving white opinion makers a heavy dose of what they want to hear. Gates didn't get to be a world-class Black Voice until he denounced the bogey of "black anti-Semitism" all over the op-ed page of *The New York Times* and went on to reassure *Forbes*'s readership, that "yes, there is a culture of poverty," calling up the image of a "sixteen-year-old mother, a thirty-two-year-old grandmother and a forty-eight-year-old great-grandmother," noting for good measure that "It's also true that not everyone in any society wants to work, that not all people are equally motivated. There! Was that so hard to say?" He has since secured his public intellectuality in a series of essays in *The New Republic* and elsewhere whose main point is to endorse the "vital center," and he extols the lost Jim Crow world in *Colored People*, a memoir that could have been titled *Up From Slavery on Lake Wobegon*. West's conservative moralism and victim blaming has made him Bill Bradley's favorite conduit to the Mind of the Negro and a hit on the business school lecture circuit.

Most insidious, though, is the retrograde sham that masquerades as a leftist "cultural politics." Rather than an alternative, deep structural "infra" politics, as Kelley and others contend, the cultural politics focus is a quietistic alternative to real political analysis. It boils down to nothing more than an insistence that authentic, meaningful political engagement for black Americans is expressed not in relation to the institutions of public authority—the state—or the workplace—but in the clandestine significance assigned to apparently apolitical rituals. Black people, according to this logic, don't mobilize through overt collective action. They do it surreptitiously when they look like they're just dancing, or as a colleague of mine ironically described it, "dressing for resistance." In a *Journal of American History* article, supposedly about black working-class opposition, Kelley asks rhetorically: "If a worker turns to a root doctor or prayer rather than to a labor union to make an employer less evil, is that 'false consciousness'?" He compares a conjuror's power favorably to that of the CIO, the Populists, and the NAACP.

This is don't-worry, be-happy politics. Resistance flows from life by definition. There is no need to try to create it because it's all around us; all we have to do is change the way we define things. Then we can just celebrate the people's spontaneous infrapolitics and show white people how to find it and point out to them that Gramscianism is an African survival. We can make radical politics by climbing the tenure ladder and feeling good about our collective black selves through the pride of vicarious identification with the embedded theoretical sophistication of the folk.

Worst of all, though, the black public intellectual stance derives from and presumes a condition of political demobilization. And for good reason. The posture of the Racial Voice requires—and, as the centennial of Washington's perfidy should remind us, helps to produce—a black population that is disfranchised and incapable of articulating its own agendas as a citizenry. Thus the black intellectuals' insistence on defining politics centered in the exercise of state power as inauthentic, which in turn underwrites all the Aesopian interpretive twaddle in black cultural studies. (Interestingly, in chastising proponents of codes prohibiting hate speech, Gates has complained self-righteously about an identity politics that pays no attention to public policy. His point would go down better if it came with a little self-criticism from one whose scholarly reputation—supposedly the source of his prominence—is based on precisely the view that he disparages.)

Before disfranchisement in the South black people didn't have to express their politics surreptitiously; they crafted and fought to realize their agendas through public policy, and after disfranchisement they fought for sixty years to be reenfranchised so they could do it again. And the record of overt black political action outside the South is unbroken. What the current environment demands from black intellectuals who would comment on public affairs is not more whining about disparagement of the "black body" in Western culture (as if that were news) or examination of representations of representations or noodling about how, if we apply the right spin, everything black people do is resistance to oppression. And most of all there is no need for interpretations that presume an uncomplicated, conveniently mute black reality; there's already a surfeit of analysis propelled by the collective black subject—"black people want, feel, etc." As is true on the left generally, what is desperately called for is stimulation of informed discussion among black Americans, and between blacks and others, that presumes proprietorship of the institutions of governance and policy processes on an identical basis with other citizens and aims at crafting agendas that define and realize black interests accordingly. We should be in the forefront of the fight against ratification of the balanced budget amendment, crafting responses to so-called tort reform, fighting corporate globalization, and finding ways to counter the assault on the Bill of Rights.

The cultural politicians' fixation on youth definitively illustrates their bankruptcy. Not only are young people the least connected, the most alienated, and the least politically attentive cohort of the black population, they're also the ones whites are most interested in. "Willie, why do they have those welfare babies? What must we do so that they won't take my car stereo?" What a felicitous coincidence.

*—Part Two*

# EQUALITY &
# IDEOLOGY IN
# AMERICAN POLITICS

# —The Underclass Myth

In recent years the image of an urban "underclass" has become the central representation of poverty in American society. In less than a decade the underclass took hold of the public imagination, and came to shape policymakers' agendas concerning issues of race, urban decay, and social welfare. But what is the underclass? What is so compelling about that image? What is its significance in American political life?

The underclass idea rests on fuzzy and disturbing assumptions about poor people, poverty, and the world in which both are reproduced. Those assumptions amount to tacit—and sometimes explicit—claims regarding the defective nature of poor people's motivations, moral character, and behavior. They appeal to hoary prejudices of race, gender, and class which give the upper-class image instant acceptance and verisimilitude even though it is ambiguous and inconsistent on its own terms.

Right-wing, mean-spirited beliefs about poor people have come to suffuse even self-consciously liberal, technocratic policy discussion. Such supposed "friends of the poor" as Charles Murray, Lawrence Mead, Nicholas Lemann, Mickey Kaus, Thomas Sowell, Walter Williams, Robert Woodson, and Glen Loury assume the need to correct, or at least to take into account, poor people's defective tendencies as an essential limit on social policy. The reactionary, purely ideological foundation of the underclass idea becomes clear on close examination.

Although the term has been around for longer, it caught fire in popular and academic circles after Ken Auletta canonized it in 1982 in *The Underclass*, a journalistic, mock-ethnographic essay originally serialized in *The New Yorker*.

Auletta began by joining "poverty" and "antisocial behavior" as equivalent qualifications for underclass status. "The underclass need not be poor—street criminals, for instance, usually are not," he wrote. "The underclass usually operates outside the generally accepted boundaries of society. They are often set apart by their 'deviant' or antisocial behavior, by their bad habits, not just their poverty."

Auletta mused that we might not want to include those who "actually earn a living in the underground economy" and maybe "add illegal, or undocumented aliens," and he wondered whether "those with serious mental illness [should] be counted." In a pinch, for a quick, quasi-empirical referent, however, he called up the holy trinity of "welfare mothers, ex-convicts, and drug addicts."

For Mickey Kaus, writing in *The New Republic*, the underclass is the "black lower class" for whom "the work ethic has evaporated and the entrepreneurial drive is channeled into gangs and drug-pushing." Culture figures prominently in Kaus's outlook. In addition to the culture of poverty, he asserts the existence of a "single-parent culture," a "welfare culture," a "culture of single motherhood" (presumably a more specific articulation of the single-parent culture), a "working, taxpaying culture," and a "work-ethic culture."

Nicholas Lemann never tells us exactly how we can identify a member of his underclass. In his nearest attempt at definition, he simply announces that "blacks are splitting into a middle class and an underclass that seems likely never to make it." He tells us that the underclass suffers from a "strongly self-defeating culture" which has its roots in the sharecrop system and whose centerpiece seems to be out-of-wedlock birth. That, however, is as precise as Lemann gets. He does volunteer, though, that this ghetto culture is "venerable" and "disorganized" and that its members need training in some equally vague "bourgeois values."

Within four months of publication of Kaus's and Lemann's articles, Richard Nathan, then of Princeton's prestigious Woodrow Wilson School, declared it was time to shut off debate about the usefulness, empirical soundness, or implications of the underclass notion. We should, he suggested, follow the media in using the term "as a shorthand expression of the concentration of economic and behavioral problems among racial minorities (mainly black and Hispanic) in large, older cities." This underclass is "not just a function of being poor. It involves geography and behavior."

Isabel Sawhill, senior fellow at the Urban Institute, similarly proceeds from the authoritative imagery of "television and newspaper stories" which document the existence of the underclass. Again, the underclass's behavior is its "most distinctive, most interesting, and most troubling" characteristic.

The underclass appeals entirely as a powerful metaphor; its resonance has far outpaced its empirical content, and it has thrived as a concept in search of its object. Most who find the notion attractive agree that the underclass is mainly urban and largely nonwhite. They typically agree as well that it constitutes approximately 10 to 20 percent of the poverty population. That percentage, however, is produced by sleight of hand. The number, glibly repeated by journalists and professional statisticians of poverty, has become the consensual estimate without justificatory argument.

The ultimate source of this estimate, instructively, may be Oscar Lewis, *auteur* of the "culture of poverty," the last generation's effort to ground a behavioral focus on poverty in the authority of social science. Lewis speculated that "about 20 percent of the population below the poverty line" fell into his poverty culture. But his speculation had no sounder basis than contemporary punditry. He characterized it as a belief and a "rough guess" and offered no supporting evidence or argument.

Despite the consensus on the size of the underclass, it is not clear exactly what joins the various aggregations of people said to constitute the underclass. What makes street crime and teen pregnancy signifiers of a common population? Does participation in an underground economy not suggest just the opposite of an evaporated work ethic? How exactly does out-of-wedlock birth become an instance of social pathology?

If a thirty-five-year-old lawyer decides to have a baby without seal of approval from church or state or enduring male affiliation, we do not consider her to be acting pathologically; we may even laud her independence and refusal to knuckle under to patriarchal conventions. Why does such a birth become pathological when it occurs in the maternity ward in Lincoln Hospital in the South Bronx, say, rather than within the pastel walls of an alternative birthing center?

If a woman's decision expresses pathology because she makes it in poverty, then we have fallen into a tautology; she is poor because she is pathological because she is poor.

Part of the problem stems from reliance on mystical assumptions about class, attitudes, behavior, values, and culture. Underclass constructions revise the old nature/culture dichotomy, in which "culture" stood for the principle of human plasticity and adaptation—in the old, Enlightenment view, the agency of progress. Instead, the power of the underclass idea derives from its naturalization of "culture" as an independent force that undermines adaptability and retards progress.

Culture-of-poverty ideology resuscitates the idea of cultural lag, itself a vestige of antique notions of racial temperament.

The underclass image proceeds from a view of class in general that strikingly resembles Victorian convention. Victorians often used "class" and "race" interchangeably; each category was seen as innate. Class and race essences generally were thought to include—in addition to distinctive physiognomy—values, attitudes, and behavior. Thus, Victorian fiction commonly featured characters in humble circumstances who, though unaware of their true, genteel natal origins, always felt ill at ease or out of place among their coarse fellows, as well as other characters whose base derivations, unknown even to themselves, nonetheless brought them low in polite society.

The Victorian resonances come out in the rhetorical moves and chains of inference current culture-of-poverty thinkers employ as they seek to construct meticulous, apparently social-scientific descriptions of an objectively existing underclass.

Richard Nathan, for example, might be able to adduce evidence supporting his contentions about the prevalence of crime, prostitution, drugs, long-term welfare use, and homelessness, but "lack of will and commitment to get an education or a regular job" cannot be ascertained from the data at his disposal. On what does he base that inference? He avoids justifying it by slipping it into a list of categories for which he could marshal plausible evidence. Isabel Sawhill suggests that as dysfunctional behaviors "become commonplace, they are likely to become more acceptable." Both scholars presume to know people's motivations without interviewing them or taking account of their self-understandings.

The problem is compounded by another subtle but critical elision: the assumption that census tracts are synonymous with neighborhoods. Analysis of aggregate socioeconomic and demographic characteristics from census tracts does not inform our understanding of patterns of interaction or the character of norms, values, and aspirations in a group of people who live together. Nevertheless, the elision has become institutionalized in the poverty-research industry, and debate occurs now only over which batches of indicators and what thresholds of them most satisfactorily mark an underclass area.

Those laundry lists of characteristics also entail a questionable extension of the category "behavior" to phenomena that might only indirectly be products of human agency. Female household-heading, for example, can result from a number of circumstances entirely beyond the control of women whose lives are compressed into that label. The same applies to unemployment or underemployment, and even long-term status as a welfare recipient can stem completely from impersonal forces. Characterizing those phenomena as behavior reveals a zeal for validating the underclass concept, and a fundamental inclination to seek the sources of poverty in deficiencies of individuals.

All versions of the underclass notion center on the behavior of its categorical members, though liberals typically hedge with genuflections toward the ultimate weight of historical or structural forces. (The differences on that score, however, are not great. Conservatives also frequently genuflect toward structural pressures and past oppression before enunciating one or another brand of tough-love remedy for the present.)

Why, though, does the underclass idea appeal so powerfully to people—including disciplined scholars—even as they must perform elaborate, dubious maneuvers to define it?

Some of the notion's popularity is driven by the sociology of the policy research community. Technocratic discourse and methods nurture ideas that depoliticize the frame for examining social problems. The underclass formulation is attractive precisely because it does not exist as anyone's self-description. It is purely a statistical artifact, and therefore exclusively the creation and property of its chroniclers.

The underclass notion also appeals to several ideological dispositions. Most immediately it resonates with the ahistorical individualism rampant in the Reagan/Bush/Clinton era. As a corollary, it is attractive to many petit bourgeois blacks because it flatters their success by comparison and, through the insipid role model rhetoric, allows fawning over the allegedly special, tutelary role of the black middle class.

The idea of a behaviorally defined underclass also affirms an ensemble of racial and class prejudices that lurk beneath an apparently innocuous, certainly stupid tendency to reduce the social world to aggregates of good people and bad people. Simply, good people are people like "us"; bad people are not, and the same behavior is assessed differently depending on the category into which the perpetrator falls.

An eighteen-year-old drug courier with a monogrammed BMW is pathological; an arbitrageur who strays too far onto the wrong side of legality, is too clever for his own good—the stuff of tragedy. Dependency on AFDC breeds sloth and pathology; dependency on military contracts, tax abatements, or FHA loans does a patriotic service for the country, incubates family values, and so forth.

Finally, the underclass notion may receive the greatest ideological boost from pure sexism. For drug-crazed, lawless black and Hispanic men, the companion image is the so-called "cycle of poverty," which focuses on women's living and reproductive practices as the transmission belt that drives the cycle.

The rhetoric of "family values," and of "disorganization," "deterioration," and "disintegration" stigmatizes female-headed households, which now are home to a majority of American children, and applies a hierarchy of propriety to the conjugal arrangements within which women might give birth. Of the master list of empirical indicators of pathology, most are observable only in women.

We are already seeing the policy fruit that this imagery bears. A judge in Kansas City has ordered children to use their absent fathers' names, presumably to strengthen obligation by establishing ownership. A Kansas state legislator has argued that impoverished women should be induced to accept Norplant birth-control implants as a way to hold down welfare costs and cut the size of the recipient population.

State welfare departments have taken up marriage brokering, as in a Wisconsin plan to offer cash inducements for women who marry their way off AFDC and to cut benefits for "unwed teenage mothers." These moves demonstrate unambiguously the repressive, antifeminist outlook lurking beneath the focus on family. (In 1996, this repressive impetus culminated in Congress's passage of the Personal Responsibility and Work Opportunity Reconciliation Act, which eliminated AFDC. The Act was signed by President Clinton, who boasted that it was the fulfillment of his 1992 campaign pledge to "end welfare as we know it.")

How, then, should we talk about those who are stigmatized as the "underclass"? First, it is imperative to reject all assumptions that poor people are behaviorally or attitudinally different from the rest of American society. Some percentage of *all* Americans take drugs, fight in families, and abuse or neglect children. If the behavior exists across lines of class, race, and opportunity, then it cannot reasonably be held to produce poverty. If it does not *cause* poverty, therefore, we do not need to focus on it at all in the context of policy-oriented discussion about poverty.

We should also fight against lurid, exploitative journalism that reproduces obnoxious class and racial prejudices. And we should be prepared to recognize the extent to which such prejudices infiltrate even ostensibly more careful, allegedly sympathetic depictions and expose them for what they are.

Affirmatively, we should insist on returning the focus of the discussion of the production and reproduction of poverty to examination of its sources in the operations of the American political and economic system. Specifically, the discussion should focus on such phenomena as the logic of deindustrialization, models of urban redevelopment driven by real-estate speculation, the general intensification of polarization of wealth, income, and opportunity in

American society, the ways in which race and gender figure into those dynamics, and, not least, the role of public policy in reproducing and legitimating them.

Moreover, we should fight for policy changes that will open opportunity structures: support for improving access to jobs, housing, schooling, real drug rehabilitation of the sort available to the relatively well-off. A focus on behavior, after all, leads into a blind alley in policy terms. If we say that poor people are poor because they have bad values, we let government off the hook, even though conscious government policy—for example, in the relations between support for metropolitan real estate speculation and increasing homelessness, malnutrition, and infant mortality—is directly implicated in causing poverty.

Finally, with respect to the litany of moral repressiveness that seems to be obligatory these days, I want the record to show that I do not want to hear another word about drugs or crime without hearing in the same breath about decent jobs, adequate housing, and egalitarian education.

# —Pimping Poverty, Then and Now

On May 20, 1994, we saw the creation of a new avatar of welfare fraud, a black woman in New York City accused of receiving $450,000 in public aid illegally (through a number of fictitious identities and nonexistent children) over a seven-year period. The story of the alleged culprit—complete with photos and videotape of her being led, handcuffed, to her arraignment—was splashed sensationally over *The New York Times* and television network news, as well as local media. Several aspects of this spectacle, which seems to have evaporated as suddenly as it appeared, are worthy of note.

For one thing, the media representations update the old "welfare queen" imagery. A decade of underclass rhetoric has melded black poverty and criminality. The "welfare queen" no longer rides, Amos 'n' Andy–like, joyfully in her Cadillac; she is now sullen, foreboding, and shackled, like her brother, Willie Horton.

The episode also highlights the way the news industry and government institutions can collaborate to shape public consciousness. How did the news media get videotape of the suspect in police custody? How did they even know about the arrest so soon?

The incident coincided with Mayor Rudolph Giuliani's and Manhattan District Attorney Robert Morgethau's efforts to install a mandatory system of electronic fingerprinting of welfare recipients in New York. A willing news industry thus becomes part of the public-relations campaign in support of such initiatives.

There is also the matter of definition of welfare fraud. Ultimately, any public policy is intended to enhance or preserve the social welfare. Yet only certain policy areas and programs—usually those that disproportionately benefit stigmatized groups—attain the social-welfare label. When we expand the definition of social welfare to include the billions siphoned off routinely in sweetheart contracts, pork-barrel projects, special tax breaks, and the like—not to mention Pentagon waste and the scandals in the banking and savings-

and-loan industry and the Department of Housing and Urban Development—the magnitude of the fraud in this sensationalized case scarcely warrants a blurb in the B section.

A one-on-one comparison is also revealing. Less than two weeks after the welfare-fraud story, Representative Dan Rostenkowski, Democrat of Illinois, was indicted for having defrauded the Federal Government of at least $760,000 over two decades. Unlike the new welfare queen, Rostenkowski was neither handcuffed nor denied bail. His situation has been framed in the media as a tragedy as much as a crime. Coverage has devoted considerable attention to the complexity of his character, a humanizing and mitigating focus absolutely missing from the other case.

Discovery and propagation of the new welfare-fraud story stimulate another comparison. Shortly after I began teaching at Northwestern University, I attended a long-range planning meeting at the Center for Urban Affairs and Policy Research, of which I had been a fellow since joining the faculty there. As the discussion among my new colleagues focused on the need to anticipate and craft projects fitting funding agencies' research priorities, I found myself overtaken by a curious sense of déjà vu. Gradually, I realized that the discussion reminded me almost exactly of Community Action agency staff and board meetings in the late 1960s and early 1970s. It reminded me, that is, of the mindset and practices that gave rise to the phrase "pimping poverty."

Poverty pimping, generally speaking, was another form of at least de facto welfare fraud. It connoted the pursuit of narrow personal gain under the guise of fighting poverty. It implied the hypocritical appropriation by relatively well-off people, usually as program functionaries or putative spokespersons, of public and philanthropic resources designated for improving the lives of the poor. It was more or less tawdry, distasteful, and reprehensible. In an imperfect world, it was also inevitable that some people would seek out opportunities for corruption.

And that corruption included a political opportunism and dishonesty that, beneath superficially militant rhetoric (the "mau mau" scam immortalized by Tom Wolfe), actually impeded and undermined advancement of poor people's interests. The typical move was to demand payoffs in exchange for acquiescing to ruling elites' regressive agendas (for example, urban renewal plans that would displace poor people, or cuts in public spending). The legitimacy and visibility derived through connection to official antipoverty institutions, moreover, made it easier to enforce that kind of acquiescent politics.

Poverty pimping required collusion by the government and philanthropic elites who controlled purse strings and defined both the nature of material incentives and the rules of the game. Arguments from such apologists for the Democratic Leadership Council as Theda Skocpol, Thomas Edsall, and William Julius Wilson that black militants hijacked Federal antipoverty efforts are absurd, disingenuous attempts to justify retreat from egalitarian ideals.

The style developed because granting agencies allowed it to. They rewarded poverty pimping while at the same time rejecting more genuinely redistributive initiatives. Having steered antipoverty politics relentlessly toward narrow opportunism, those elites and their intellectual housepets now cite that narrow opportunism as the all-purpose cause of the failure of 1960s activism, the collapse of the Democratic coalition, white racism, and whatever else comes to mind.

The key characteristic of 1960s poverty pimping—apart from its venal substance, of course—is that it was a fundamentally accommodationist politics that sought credibility through a racial or activist patina. The world of official antipoverty programs developed as a response to popular activism and agitation for democratic redistribution of wealth. Poverty pimps' spurious claims to broker the interests of "the people" were therefore important for elites' legitimacy as well.

Not anymore. The climate of the 1960s and the structure of antipoverty programs dictated that the benefits of poverty-pimping trickle down a tad. Cooptation of grass-roots activists meant that the occasional AFDC recipient or public-housing resident would enjoy real upward mobility. Right-wing state legislator Polly Williams in Milwaukee is one example of that trickle-down effect. Democratic Representative Maxine Waters of Los Angeles is another. Similar, if less dramatic, cases exist in virtually every big city.

In the sixties, poverty pimping enacted a perverse model of egalitarian redistribution that was both extremely limited and predicated on leaving larger structures of inequality intact.

Sitting in that seminar room in the fall of 1991, I realized that I was witnessing the familiar impulse to turn poverty into an opportunity for personal gain. But it was also immediately clear that the minions of the poverty-research industry have redefined poverty pimping. No longer does the pimp claim to be an authentic representative of the poor. No one cares much anymore what poor people think or want or need. Again, a decade of underclass ideology has denied poor people any human agency in social-policy discourse. They exist only as a problem to be handled, more or less dangerous and alien objects of administration.

What we have now is neoliberal poverty pimping. Technical expertise is the new criterion of authenticity; policy-wonk technospeak has replaced the mau mau. That means, of course, that the qualifications for entry into the pimping profession have changed. One now needs to hold a doctorate, preferably in economics or the quantitative branches of sociology—or at least to be conversant with them and to have mastered the four essential hedging judgments of poverty research: 1) some do, some don't; 2) the differences aren't all that great; 3) it's more complicated than that; and most of all, 4) further research is needed.

I remember an earlier seminar—my first real exposure to the inner circles of the poverty-research biz—on scholarship in progress on teenaged childbearing, held at the Commonwealth Fund in New York, which was funding the research. Frank Furstenberg, a University of Pennsylvania sociologist and captain of the teen-pregnancy industry, and Gilbert Steiner, Mr. Family Policy at the then–nominally liberal Brookings Institution, responded to every single attempt to make general statements about the issue (presumably a necessity for crafting any social policy) with haughty combinations of hedging responses 3 and 4. All roads, it seems, lead to poverty researchers getting paid, and not very far beyond.

As I looked around the room at Northwestern during my epiphany, it was striking that the group was almost all white, almost all male, and all middle-class. And Northwestern's cohort accurately represents the social composition of the larger poverty-research industry. The neoliberal poverty pimps' status underwrites the disgustingly smug, self-righteous, third-person discourse that dehumanizes and disparages poor people. It also reflects the elimination of even the perverse egalitarianism of the old school of pimping.

Long gone are the days when a clever, entrepreneurially inclined person might use antipoverty programs and rhetoric as an individual route up from the projects or AFDC. Apart from a very small handful of Potemkin success stories cynically propagated by Republican ideologues (sometimes operating under the Democratic label), the field now belongs to the academics. Antipoverty money now trickles no further down the class ladder than to graduate student neophytes, who by and large go on to reproduce the industry on the same terms.

The stakes in this game are high. And challenges to the regular players—while no longer met with fistfights or gun battles, as in the days of Community Action turf disputes—are dealt with ruthlessly in a new way.

University of Michigan Professor Arline Geronimus, whose research has challenged the orthodoxy that teenaged childbearing *causes* rather than reflects poverty, has been the target of a concerted and vicious campaign of misrepresentation and character assassination. Marian Wright Edelman's Children's Defense Fund has stooped to race-baiting Geronimus, who is white. Frank Furstenberg, who patrols trademark integrity for the Guttmacher Institute (formerly Planned Parenthood's research arm), has led the charge in academic circles.

I attended a crudely staged attempt to discredit Geronimus, then an untenured assistant professor, orchestrated by Furstenberg and others and suffused with sexist condescension. Geronimus was invited to present her work at a joint Northwestern/University of Chicago poverty seminar in 1992, which turned out to be a staged attack.

Large grants and the credibility that access to them requires are at stake in this business, and the pimps act accordingly. How lucrative is this new form of welfare fraud? Keep in mind that the 1994 welfare queen allegedly grossed on average just under $65,000 per year.

Now consider: At Northwestern's Center for Urban Affairs and Policy Research, affiliated faculty received a total of at least $4,800,000 for poverty research in 1992 and 1993 alone. The big hitters include professor Thomas D. Cook, who got $1,997,700 for projects on adolescence and schools, teen pregnancy, and racial-identity formation in the schools. John McKnight, who has retained high levels of public and private funding through Democratic and Republican administrations, received $499,200 for work on mi-crolevel "community innovations"—nonpolitical accommodations to systematic dispossession. Professor James Rosenbaum acquired $422,200 for studying school/employer linkages. (He thinks they're good, by the way.) Economist Rebecca Blank received $394,200, mainly for a joint project with Christopher Jencks to reproduce neoliberal poverty pimps' professional DNA by "training" graduate students as specialists on the underclass. Sociologist Roberto Fernandez received $237,400 for yet another rehash of the thesis that inner-city unemployment is so high mainly because black and brown poor people live too far away from the jobs for which they'd qualify.

I don't mean to suggest that my colleagues are unique or even distinctive perpetrators of this upscale welfare fraud. I focus on them only because I have ready access to the figures. The same pattern could be seen at Princeton's Woodrow Wilson School, the University of Wisconsin's Institute for Research on Poverty, the University of Chicago's Harris School of Public Policy, the School of Public Policy at UC-Berkeley, Harvard's Kennedy School, the University of Michigan's Institute for Public Policy Studies, and in smaller doses elsewhere. In addition, such nonacademic think tanks as the Manpower Demonstration Research Corporation, the Urban Institute, Brookings, and even such rightist front groups as the American Enterprise Institute, suck up even greater sums of poverty-research money.

For a sense of the industry's magnitude, during 1991 and 1992, the Rockefeller Foundation awarded approximately $17.8 million in grants to support research on urban poverty in the United States.

During the years when our welfare queen pilfered her $450,000, the Ford Foundation gave out $30.3 million—an average of $4.3 million annually—in the Policy Research and Program Evaluation component of the U.S. section of its urban poverty program alone. And this is a most conservative estimate of Ford's total poverty-research budget. It doesn't include expenditures on international policy research and program evaluation. Much of the activity supported under other components of the urban poverty program—for example, "Welfare and Teen Pregnancy," "Secondary Schools and Youth Employment," and "Crime Prevention and Neighborhood Security"—also is primarily research-related. Nor does it take into account Ford's comparably funded and organized rural poverty program. This quick glance also doesn't consider the scores of millions in poverty-related research funded annually either by other foundations or by the U.S. Departments of Labor, Health and Human Services, and Housing and Urban Development.

The point is that poverty research is a huge academic business. Of course, some of the output of this industry is useful. (Geronimus's research is one important and significantly disregarded example.) And many of its practitioners are motivated by benign intentions. Nevertheless, the bottom line is that they make money off the existence of poverty, and those good intentions often seem to be just so much petit-bourgeois self-aggrandizement.

Endlessly cooking and rehashing data to fine-tune minute interpretations of aggregate statistical relationships in a self-consciously depoliticized way are alternatives to clear and direct arguments about inequality. As studying poverty comes increasingly to substitute for fighting inequality, the 1960s poverty pimps look less bad in comparison. The old pimps, like the new welfare queen, were more marginal economically and therefore likely to be driven by the somewhat more forgivable desire to escape their own impoverishment. They were also less implicated than the contemporary poverty pimps in defining the limits of the possible and the thinkable with respect to social policy in general. Poverty researchers' invocations of expertise and specious posture of neutrality canonize the most mean-spirited, victim-bashing prejudices about poor people.

The originators of poverty pimping as a form of welfare fraud

were creatures of a system of dispossession. The new academic perpetrators are also its active agents. They should be fingered as such
publicly, since that's what we do with welfare cheats. They can take
heart, though—at least they'll never suffer the police-station mug
shots and handcuffs.

# —Liberals, I Do Despise

After years of crafting and rationalizing Bill Clinton's version of the attack on poor people, high-ranking, Department of Health and Human Services officials Mary Jo Bane and Peter Edelman resigned several weeks after the president signed the hideous "welfare reform" bill. David Ellwood, another architect of the welfare overhaul, left a year earlier. I'm sorry, but their grand gesture, tastefully skirting direct criticism of Clinton's action, seems too much like a self-righteous attempt to escape responsibility for their own involvement in bringing this savagery about. To that extent, their crocodile tears underscore the ugly truth of American liberalism.

Sometime early in Ronald Reagan's first term, I decided to forget everything I'd always disliked about liberals. I took pains to subordinate what put me off about them to the larger objective of unity against the right-wing onslaught. I decided to overlook their capacity for high-minded fervor for the emptiest and sappiest platitudes; their tendencies to make a fetish of procedure over substance and to look for technical fixes to political problems; their ability to screen out the mounting carnage in the cities they inhabit as they seek pleasant venues for ingesting good coffee and scones; their propensity for aestheticizing other people's oppression and calling that activism; their reflex to wring their hands and look constipated in the face of conflict; and, most of all, their spinelessness and undependability in crises.

But during the '80s, liberal opinion gradually accommodated to Reaganism by sliding rightward. Two rhetorical justifications emerged for this adaptation. The Democratic Leadership Council called for a new centrism, jettisoning egalitarian politics and the constituencies identified with it. Additionally, an excesses-of-the-'60s-as-fall-from-grace fable propelled this slide and justified the smug dismissal of those of us who didn't want to go along. This new liberalism curtly demanded that we grow up and accept the *realpolitik*; Reaganism was all our fault for going too far anyway.

Bill Clinton's genius is that he managed to embody both the neoliberal and DLC variants of the rightward shift, and combined them with a superficial earnestness that mitigates whatever egalitarian thoughts may linger among those who will to believe in him. So liberals have followed and rationalized and pimped for him through the debacle of his half-assed, insurance company-led health-care reform, NAFTA and GATT, his horribly repressive crime and anti-terrorism legislation, and his conspicuous retreat from support of civil rights enforcement.

Clinton's apologists even attempted to justify his embrace of the abominable welfare-reform bill, stooping to a Flip Wilson defense (Gingrich made him sign it) and using the bill's passage as a reason to vote for Bipartisan Bill (so that he can "fix" what he just did). Talk about will to believe. Or is it will to get paid?

Their lapdog defense of Big Bill highlights liberals' willingness to sacrifice the poor and to tout it as tough-minded compassion and an act of courage. Even before Clinton won the Democratic nomination in 1992 this trait was visible, especially among those policy-jock types who had begun to sense the possibility of a Clinton victory and their impending opportunity to consort with power. I got my wake-up call from a poverty-researcher colleague who, on the eve of the Illinois primary, impatiently dismissed my objections to Clinton's having just executed black, impoverished, and brain-damaged Rickey Ray Rector. She blew me off as naïve for not recognizing that any Democrat would have to support capital punishment. "Easy for you to say," I thought, but, regrettably, was too polite to say out loud.

Nowhere have the moral and political deficiencies of this liberal notion of *realpolitik* been more clearly exposed than around the Clinton administration's welfare-reform politics. William Julius Wilson, who set the tone with *The Truly Disadvantaged*, proposed a sleight-of-hand approach to helping the poor schmucks through "universal" programs that wouldn't antagonize the better-off by appearing to do anything for poor people in particular. Fittingly, he became a major Clinton apologist in 1992.

Following Wilson, David Ellwood, a highly regarded liberal poverty researcher at Harvard's Kennedy School, invented the "two years and off" notion, which he publicized in his 1988 book, *Poor Support*. Ellwood eased his provocative idea with calls for a battery of support services that would accompany expulsion from the welfare rolls. Like Wilson, he blew off the critics on his left who argued that his costly bundle of safeguards would go nowhere without a forceful challenge to the right-wing climate that his get-'em-off-the-dole slogan accommodated. The fear, now realized, was that his liberal credentials would legitimize the two-years-and-off idea as a programmatic goal without including any of his finely crafted hedges.

Attracted by Bubba's call to "end welfare as we know it," Ellwood and his Kennedy School colleague Mary Jo Bane headed south to become part of official Washington. They would be the main players in the administration's overhaul of welfare, using two-years-and-off as their centerpiece. Joining the team later was Peter Edelman, the perennially up-and-coming liberal lawyer. He had assailed welfare as early as 1967, employing the coded attack phrase *fostering dependence* (read: poor folks are lazy bastards).

Beneath all this idiotic coyness lie liberals' long-standing aversion to conflict and their refusal to face up to the class realities of American politics. They avoid any linkage of inequality with corporations' use of public policy to drive down living standards and enhance their plunder.

So Marian Wright Edelman (Peter's wife) of the Children's Defense Fund concocted the strategy of focusing on children. This save-the-babies politics is not only maudlin (notice how her pal Hillary's "whole village" went so easily from raising a child to stoning poor families in her support of hubby's welfare travesty), it also gives in to the right's demonization of poor adults by conceding their worthlessness in order to focus on their presumably innocent kids.

Roll ahead to the summer of 1994. Ellwood and Bane, representing HHS, sat at Daniel P. Moynihan's Senate Finance Committee hearing on Clinton's welfare-reform package (which, by the way, wasn't all that different from the Republican thing he signed). Alongside them was their boss, another liberal stalwart, HHS secretary Donna Shalala. As chief Clintonista, Shalala proclaimed that the purpose of the president's welfare-reform initiative was to eliminate out-of-wedlock births. Her underlings nodded in agreement—

thus playing into one of the ugliest right-wing canards about social provision. As if that wasn't disgusting enough, when Moynihan invoked the specter of "speciation"—the notion that generations of out-of-wedlock breeding in isolated, impoverished city pockets has created a new "species" of human beings—each of the HHS folks nodded again.

I'm sure that these good liberals would have explained away their participation in that dehumanizing characterization as a strategic move; their intention being the advancement of humane social policy within an unfavorable political climate. However, their behavior exposes a deeper truth about the political commitments on which this strain of liberalism rests: This is a politics motivated by the desire for proximity to the ruling class and a belief in the basic legitimacy of its power and prerogative. It is a politics which, despite all its idealist puffery and feigned nobility, will sell out any allies or egalitarian objectives in pursuit of gaining the Prince's ear.

In a few short years, liberals of this sort have reminded me of all that had troubled me about them, and more. I'd just about convinced myself that my earlier scorn was a function of youthful hotheadedness. Some was, but not that much. In the end, it is the poisonous mix of self-righteousness and hypocrisy—as illustrated by Ellwood, Bane, and Edelman—that earns my contempt.

# —Kiss the Family Good-bye

L et's forget about the family. It's one of those concepts the left has been harping on for some time, without getting anywhere. I'm proposing a list of such terms that, as far as I'm concerned, the right can have.

My main group of what we might call negative keywords includes the following: "family," "community," "neighborhood," "grassroots," "empowerment," "the people."

"Family" heads the list because it is both the most seductive and the most insidious. The seductiveness makes sense—after all, who actually opposes the idea of family? We're all aware that the right looks to demonize us as a fringe element of freaks, alien from and hostile to the values of a supposed mainstream. Pointing out that we have families counters the image of the left as rootless kooks or demons. So the temptation to try to "take the family back" from the conservatives is powerful.

The desire to make a left program symbolically consonant with "ordinary" Americans' attitudes isn't new. It's what prompted Eastern European immigrant Communists in the 1920s and 1930s to adopt "American" surnames. It also has undergirded a lot of sectarian groups' fetishes for stereotypes of working-class behavior—beer-drinking, homophobic, macho style. And, as comes through most clearly among defectors from the Democratic Party's liberal wing, it's a slippery slope.

There are two main problems with the "take back the family" stratagem. First, the "family" in American political debate still means the patriarchal, nuclear household. So we must load cumbersome qualifications onto family imagery. We have to point out, for instance, that by "family" we mean any set of individuals who understand themselves to be committed to one another in a primary, durable way. We have to do that, rightly, to make clear that we don't want to diminish the legitimacy of a wide variety of nonheterosexual, nonnuclear household arrangements.

It's certainly necessary to combat the use of family rhetoric, which the right uses as a weapon against anyone who doesn't conform to conservative patriarchal ideals. Contesting for ownership of a label whose popular usage is saturated with evocations of a narrow, conservative moralism, however, is not obviously the most effective way to battle. The real issue, after all, isn't whether "families," by whatever reckoning, are suffering or being undermined by rightwing policy initiatives. It's that the right's program impoverishes and otherwise endangers large numbers of individuals—without regard to their household arrangements and patterns of intimate attachment.

A simpler, more direct approach is to point out that the thrust of a progressive, egalitarian policy agenda is to make certain that individuals have access to the resources—among other things, decent education, health care, a safe environment, a living wage, freedom from discrimination—that they need to realize their capacities as autonomous members of the society. Under those conditions, the family issue will largely take care of itself. Autonomous individuals can choose whatever domestic arrangements they wish, with whichever specific partners they wish, free from the sting of bigotry or the lash of the market.

The best single "family policy" would be to end wage discrimination and labor-market segmentation by race and gender. Only when women are free, without fear of impoverishment, to order their intimate lives as they choose on an equal basis with men will we have a sense of what a "natural" family form might be for our society. This is also a key component of the struggle against domestic violence.

Charles Murray and other reactionary bemoaners of the demise of "the family" know what's up. They object forthrightly to the system of social support—not just social welfare spending, but even housing patterns that make smaller units available, thereby reducing the cost of living alone—that makes it possible for women to live independently. They recognize, in principle at least, that Engels knew what he was talking about in the late nineteenth century; that the economic and political subordination of women is the *sine qua non* of the sacrosanct nuclear family as we know it.

This connects with the second disturbing feature of the "take back the family" strategy. It often masks a fundamentally left-inform, right-in-essence acceptance of conservative family ideology. I've learned from responses to my criticisms of underclass ideology in *The Progressive* and *The Nation* that all too many people who identify with the left nonetheless maintain blind spots about the intrinsic superiority of the two-parent, "intact" nuclear form of household organization.

Jacqueline Jones's well-intentioned book, *The Dispossessed*, is a clear example of how a misty-eyed concern for family can produce blindness to the abusive and exploitive relations that frequently characterize real families. This blindness is also why William Julius Wilson's silly idea that we should direct employment programs to inner-city men to make them "marriageable" (his macroeconomic dating service) hasn't ruffled more feathers on the left, despite its blatantly anti-feminist premise that women should marry their way out of poverty.

"Family" has the aura of a natural relation that occurs outside the system of hierarchies associated with a particular social division of labor. But what we tend to reify—even to the extent of imputing it to other animals—as The Family is more usefully and accurately seen by anthropologists as only one of a very large variety of actually functioning kinship and household systems.

"Community," "neighborhood," "grassroots," and "the people" work the same way. Like "family," these notions appeal partly as a counter to the right's charges that we're marginal. Each is supposedly popular, authentic, collective, and organic. Each appeals to the image of a group that exists apart from—and prior to—external identities and interests, including larger institutions like government. Each is construed as a direct pipeline to the general will. Invoking the community, the neighborhood, the grassroots, or the people is a self-contained political justification.

There are at least two other problems with this view as well. One is that each of the four categories is too neat an abstraction. There is no pure, organic solidarity. Communities and neighborhoods are not pristine with respect to their alliances, nor are they joined by general will. Each category (really four versions of the same category) exists at best as what Hungarian Marxist philosopher Georg

Lukács in his 1923 book, *History and Class Consciousness,* described as a unit of "objective historical possibility." It is invoked as part of an attempt to create it, as part of the effort associated with generating constituencies for specific political interpretations and programs.

Communities and neighborhoods are sites of political disagreement and contest just like every place else: "the grassroots" and "the people" are only more abstract and diffuse forms of the same imagery. They aren't pure, and they don't act with one mind. Their political affiliations are defined by the same kinds of struggles and negotiated meanings that occur in households, workplaces, co-ops, union locals, or editorial boards.

The disposition to appeal to that imagery for political validation reflects a naive, Jeffersonian romanticism that equates smallness and informality with democracy and justice. And that's the second problem with this imagery.

Presumption of that kind of organic collectivity as the font of political legitimacy is a double-edged sword. Ever since the anti-abolitionist riots in the Jacksonian era, racist whites have justified their exclusionist, anti-egalitarian politics in terms of appeal to the collective will of "the community," "the neighborhood," "the grassroots," and "the people." In fact, this rhetoric has been a staple among those seeking to promote all manner of illiberal and repressive agendas.

As anyone who has lived in a small town knows, the small community can be ruthlessly oppressive for those defined as outsiders, and internal democracy is by no means necessarily the norm for establishing the "community's" dominant points of view. Think of the Jim Crow South.

"Empowerment," like the other negative keywords, speaks more of process than of program. This notion is perhaps the emptiest of them all, as the ease with which the Reaganauts appropriated it attests. It covers the waterfront: from self-help psychobabble to bootstrap alternatives to public action, to vague evocations of political mobilization. It's currently particularly seductive because its vagueness provides an apparent basis for broad agreement.

The allure of these symbols points to serious conceptual problems among progressives, who—especially in this perilous time— must think more clearly. Philanthropic foundations now routinely promote community "leaders" whose appeal rests almost entirely on clever deployment of a rhetoric driven by these keywords. Their substantive programs typically reduce to bootstrap economic development, victim-blaming, corporate-partnership stuff. Surprisingly, many progressives have shown themselves incapable of looking beyond such patter about empowering the grassroots, mobilizing at the community and neighborhood levels, and so on.

Our response as leftists to such rhetoric should always be to ask. "Empowering whom? To do what? Mobilize which communities in support of what programs?"

Least of all now can we afford to become victimized by our own propaganda or to fall prey to wish fulfillment. Our politics must always proceed from a clear-headed analysis of substantive programs and a determination of who benefits and loses from them.

Of course, we invoke those contested symbols in our propaganda as do all other interested forces in the society (though I am convinced that "family" in particular is at best a dead end), but we must be clear that they are rhetorical, not analytical, categories. They help us advance and sell a vision and program; they don't define, clarify, or substitute for them.

A final irony about these counterproductive keywords is that their attractiveness stems from our own sense that we are fundamentally alien from the American population, that our politics can be validated only by showing that we have support from supposedly more authentic, popular constituencies.

There's a subtly anti-democratic undercurrent to this view. It amounts to defining ourselves as outside the political culture, and it feeds a reluctance to be forthcoming and direct about our politics with others. This is an understandable reflex, given the isolated and demoralizing position we're in (which also leads to flights into irrationalism and the make-your-own, virtual world of "cultural politics"). It's a variation of liberals' current ideas about slipping decent social policy past the electorate by dressing it up in different rhetorical clothes.

As any decent organizer knows, however, such stratagems inevitably backfire. People can sense that they're being sold a bill of goods, and the result is a further discrediting of the left. Our only hope is to hold firmly and self-confidently to our politics, approach others as equal citizens, and stand or fall on the strength of our analysis and practice.

We have to recognize that we are the people as much as anyone else. Our job is to propagate our vision of how the world should be, reshaping the vision (and in the same process, the world) along with those who join us. That's what a progressive, democratic politics looks like.

# —A Polluted Debate

No one should be surprised that the affirmative action debate surged toward a crest in 1994. The momentum had been building since the Gingrich electoral putsch. Almost immediately after the elections, mainstream pundits began to speculate on when and how the new Gingrich Congress would draw a line in the dirt on "racial preferences" and to what extent "voters" had been expressing their frustration with such "entitlements."

Phil Gramm rolled up his brown shirtsleeves to announce the impending death of "race-based" initiatives as he declared himself a candidate for the presidential nomination. One after another, the GOP hopefuls slithered forth to declaim on their noble hatred of "preferences," one-upping each other with gleeful venom and making President Big Bill squirm in his tight space between the Democratic Leadership Conference's program of catering to white racism and his electoral need not to drive black voters completely away. (To his credit, Clinton's official response in his July 19, 1995 speech was a firm defense of affirmative action.)

This assault no doubt expressed its militants' unapologetic racism; but it also reflected an electoral strategy that constructs what the news-chat guys and dolls euphemistically call "hot button" issues and milks them for advantage. The GOP had been playing on white racial panic since at least the 1964 Goldwater campaign (Lyndon Johnson, who took a fairly aggressive stand on racial equality, trumped the opposition with a crude appeal to Cold War fear of nuclear conflagration). The attack on affirmative action was part of a larger program of scapegoating that both diverted attention from the question of who actually benefited and lost in the Contract on America and fed the fiction that assaults on the rights of some groups won't be extended to others. (First they suspended the Bill of Rights in the inner cities . . . )

When California governor Pete Wilson, therefore, decided to distinguish himself from the field by being the most single-mindedly focused on affirmative action as the source of America's problems, he didn't exhibit much imagination. The Republicans have worked for more than a decade on reformulating for the national stage the time-honored stratagem of Southern demagogues: pursue an agenda that reduces government's role to concentrating advantages among the rich and powerful and deflects suspicion by screaming "NIGGER!" Nowadays, reflecting our multicultural, diverse sensibilities, the scapegoating extends as easily to poor people, gays, non-white immigrants, women who want to control their reproduction or earn a decent living without depending on a man, liberals and other secular humanists, but the point is the same. Wilson was reading the cues in California politics, where Proposition 187 had just won and a couple of right-wing Beavis and Butthead academics had announced their campaign for the "California Civil Rights Initiative," a ballot measure to outlaw "preferences." (It's curious how the state retains its liberal image despite having infected national politics with Richard Nixon, tap-dancing senator George Murphy and his reincarnation in Sonny Bono, S. I. Hayakawa, Ronald Reagan, Ed Meese and company, William Dannemeyer, Robert Dornan, Howard Jarvis, and Proposition 13.)

Now California has given us a new black anti-affirmative action celebrity in Ward Connerly, the University of California regent who proposed and pushed through the elimination of "race-based preferences" for admission, hiring, and contracting throughout the system. Connerly is an interesting figure, but not for the reasons that *Newsweek* and the like have been hyping. Indeed, you'd think that by now the anti-affirmative action minority shtick would be old news. That it isn't serves to remind us that the so-called liberal media are forever in thrall to the *Zeitgeist*—they follow power, and the power is now with the right. What's interesting about Connerly is that his career and public persona make a nice entry point for a discussion of affirmative action. His history, which hasn't been much discussed outside California, highlights some of the patterns of exclusionary privilege that affirmative action is intended to break down.

Wilson appointed Connerly to the UC Board of Regents in 1993 in response to pressure to diversify the body. His main qualification was his twenty-five–year friendship with Wilson. He's had a long involvement with state and local government, including a stint as chief deputy of the state Department of Housing and Community Development when Reagan was governor. (In that capacity his leasing of low-cost housing units to the Sacramento Development Authority provoked serious questions of conflict of interest in 1972.)

Connerly lists his profession as "consultant" or "land-use consultant," and his firm specializes in administering government contracts, particularly federal Community Development Block Grants. In May 1995 there was a mini-tempest in the California press about Connerly's allegedly receiving almost $1.25 million in minority set-aside contracts. It turns out, however, that of that sum only about $140,000 came strictly via the set-aside route. His defense is that he was forced by circumstances to apply as a minority and was offended by having to do so. To prove his commitment to principle, he has pledged to sue to eliminate the set-aside program.

Critics have called Connerly a hypocrite for taking set-aside money only to complain afterward, but there are two more significant ways that he is an affirmative-action baby. First, like all government contractors who were formerly employed by the state, he enjoys personal and informal contacts that give this enemy of "preference" a competitive advantage, just as his friendship with Wilson helped him win the Regents appointment. (True to sleazy form, Connerly has failed to list his major clients as required on annual income disclosure reports that all UC regents must file with the state's Fair Political Practices Commission.) That is, he has consistently profited from precisely the sort of old-boy network that operates to exclude minorities and women in pursuit of contracts, employment, and even university admissions. Affirmative action arose in part to compensate for the discrimination perpetuated by this kind of cronyism.

Second, Connerly's only other manifest qualification for the board is his race; he was nominated to boost minority representation. In that respect, he's yet another version of a contemporary right-wing cliché: the anti-affirmative action affirmative-action appointment, a group headed by Clarence Thomas. Their mission is to lobby against the criteria of their own claims to our attention. The substance of their arguments undermines the legitimacy of their voices in making them. If, as Connerly contends, race-based appointments are by nature flawed, why should we accord him credibility as a public spokesman when the only credible thing he could do is resign?

The Connerly case underscores the extent to which public debate on affirmative action is driven by specious abstractions and empty pieties that only mystify the issues at stake. The terms of this polluted debate have been set by the DLC/GOP consensus, with the aid of willing media. Among these are the supposedly necessary trade-offs between merit and quotas, equality of opportunity and equality of results, and fairness and racial preferences. These premises are not only simplistic and wrong; they also stack the deck in favor of those who oppose antidiscriminatory intervention. Who would endorse quotas over merit, preferences over fairness?

Other formulations help to skew this debate further. One is the contention that affirmative action seeks to provide recompense not for current exclusionary practices, but for past grievances—slavery and/or Jim Crow segregation. Another is that it is a pointless failure because it helps mainly the already relatively well-off rather than those in poverty. Still another is that, by lowering standards, affirmative action undermines productivity for both individual institutions and the economy as a whole.

Finally, there is a set of intrinsically illogical arguments that emanate from the idea that affirmative action is actually self-defeating. One such claim asserts that it stigmatizes its beneficiaries as unqualified and therefore creates racist stereotypes, resentment, and thus discrimination. (This view sometimes supports a charge that affirmative action is responsible for the "glass ceiling" that denies minorities and women access to the highest levels of government and corporate power.) Another argues that it instills in its beneficiaries debilitating doubts about their competence and their white male colleagues' perceptions of their abilities. Yet another is that affirmative action actually restricts opportunity for minorities and women by slotting them into narrow quotas.

Another troubling feature of the contemporary political landscape that Ward Connerly's momentary prominence demonstrated: the thorny politics of racial representation, the problem of determining group interests and who actually express them. This problem is embedded in the presumptions on both sides in the affirmative action debate. A serious debate on affirmative action would at least address these issues.

Briefly, although it's commonly so described by both opponents and supporters, affirmative action does not rest on a principle of compensation for slavery and prior discrimination. Its target is current discrimination and current patterns of inequality or disadvantage that are the effects of prior exclusion and discrimination. The objection that affirmative action disproportionately helps the relatively well-off also rests on a misrepresentation. Affirmative action is not an antipoverty initiative. Claiming that it has failed because it doesn't target the worst-off is like claiming that highway spending and environmental regulation have failed because they don't primarily attack poverty.

No evidence supports the contention that affirmative action undermines productivity. This claim is based on a premise that affirmative action advances the less competent over the more competent. This presumes that arrangements favoring whites and men over others automatically represent the optimal distribution of talent. This presumption is exactly what makes affirmative action necessary in the first place.

Likewise, arguments that affirmative action harms its putative beneficiaries are just sophistry. Each denies the very situation that produced the need for affirmative action. The alternative, after all, is not open access without stigma; the alternative is restricted opportunity.

# —Nasty Habits

I started this essay intending to dissect the spurious premises that dominate the current debate on affirmative action. But after laboring over a draft that read depressingly like a law review article, I realized my problem: I was imagining a dialogue with liberal apostates and wannabe apostates. The discussion—as it has been framed by frankly hostile conservatives with the queasy cooperation of apologetic liberals—is less a vigorous argument over the pros and cons of affirmative action than an intramural squabble over just where affirmative action has gone wrong. In this so-called debate, all the participants are on the attack.

It seems increasingly clear that all the public to-ing and fro-ing over preferences, merit, quotas, fairness, and equality of opportunity versus equality of results is a smoke screen. No one would support a bean-counting quota system that ignores merit in hiring, promotion, or university admissions. And indeed—conservative mythmaking to the contrary—no one has to, because no such system exists. By the same token, how can you assess compliance with antidiscrimination laws unless you examine the actual results? And yet the conservative-dominated courts of the Reagan-Bush-Clinton era refuse to permit such examination; results be damned, discrimination only occurs if you can prove a conscious *intent* to discriminate. But shouldn't the very heart of the debate over affirmative action be what constitutes fairness and how best to overcome long-standing patterns of exclusion that favor whites and men?

No, the debate's real basis is nothing so lofty. It is positional warfare in an ideological struggle about race and social justice in American politics. At issue is the legitimacy of nonwhites and women of all sorts as citizens with equal claims on the polity as white men.

The most revealing feature of the discussion of affirmative action may be its opponents' refusal to accept existing inequalities as evidence of the likely workings of discrimination. There are only two conditions under which that refusal would be reasonable. Disproportionate concentrations of social benefits among whites and men must either (1) arise purely at random, through uncommonly good luck, or (2) reflect whites' and men's natural, and therefore justifiable, superiority. The first condition is absurd on its face, although it is currently the anti-affirmative action crowd's contention of choice. In fact, the courts' insistence that specific intent to discriminate must be demonstrated to sustain each charge of discrimination is a bit of sophistry aimed at forcing attention away from this absurdity. Only by demanding that each case be treated as if it arose in isolation from history and social context is it possible to maintain that white guys repeatedly finish first by serendipity.

Of course, no one is stupid enough really to believe that—except maybe Associate Supreme Court Justice Clarence Coon. The argument is a front. I suppose we should be thankful that it's still unpalatable to embrace fundamental racial inequality in public, though thinly coded language seems to work very well toward the same end. However, a GOP presidential campaign featuring Buchanan, and others of that ilk, in a rush of racist one-upmanship could strip away the remaining veneer of embarrassment at making explicitly racist appeals. It's not farfetched to imagine Buchanan, for instance, proclaiming to cheering crowds that this is a white man's country, and everyone else had better shut up and get with the program. After all, there is *The Bell Curve*'s racist pseudoscience to mine for a rationale.

If this seems paranoid, consider that the modes of argument—and often the very arguments themselves—currently advanced by affirmative action's foes have a long, dismal pedigree. Justice Henry Billings Brown's infamous majority opinion in *Plessy v. Ferguson*, the 1896 case that legitimized the "equal but separate" justification for codified segregation, also refused all reference to history and context. The arguments against the creation of the Freedman's Bureau after the Civil War centered on a contention that the agency went beyond the dictates of equality of opportunity and used state power to produce equal results. Supreme Court Justice Joseph Bradley's opinion in the 1883 decision overturning the 1875 Civil Rights Act proclaimed—eighteen years after the end of slavery and in the midst of the terrorist reimposition of white supremacy in the South—that it was time that the black American "takes the rank of a mere citizen, and ceases to be the special favorite of the laws." Then as now, liberals recoiled from a resolute defense of black Americans' pursuit of justice and equality, and in both eras their reluctance stemmed from racial bad faith. This willingness to give ground before the right's rhetorical canards betrays the unspoken suspicions of some white liberals — and perhaps some black ones as well — that white primacy may be inherently justified. The plain fact is that beneath a pro forma, often condescending public discourse suggesting otherwise, black inferiority remains at least an open question in the minds of many white Americans regardless of political persuasion. (Even some who support affirmative action may do so because they suspect that blacks are functionally defective and therefore need special assistance. That is the grain of truth that lurks within black conservatives' steady laments that the programs demean beneficiaries by impugning their capacities.) The vicissitudes of intelligence testing illustrate this grim reality.

Early twentieth-century psychometricians interpreted the finding that women performed better than men on some elements of I.Q. tests as evidence of poor design and adjusted the tests accordingly. Why? Because they presumed from the outset that men were smarter than women and, therefore, a test showing the opposite had to be flawed. Although belief in inherent sex inequality has hardly disappeared from American society, the notion that women may be dumber than men doesn't currently have the force of common sense, at least not among opinion-leading elites and academics. Thus, intelligence testers have for some time crafted tests to correct for gross gender differences in results. The idea of racial equality in intelligence is not yet that sort of commonsense presumption. So differences in test scores between blacks and whites become grist for claims that existing inequality may just be natural and unavoidable. That *The Bell Curve* sold 400,000 copies in its first four months indicates that a significant segment of the literate white public is at least willing to entertain arguments about black inferiority.

Sure, to some extent the current assault on affirmative action reflects politicians' willingness to cultivate the worst strains of white populism for electoral advantage. But that only begs the question as to why the "race card," as it is now euphemized, has such appeal. This was true in the late nineteenth century as well. The overturn of

Reconstruction by the Southern white politicians who called themselves the Redeemers derailed interracial southern populism as well. (Through the use of poll taxes and property and literacy requirements, the Redemption's program of political disfranchisement took back the vote from a substantial segment of the Southern white electorate and nearly 90 percent of blacks.) And the historical comparison underscores a crucial point. Like Reconstruction, affirmative action is under attack not—despite its critics' claims—because it has failed but because it has succeeded. The success, also like that of Reconstruction, is partial and not always on the most desirable terms, to be sure. But it is real. There are no conclusive assessments of the statistical impact of affirmative action, but studies by Martin Carnoy, in his 1994 book *Faded Dreams*, and Jonathan Leonard, in the August 1984 issue of *Review of Economics* and the Spring 1984 issue of the *Journal of Human Resources*, find a significant mitigating effect on job discrimination at all skill levels among black Americans. Abundant anecdotal evidence supports those findings.

The current assault on affirmative action lies within a longstanding and wretched pattern of racist reaction in American politics. It thrives on economic insecurity, on fears of lost privilege, and on the liberal bad faith that shrinks from principled defense of an egalitarian vision. Because of that bad faith, we don't know how deep or broad the racist strain is in white America; no one challenges it head-on, forcing the debate beyond the morally vacuous platitudes on which hack politicians and their journalistic helpmeets feed.

# —A Livable Wage

In 1997, the newly christened Labor Party launched a major national undertaking: a campaign for a constitutional amendment that will guarantee every resident the right to a job and a livable wage. The wage floor for the amendment was defined as $10 per hour, with regular cost-of-living adjustments.

The campaign's centerpiece was a door-to-door petition drive. The petitions targeted state and local officials, calling on them to exhort Congress to pass a simply worded amendment establishing the guarantee. But a more significant, yet subtler, aim of the drive was to foster a national discussion of government's basic responsibilities to its citizenry.

Progressive activists have been on the defensive for more than a decade, but the recent wave of local campaigns around livable-wage ordinances has been one of the more inspiriting developments for them. These drives, usually led by local ACORN activists and the AFL-CIO's Jobs With Justice Coalition, have concentrated on mobilizing public support around a legislated, humane wage minimum for public employment and contracting. The dollar figures vary, but they oscillate around the local poverty threshold for a family of four.

In Baltimore, an early success story for the movement, the level fought for and won was $6.60 per hour. In Chicago, where the mayor's opposition has stalled the campaign, the target is $7.60, New York's City Council had to override a Giuliani veto to pass its "prevailing wage" law. That legislation sets several different wage floors, the highest of which is $12. The reach of the ordinances varies as well—in some cases covering anyone hired by any firm contracting with or receiving subsidies from local government, and in others imposing more complex or limited restrictions.

Aside from their direct effects, these campaigns are important in that they inject two important propositions into public discussion: (1) that a job is only worthwhile if it pays enough to live on, and (2) that government, which is responsible for the general public welfare, should not be implicated in employment at sub-poverty-level wages. It says something about how much ground we've lost politically that these should seem like bold or controversial ideas. But the fact is that extraordinary action is necessary to get a public hearing for the notion that work should provide a decent livelihood and that one of government's responsibilities is to provide living wages to its employees.

The municipal ordinances have their limitations, though. Chief among them is that local governments are the weakest, least influential links in the federal system. They are vulnerable, among other things, to threats of capital flight, and their potential revenue sources are severely constrained by state constitutions. Therefore, the wage demands must be relatively modest, and elected officials' support of them tends to be tenuous at best. Baltimore's Kurt Schmoke, for example, has a reputation as a pro-labor mayor, but he began undermining that city's ordinance by bringing workfare assignees into the municipal workforce.

What is needed, as a next logical step, is for the livable-wage demand to be framed at the national level. At that stage, there is greater latitude for enforcement. The Labor Party's campaign takes that crucial step. (Full disclosure: I am a member of the party's Interim National Council.) Because of its nationwide scope, the constitutional-amendment approach eliminates the vulnerability to competition from noncomplying jurisdictions. Contractors won't be able to boycott one municipality in favor of another with a lower wage scale. It is comprehensive, covering both public and private employment, eliminating the threat to forsake government contracting for a more "competitive" private-sector labor market. Also, the national focus avoids the problem of the limited revenue capacities of local governments, undercutting a central argument against establishing a decent income level as the minimum.

Proposing such a constitutional amendment could force a discussion of government's basic responsibilities to the populace, and this is an important prospect. This campaign is a way to shift the terms of political debate away from the smoke-screen issues—balanced-budget hysteria, drug and crime furor, and family-values idiocies—that have become dominant in this increasingly bipartisan climate.

The political initiative needs to be seized so that activists aren't always occupied with defensive efforts and responding to corporate and right-wing agendas. As important as the struggles are to preserve the social security system and Medicare, for example, they must be linked with an effort to mobilize around a broader, alternative social vision. The drive for a livable-wage amendment can forge a political outlook in which those connections become obvious.

I attended an eastern district meeting of the Oil, Chemical, and Atomic Workers Union (now Paper, Allied-Industrial, Chemical and Energy Workers) at which the constitutional amendment campaign had its first public hearing. The response it generated was very exciting. Workers there were clearly provoked by it. Those who commented acknowledged that it sounded like a good idea but thought it raised several critical questions: How would we pay for it? How would we keep capital from running overseas? What would the amendment mean for people who already have jobs? Wouldn't the mandate to provide jobs for all require redefining what we mean by work?

These questions, in turn, led to a broader political discussion in which an alternative social vision was laid out. Much of that vision intersects with the Labor Party's political program, which is based on economic justice for all. And in that program answers can be found to people's concerns about the implications of a livable-wage amendment.

How would the amendment's mandate be paid for? By eliminating all corporate tax breaks and subsidies; a higher income tax rate on the rich; a wealth tax on those with personal assets over $2 million; a tax on all mergers and acquisitions over $1 billion; a tax on all stock options over $1 million; a tax on nonprofit institutions with $100 million or more in assets; and a 100 percent tax on the portion of executive salaries that exceeds 20 times the average worker's salary in the firm.

How would this program counter capital flight? By raising the costs of disinvestment and therefore reducing the incentive to flee. The Labor Party program calls for a Job Destruction Penalty law, which would require any firm with at least 100 employees working worldwide to pay each laid-off worker two months severance for every year of service. It also requires payment of $25,000 to the community for each severed worker in order to cover the social costs of dislocations. (The one exception is for those in hiring-hall situations.) The party program also calls for renegotiating NAFTA and WTO agreements, establishing the strongest possible international labor and environment standards. In any event, the amendment would place the responsibility on the government to compensate for the private sector's inadequacies regarding job creation.

What would the amendment mean for those with jobs and in redefining what we think of as work? It certainly would mean finding ways to absorb many new people into the workforce. Among other things, this could mean a shift to a 32-hour, four-day work week (at 40 hours pay) with a double-time minimum for all overtime, one hour off, with pay, for every two hours of overtime; and 20 mandatory paid vacation days a year. It could also mean implementation of a sabbatical for all workers.

Other possibilities opened by this mandate could include recognizing all full-time post-secondary students as workers eligible for the minimum livable wage. Other ways to spread work around — and free up workers to live other facets of their lives — could include a mandatory minimum of twelve weeks paid leave for each newborn or adopted child, and provisions for high-quality pensions could expand the pool of viable jobs by enabling people to retire early. Also, the amendment's mandate could be, must be, enforced by restoring and extending workers' rights to organize, bargain, and strike.

These possibilities are all drawn from the Labor Party program. When laid out in full, it constitutes a coherent vision of how the society could be organized — one that diverges sharply from the pro-corporate, free-market theology that dominates political debate, and stands in start contrast with what the pundit classes have validated as thinkable.

If we are to have any chance to enact a model of a decent and just world, we must find ways to shift the terms of public discussion. And the best way to do so is to take a clear alternative out to the people on a face-to-face, door-to-door basis. In that way, we can begin a national conversation that leads to a challenge of the seemingly unmovable forces that drive the nation. Amending the Constitution is a daunting prospect. It certainly won't happen anytime soon. The struggle to do so could, however, help build the political force we need to meet the real challenges that confront us every day. And, of course, building such a force would make the prospect less daunting.

# —Token Equality

For Bill Clinton, egalitarianism is a token issue. From Janet Reno, Henry Cisneros, and Ron Brown in the first Cabinet, through Madeleine Albright, Rodney Slater, and Alexis Herman in the second (with Federico Peña a telling holdover), Clinton has played photo-op politics. He's maintained his egalitarian bona fides with the identity-politics crowd by constructing a Cabinet to "look like America."

But what difference does it make what it looks like? All his appointees are centrist insiders, committed to his neo-imperialist foreign policy and his "bipartisan," pro-corporate retreat from a program of democratic redistribution.

Still, feminists actively lobbied for Albright's nomination as Secretary of State, and civil-rights groups threw their weight behind Herman as Labor Secretary, despite the fact that she is a longtime Democratic Party and White House functionary and hardly likely to be a forceful or independent advocate of labor's interests.

Clinton points up the limit of identity politics. The term refers most generally to a political approach that gives priority to advancing the perspectives and interests of specific groups defined in ethnic, racial, or cultural terms—that is, as explicit alternatives to class. And it implies a belief that asserting and demanding recognition of the distinctiveness and independent cultural legitimacy of one's group is a crucial political objective in its own right.

Identity politics is sometimes a term of scorn, suggesting a parochial, maybe even frivolous politics that either distracts from some more substantive focus or undermines the idea of common purpose. This perspective has adherents on both left and right.

Todd Gitlin is prominent among those on the left who complain that the turn to identity politics undermines possibilities for building broadly based progressive coalitions and diverts attention from fundamental class concerns in favor of demands for symbolic statements of group worth. Arthur Schlesinger, Jr., who apparently still thinks of himself as a centrist liberal, and a host of rightwing pundits kvetch about the threat that identity politics poses to our "common culture"; they sound the tocsin against it as a harbinger of the new barbarism.

Others defend identity politics as an expression of the concerns of populations whose interests are otherwise submerged or ignored. From this perspective, the focus on identity is a necessary corrective to a long-standing tendency on the left to subordinate struggles against sexism and racism to a narrow, idealized notion of class politics. Historically, this tendency has declared such injustices to be "epiphenomena" of capitalism and therefore secondary to workplace-based struggles—or just plain outside the domain of radical politics.

Some defenders argue that identity politics constitutes the basis for "new social movements" that reflect the character of a post-industrial society. In this view, the breakdown of large-scale industrial production has rendered class less important as a primary identity, and people find other identities—like race/ethnicity, gender, sexual orientation, or age—to be more meaningful bases for political mobilization.

As is often the case, the debate about identity politics doesn't provide much clarity. The contending positions are defensive or sanctimonious, and they're too abstract; as a result, they talk past each other. For instance, it's certainly true that there's a long history in American politics—even on the left—of using calls for unity and solidarity to silence the concerns of women and minorities. At the same time, it's difficult to believe that anyone committed to progressive political change would, as a matter of principle, oppose the idea of building broad-based movements.

So how are we to make sense of identity politics? How do the tendencies or movements that are summarized by that label connect with the strategic objective of building a progressive politics in the contemporary United States?

The ideological roots of what is now called identity politics lie in a sensibility that emerged during the New Left and the civil-rights movement, the sensibility captured pithily in the statement, "the personal is political." It arose as part of a brief against sexism in the movement itself, as women in SNCC (the Student Nonviolent Co-ordinating Committee) and SDS (Students for a Democratic Society) rebelled against the gender politics of those organizations. In this sense, it was part of a developing critique of the ways that larger patterns of oppressive and inegalitarian social relations can permeate every sphere of the society, even the movement. This critique was also part of the Black Power argument for the need to organize on explicitly racial lines.

The assertion resonated as well with those who believed in a kind of "prefigurative" politics: that radicals should seek to enact models of the world we would create. This strain emphasized the need to provide space for voices of relatively powerless groups and individuals who are typically pressed to the margins of public life. And it also evoked a call to value political action for its qualities of self-transformation and personal enrichment. To that extent, it connected with the period's countercultural notions of personal liberation that stressed the political significance of pursuing and embracing alternative lifestyles, which is one of the reasons this radical sensibility was less radical than it appeared.

Lifestyle politics shared a mindset with youth-oriented consumerism and became the foundation for the hip, boutique-style capitalism associated with firms like The Body Shop, Benetton, or Whole Foods. Freedom to choose one's own lifestyle slides easily into freedom to purchase the accoutrements of a merchandised lifestyle: freedom to express an identity becomes freedom to purchase commodities that symbolize an identity. The signs were already present in the 1960s, when styles of hair and dress and other paraphernalia—peace symbols, or red, black, and green buttons and patches—took on automatic significance and marketability as easily attainable and fashionable expressions of supposedly deep existential and political commitments.

During the 1980s and 1990s, we've seen stark evidence of the inadequacy of this kind of politics. Firms like Nike and Reebok go out of their way to project corporate images that advance, sometimes even provocatively, a multicultural sensibility—as they amass huge profits from the exploitation of nonwhite labor. In hip-hop culture, we have a youth movement that collapses its notion of political critique and practice so completely into adolescent consumption that the movement's adherents often seem incapable of recognizing any other notion of politics.

One irony about identity politics is that it's nothing new: It's a form of interest-group activity that has been an organizational principle of the American political system for decades (a point lost in the overheated objections of the Gitlin–Schlesinger crowd). It has functioned in part to open up the political system to neglected populations. This is not to be sneezed at, of course, from the standpoint of expanding democratic interests; for example, the electoral empowerment of racial minorities through the enforcement of voting rights was a significant improvement. However, we should not gloss over the contingent and partial nature of the victories that come with greater inclusiveness.

At bottom, identity politics rests on problematic ideas of political authenticity and representation. These derive from the faulty premise that membership in a group gives access to a shared perspective and an intuitive understanding of the group's collective interests. This leads to two related beliefs that are wrong-headed and politically counterproductive: that only a group member can know or articulate the interests of the group, and that any group member can do so automatically by virtue of his or her identity.

Clarence Thomas should have been evidence enough to invalidate the premise linking group membership and perspective. Embarrassingly, people like Maya Angelou and Catharine MacKinnon initially cut Thomas slack based on the silly belief that because he's black and once was poor, putting him on the Supreme Court would turn out OK.

The simplistic belief that any credible member of a group can automatically represent that group's interest feeds a tendency to reduce political objectives to a plea for group representation on decision-making bodies or in other councils of power. That's the Clinton trick: to accept pleas for group representation or "access" while repudiating demands for an issue-based program. The dominant elites can happily satisfy such pleas; token egalitarianism is no threat at all.

\*   \*   \*

I've been startled by the reaction I've encountered to the Labor Party from many of those committed to identity politics and the "new social movements." They've objected to the Labor Party's formulation of our constituency as people who have to, or are expected to, work for their living. This is an explicit attempt to project a collective identity that can help to break down the ultimately artificial distinction between "economic" and "social" issues; it's an attempt to establish a broad and inclusive definition of the working class.

To be sure, some of the resistance reflects a healthy skepticism: The labor movement has hardly been always heroic and often has been just as bad as any other institution in American society with respect to racial and gender justice. But some of the resistance stems from the knee-jerk insistence on stressing distinctiveness and difference.

The claim that being a worker is not the most crucial identity for members of marginalized groups is debatable, to say the least. But even if that claim were true, what it means simply is that people see themselves in many ways simultaneously. We all have our own sets of experiences fashioned by our social position, our family upbringing, our local political culture, and our voluntary associations. Each of these goes into the mix, modifying, cross-cutting, even at times overriding identities based on race or ethnicity, gender, or sexual orientation.

Our identities are fluid, and they encompass competing claims, each vying for the mantle of universality. There's no such thing as authenticity; it's only a marketing ploy. No coherent group perspectives are decreed automatically by nature or by social and economic "law," and this applies to class consciousness as well as identity politics. The fact of the existence of a capitalist economic order doesn't automatically tell us how people interpret their positions within it. Class consciousness, no less than other identities, is contingent, the product of political debate and struggle.

So, in the Labor Party, we are trying to offer an umbrella for all those who want to engage in class politics, no matter what their other identifications are. There doesn't seem to be anything wrong with that, if you ask me. The view that it is wrong to identify on class grounds betrays a fundamentally conservative group outlook, which is a conceptual relative of racism. It has been disturbing to see this reflex in action, rejecting the premises necessary for building an effective political force that can challenge the juggernaut of corporate power.

That's the point, after all, of the Labor Party's broad definition of a working-class constituency. We need to establish the basis for an identity that unites us by showing how the same forces affect us all, albeit in somewhat different ways. This is not to diminish the reality of sexism, racism, or homophobia. But we have to come together to fashion a concrete alternative both to narrow, exclusivist forms of identity politics and to the false universalism that denies the reality of other forms of injustice. If we don't organize on a class basis, we'll be picked off one at a time, as we were with "welfare reform."

# —Skin Deep

A few years ago, in seminars within weeks of each other at two different Ivy League universities, colleagues queried me about the difference between race and ethnicity. I was a little surprised by the genuine puzzlement that motivated their questions, but I was struck still more by the good-natured querulousness that greeted my answer.

I said that race and ethnicity are simply categories of social hierarchy; they are just labels for different magnitudes of distance from the most desirable status on a continuum of "okayness." The farther out a population is on that continuum, the more likely it will be seen as a "racial" group; if it's somewhat nearer in, it'll more likely be understood as an "ethnicity." Several people were skeptical and unsatisfied with this characterization, thinking that there must be something firmer that distinguishes race from ethnicity, that *racial* difference must be in some way objectively more extreme. Then came the old chestnuts: more dramatic phenotypic difference, more remote common ancestry, and so on.

I mentioned historian Barbara Jeanne Fields's exercise inducing Columbia undergraduates to note whether they're sitting in class next to individuals of their same race—usually they are—and then whether those individuals look just like themselves, which they don't. Fields's point is that human populations vary in myriad ways, only some of which become racialized, based on specific histories of political economy and the facts of political power. Some superficial differences, like skin color, stand out to us because we perceive them in a context in which they're already laden with significance as markers of social status, while others, like, say, eye color, height, or head shape, don't. W. E. B. Du Bois put in succinctly in 1940, in a hypothetical dialogue with a foreigner seeking a road map of American racial classification. After considering and rejecting all the usual biological or morphological criteria, Du Bois concluded that a black person is most accurately "someone who must ride Jim Crow in Georgia." My son, Touré (who insists that I note for the public record that he is not the guy who writes about hip-hop in the *Voice*), suggests a variation of Du Bois's formulation that holds for the post-Jim Crow era: you are what the police think you are.

Those apothegms go to the heart of the matter. "Race" is purely a social construction; it has no core reality outside a specific social and historical context. That is not to say that it doesn't exist or that it is therefore meaningless, but its material force derives from state power, not some ahistorical "nature" or any sort of primordial group affinities—the nineteenth-century racist mush that has never lost its appeal as a simpleminded journalistic frame. Racial difference is not merely reflected in enforced patterns of social relations; it emerges exclusively from them.

This point typically elicits a string of anxious, incoherent yes-buts from people all over the official racial map, inside and outside the academy, across the political spectrum. The hesitancy about accepting race's contingency and fluidity shows just how thoroughly racialist thinking—which isn't just bigotry but all belief that race exists meaningfully and independently of specific social hierarchies—has been naturalized in American life, the extent to which we depend on it for our conceptual moorings. However, the conviction of race's solidity is undone by the ephemerality of the very categories that support it.

Take the race/ethnicity distinction, for instance. It didn't exist less than a century ago. There were only races, and there were a lot of them—Gallic, Nordic, Mediterranean, Slavic, just to name a few from the list of those now homogenized as white. And each of those categories yielded other, more discrete "races," such as Greeks, Armenians, Poles, the English, Welsh, Irish, and the like. (A "Racial Adaptability" chart prepared by industrial relations experts for employers in the 1920s listed 36 distinct races). For most of the nineteenth century, even the Anglo-American lower classes were often characterized as racially different from their social superiors. "Whiteness," in fact, evolved as a generically meaningful status only gradually over the nineteenth and early twentieth centuries, and in relation to specific issues associated with the incorporation of immigrant populations into an evolving system of social, political, and economic hierarchy.

Whiteness became increasingly significant as a kind of safety net, providing a baseline of eligibility to rights, opportunities, and minimal social position. Of course, whiteness presumed a contrast with nonwhiteness, specifically blackness, which was simultaneously becoming a monolithic category marking inferior status. As ambiguous or intermediate categories disappeared in the nineteenth century; the basically bipolar racial system that we now know took shape.

By the turn of the current century, immigrants came quickly to understand the material advantages of being declared white; among other things, they couldn't become naturalized citizens unless they were so classified. So federal court records from the period are littered with cases in which the swarthy flotsam and jetsam of the Mediterranean region in particular petitioned to demonstrate their legitimate claims to whiteness.

These cases were steeped in state-of-the-art "racial science," testament to the academy's voluminous history of creating and legitimizing sophistries around racial classification. Charles Murray and sociobiology are direct lineal descendants of this once hegemonic strain of scientific racism.

Besides, it didn't take much to figure out that being labeled "black" or "colored" would have a serious negative impact on economic and political opportunity. It only made sense for immigrants to try to avoid being thus hampered, and these efforts were all the more important in the Jim Crow South. Sicilians, who came from the backyard of Africa anyway, were thrust among blacks in the north Louisiana cotton fields as well as in south Louisiana — both in New Orleans and in the cane fields — where many of them were physically indistinguishable in the pertinent ways from much of the officially black population.

One of the most dramatic and revealing attempts to jockey for position involved descendants of the Delta Chinese, who had been imported into the Mississippi Delta region in the late nineteenth century to compete with blacks as plantation labor, but who eventually operated more as a stratum of commercial intermediaries. The Delta Chinese for some time occupied an ambiguous status —

including open socializing and intermarriage with blacks—that Mississippi's bipolar, white supremacist social order couldn't tolerate. Things came to a head around the issue of where Chinese should be slotted in the Jim Crow school system. No one with an alternative would have wanted to attend Mississippi's schools for black people, which were never intended to provide anything like a decent education. A group of Chinese in Jackson therefore sought to exploit the ambiguity of their "colored" designation to escape that fate. The result was *Gong Lum v. Rice*, in which the Chinese petitioners argued all the way to the Supreme Court—based once again on academic state-of-the-art "research"—that as an intermediate group they were in crucial ways racially and culturally nearer to whites and therefore should be permitted to attend white schools. (They lost the legal battle but won over Jackson's white elites, who quietly acquiesced.)

"Ethnicity"—and its corollary, the expansion of whiteness as a generic category—is the result of similar efforts at successfully negotiating the bipolar racial system to avoid the stigma of blackness. White ethnicity emerged during the New Deal and immediate postwar period, and it reflects the incorporation of previously distinct racial populations into the safety net of whiteness. This incorporation was spurred by the Democratic Party's coalition politics and the upward mobility made possible by the New Deal. As ever, academic race theory was there to provide the legitimizing conceptual frame, inventing and projecting ethnicity as a category of subracial difference.

There's a lesson here as we confront a new destabilization in the American racial system, in the face of a wave of immigration of populations defined outside the expanded universe of whiteness. Multiculturalism is partly an attempt to transcend the bipolar system. In that sense, it is an assertion that the world is more complicated than black and white, and it therefore challenges the simplistic racial discourse that has so long been a poison in American political life. However, multiculturalism also partly overlaps model-minority ideology, the current era's version of the closer-to-whites-than-to-blacks move. To that extent it's an application for a kind of contingent membership in whiteness, or for recognition of an intermediate category of okayness—both gambits that only reinforce existing racial ideology and hierarchy. We all need to be clear about which is which.

# —The Content
## of Our Cardiovascular

For some time, public health researchers have recognized that black people are disproportionately likely to die from cardiovascular disorders. Although some scholars have insisted that the effects of racism and poverty are key to understanding this phenomenon, most explanations have focused on racially based biological or anatomical causes. One leading theory, for example, is that blacks tend to have peculiarly fragile arterial walls and are therefore especially susceptible to stroke.

The November 21, 1996, issue of *The New England Journal of Medicine* contained two articles and an editorial that, at least implicitly, challenge that proposition. These articles find significant variation *within* the black population with respect to susceptibility to cardiovascular ailments. They go on to suggest that social, rather than biological, factors account for the relatively high overall black rates. When I read the report on these studies in *The New York Times*, I felt vindicated in my visceral skepticism about the racial physiology argument. The fragile-arterial-walls tale, for instance, just echoes too much of ex-L.A. police chief Daryl Gates's claim that blacks die in choke holds because of their abnormally narrow windpipes.

There's a long history of spurious claims about differences in racial biology. However, racial categories possess no real genetic legitimacy. This underscores their biological irrationality as a system for classifying people into groups. Geneticists recognize that the range of variation within a given "racial" population is usually greater than the range of variation between any two populations. This seriously undermines the notion that racial groups are clearly separated, homogeneous populations and that they can be easily generalized about. Still, researchers who work with racially defined sample populations tend to presume that what are merely political and sociological categories are also populations with biological integrity.

The tendency to seek biological explanations for black cardio-vascular problems makes sense, at least on the surface, for several pragmatic reasons. For one thing, the problem itself is a biological condition, and it's plausible to suspect that the cause would lie at least partly in the same domain as the effect. For another, medical research as a field remains biased toward treating human bodies as self-contained units, apart from the dynamics of culture and political economy. This bias has a solid historical foundation in medical training, reaching back to the mid nineteenth century. At that time, professionalization of the field demanded that doctors view patients as mere specimens on an examination table.

It's also predictable, in the current environment of genetic fetish-ism, that biological explanations would appeal. After all, medical researchers operate within the same cultural frames of reference as the rest of us: They buy the same stuff and absorb the same public information. They're concerned about their property values and jobs, crime, their kids' schools, the O.J. Simpson case, their financial security — the array of anxieties that occupy similarly situated Americans. They're no less likely than others to interpret the world through the lens of those concerns, no less likely to find comfort in the apparent clarity and constancy of biology, and no less likely to succumb to the resurgent racialism that accompanies, perhaps even drives, the popularity of biological explanations for social phenomena.

You don't have to be an editor of *Social Text* to be suspicious of the aura of transcendent, objective truth that surrounds invocations of science. It smells too much like revealed religion. A little historical perspective only reinforces the skepticism. Medical research has a long record of propping up racist ideology. Sometimes this has been done actively and sometimes indirectly, but in a way that le-gitimizes racism's common sense by associating it with science.

William H. Tucker, in *The Science and Politics of Racial Re-search*, catalogues a line of racist apologies within respectable medi-cal research that stretches back to the early nineteenth century. (One of my favorites is the 1851 discovery of something called "drapetomania." It was described as a mental disorder that drove slaves to run away to freedom.) In addition to scores of studies measuring brain weights, facial angles, motor responses, and such, mainstream public health research predicted that blacks would die out because they were unequipped to live in freedom.

More recently, popular medical research was put forth that explained why blacks excelled at sprinting but didn't do well running long distances. This theory vanished with decolonization, which ushered in an African domination of long-distance running that hasn't abated for three decades. Similarly, medical journals hypothesized that black's absence from the ranks of competitive swimmers stemmed from a physiological lack of buoyancy rather than, say, not having access to swimming pools.

These examples seem almost benign because they're so ridiculous. But they're only ridiculous after the fact. In their time they seemed plausible, and they had cultural force in the overriding discussion of essential racial difference. Many of these arguments were insidious because they weren't necessarily tied to demonstrating claims of biological difference. They just presumed it and thereby ratified that difference as an uncontroversial fact of nature.

This brings us back to blacks and cardiovascular disease as discussed in *The New England Journal*. Media reaction to the studies honed in on the social factors that cause heart and circulatory ailments. But the definition of "social factors," according to the responses, turned out to be merely personal habits; diet, alcohol and tobacco consumption, and so on. Joan Lunden punctuated the "Good Morning America" report on the studies by saying, "So, it's their choice then." This spin avoided discussion of poverty and racial injustice as causal factors. Yet, one of the *Journal* articles finds that the poverty rate accounts for more than half the racial difference in mortality in general.

That study, led by University of Michigan demographer Arline Geronimus, is exceptional in its consideration of the effects of inequality. Further, Geronimus and her colleagues find that other contributing factors may include "population density, household crowding, and correlates of residential segregation, such as residence in an area that is medically or socially underserved, one with dilapidated housing stock or a high crime rate, or one with excessive exposure to environmental hazards, chronic uncertainty, racial stress, or ongoing problems with social injustice and community disruption."

The other study, headed up by Jing Fang, an epidemiologist at the Albert Einstein Medical College, veered off into problematic territory. It concludes that birthplace accounts for the variation in cardiovascular susceptibility among black people. This explanation seems innocuous enough, until we realize what is implied by "birthplace." The study claims that Caribbean-born blacks do best and suggests that this may result from a combination of genetic factors peculiar to the region (!) and good Caribbean habits of diet and lifestyle—both biological and cultural factors.

In arguing for this environmental take on racial differences, the Jing Fang study delicately sidesteps what some, including Geronimus, would consider the most salient features of the black environment—poverty and racial injustice. In fact, Geronimus's study found that when we account for income, the birthplace differences in cardiovascular susceptibility disappear. Further, Jing Fang's suggestion of a superior Caribbean lifestyle introduces the familiar theme of the West Indian "model minority," and only reinforces the victim-blaming that dominates discussion of inequality.

The editorial accompanying the two articles, written by one Richard Gillum, M.D., of the Centers for Disease Control and Prevention, demonstrates the worst aspects of this tendency and ends up mirroring the general media spin. He basically ignores the Geronimus study's suggestion of the likely role of inequality and racism. Instead, he wonders "how protective factors in Caribbean migrants might be transferred" to counter the bad habits among less affluent black Americans, and he hopes for a new stage "in which American blacks will return to their ancestral low rates of cardiovascular disease while retaining the positive aspects of a Western lifestyle."

So at the end of the twentieth century we've come full circle and have arrived at the end of the nineteenth. Just as then, save for voices generally unheard in the public at large, respectable science now certifies the dominant argument in which racial inequality either stems from blacks' essential biological defectiveness or their essential cultural defectiveness.

# —Looking Backward

Charles Murray first slithered into American public life when he published *Losing Ground: American Social Policy, 1950–1980*, in which he argued that the cause of poverty among black Americans is the very effort to alleviate poverty through social provision. He purported to show, by means of a mass of charts and straw formulations he called "thought experiments," that the social welfare system institutionalizes perverse incentives encouraging indolence, wanton reproduction, and general profligacy. He proposed, appropriately for a book bearing a 1984 publication date, that the poor would be best helped by the elimination of all social support; a regime of tough love would wean them from debilitating dependency, on pain of extermination. (Now we have to wonder how the lazy dreck had enough sense to identify and respond to the incentives, but that was, after all, a different book for a different day.)

*Losing Ground* made a huge splash, catapulting Murray into prominence as the Reagan Administration's favorite social scientist and winning him luminary status in the social policy research industry. One can only wonder what heights of popularity Thomas Malthus would attain if he could come back into a world stocked with computers that perform multiple regression analysis!

Murray returned to the center of the public stage with publication of *The Bell Curve: Intelligence and Class Structure in American Life*, the product of a diabolical collaboration with Richard Herrnstein, the late Harvard psychologist known outside the academy—like his Berkeley counterpart, Arthur Jensen—for a more-than-twenty-year crusade to justify inequality by attributing it to innate, and therefore supposedly ineradicable, differences in intelligence.

As their title implies, Herrnstein and Murray contend that the key to explaining all inequality and all social problems in the United States is stratification by a unitary entity called intelligence, or "cognitive ability"—as measured, of course, in I.Q. This claim has surfaced repeatedly over the past seventy-five years only to be refuted each time as unfounded class, race, and gender prejudice. (See, for instance, Stephen Jay Gould's *The Mismeasure of Man*.) *The Bell Curve* advances it with the same kind of deluge of statistical and logical sophistry that has driven its predecessors, as well as Murray's opus of tough love for poor people.

Herrnstein and Murray see rigid I.Q. stratification operating through every sphere of social life. And they put two distinct wrinkles on this long-running fantasy. First is Herrnstein's old claim that I.Q. stratification is becoming ever more intense in a postindustrial world that requires cognitive ability over all else. As democratic institutions have succeeded in leveling the playing field, differences of individual merit become all the more pronounced. Second, the demonic duo back coyly away from the implications of their eugenic convictions (no doubt because cultural memory decays slowly enough that people still remember the Nazi death camps). Instead of directly endorsing extermination, mass sterilization, and selective breeding—which nonetheless implicitly shadow the book—they propose a world in which people will be slotted into places that fit their cognitive ability, in which each of us will be respected for what we actually are and can be (which will amount to more or less the same thing).

The effect of this reform will be, as they see it, to end *ressentiment* from and against those who seek more than their just deserts or aspire beyond their natural capacities. Of course, we'll need to have controls to make sure that dullards do what is best for them and don't get out of line. But that is a necessary price to stem the present tide of social breakdown. We shall, that is, have to destroy democracy to save it.

*The Bell Curve*'s message about the inevitability of existing patterns of inequality rests on a series of claims concerning intelligence. These are: (1) that human intelligence is reducible to a unitary, core trait that is measurable and reliably expressed as a single numerical entity, I.Q.; (2) that I.Q. increasingly determines (or strongly influences—Herrnstein and Murray frequently try to hide behind the weaker claim while substantively assuming the stronger one) socioeconomic status and behavior; (3) that I.Q. is distributed unevenly through the population in general and by race in particular; and (4) that cognitive ability is given and "substantially" (another bogus hedge) fixed by genetic inheritance. These claims are highly dubious. Some of them are preposterous and loony. All are marinated in self-congratulatory class prejudice and racism.

The book begins with a lengthy attempt to rehabilitate the old reductionist notion that there is a biologically based, hereditary "general factor of cognitive ability," a variant of the semi-mystical entity that Charles Spearman, a pioneer psychometrician (i.e., intelligence tester), labeled "g" in the early 1900s. The defense rests largely on protests that proponents of hereditarian I.Q. theories— for example, explicit racists like William Shockley and Arthur Jensen and the racist and fraud Cyril Burt—have been maligned and persecuted by ideologically motivated environmentalists and egalitarians. (Hereditarians, of course, are only tough-minded scientists who pursue truth courageously in the face of personal danger and ostracism.) The authors even try to sanitize psychometry's sordid history of eugenicist affiliations bordering on genocide. "[D]uring the first decades of the century," they coo, "a few testing enthusiasts proposed using the results of mental tests to support outrageous racial policies," such as forced sterilization, racist immigration restrictions, and the like. By contrast, Daniel Kevles (*In the Name of Eugenics*) and others have amply documented prominent psychometricians' active and extensive involvement in shaping eugenicist public policies in the United States that affected thousands of lives in the first third of the century and beyond. Stefan Kühl (*The Nazi Connection: Eugenics, American Racism and German National Socialism*), moreover, details the close connections and mutual admiration among American and German Nazi eugenicists throughout the 1930s and for years after. *The Bell Curve*'s tepid acknowledgment smacks of white Southerners' claims that the original Ku Klux Klan consisted of pranksters whose high jinks sometimes got out of hand—sort of the DKEs of the Reconstruction era.

Having, at least in their view, rescued psychometry's reputation from its own heinous past, the authors then offer a two-pronged, ostensibly pragmatic defense of their version of "g." They point to the tendency of tests of mental aptitude to converge, such that performance on some tests correlates with performance on others. For Herrnstein and Murray, as for Spearman and his epigones, that convergence indicates that the tests variously measure a single, fundamental property—general cognitive ability. They also adduce the authority of "the top experts on testing and cognitive ability" in support of the contention that this "g" exists.

As Gould and others (for example, R.C. Lewontin, Steven Rose, and Leon J. Kamin in *Not in Our Genes: Biology, Ideology, and Human Nature*) have pointed out, though, the numerical representation of a vector of test scores does not necessarily denote a real, empirical entity. To presume that it does it to succumb to a fetishism of numbers that inverts the relation between statistical analysis and the world it is intended to illuminate. The hard certainty of the formal mathematical abstraction imbues it with an apparent reality of its own: If a firm statistical relation exists, then it must correspond to something in the empirical world. (Gould characterizes this idealist fallacy, which lately has been resurgent among social scientists, as "physics envy.") In the absence of neurological or other physiological evidence, there is no reason to believe that the numerical "Intelligence Quotient" captures anything but a mathematical relation among a battery of test scores. This relation, in addition, is doubly arbitrary. It is not the only mathematical relation thinkable among the tests, nor are the tests themselves self-evidently measures of innate abilities that can be arrayed hierarchically. And since we can know "g" only through test scores and their correlation, determination of a test's accuracy in identifying core cognitive ability becomes to some degree a function of the extent to which the scores converge in variance. There is at least a potential for idealist circularity in this argument: We know a test is a reliable measure of intelligence because we stipulate that intelligence is indicated when the test's parts correlate well with one another.

In fact, both prongs of *The Bell Curve*'s defense of the reductionist notion of intelligence rest on circular argument. Appealing to the consensual authority of psychometricians to validate I.Q. testing is like appealing to the consensual authority of creationists to validate creationism. Psychometry by and large *is* intelligence testing, so it would be more than stunning to find a consensus of psychometricians that didn't endorse I.Q. testing. Similarly, the contention that the vector of test scores measures a core cognitive ability depends on a prior assumption that what tests measure is indeed core intelligence. As Lewontin et al., note, to determine whether a test is accurate requires some pre-existing notion of what it should measure and what results it should yield. We know that early psychometricians took girls' outperformance of boys on certain items to indicate flawed test design. And other scientific racists of that era, when confronted with blacks' greater possession than whites of some trait or thought to be desirable, simply reversed their interpretations of that trait's significance.

Herrnstein and Murray consistently bend over backward to give the benefit of the doubt to research whose conclusions they find congenial, and they dismiss, misrepresent, or ignore that which contradicts their vision. For instance, they decline to engage the work of Harvard psychologist Howard Gardner (*Frames of Mind: The Theory of Multiple Intelligences* and *Multiple Intelligences: The Theory in Practice*) or Yale's Robert Sternberg (*Beyond I.Q.*), among others, who argue for multiple fields of intelligence that are not hierarchically organized. They don't even mention the work of Gardner's colleague David Perkins, whose *Learnable Intelligence: Breaking the IQ Barrier* appears in the same Free Press catalogue as *The Bell Curve*. They also repeatedly and disingenuously accuse anti-hereditarians of contending that genes play no part in social life. Herrnstein and Murray justify their insistence on the I.Q. standard, to the exclusion of other ways of construing intelligence, primarily by pointing to the apparently strong positive relationship between I.Q. and school performance, income, and other measures of success. This presumably shows that I.Q. is the critical form of intelligence because it is such an important predictor of life chances. At the same time, they insist that I.Q. is not just or even mainly an artifact of class position. They frequently even take education or socioeconomic status as proxies for I.Q. when they lack actual test scores. This circularity reaches its zenith—and reveals the ideological motor that drives the authors' vision—in the following formulation:

The broad envelope of possibilities suggests that senior business executives soak up a large portion of the top IQ decile who are not engaged in the dozen or so high-IQ professions. . . . A high proportion of people in those positions graduated from college, one screen. They have risen in the corporate hierarchy over the course of their careers, which is probably another screen for IQ. What is their mean IQ? There is no precise number. Studies suggest that the mean for . . . all white collar professionals is around 107, but that category is far broader than the one we have in mind. Moreover, the mean IQ of four-year college graduates in general was estimated at about 115 in 1972, and senior executives probably have a mean above that average.

Let's pause a moment to marvel at the elegant precision of science.

Herrnstein and Murray seek to avoid the appearance of circularity through two strains of statistically based argument. On the one hand, they claim that the relation between I.Q. and social performance persists even when all environmental differences are taken into account. On the other, they revert to the stock-in-trade that has always underscored the hereditarian camp's sideshow quality; I mean, of course, the studies of separated twins.

I admit to not having tracked down and examined closely the research they cite to support these two lines of defense. Four points nevertheless suggest cause for skepticism. First, social environments are complex, and it is very difficult—especially in a large aggregate sample like the National Longitudinal Survey of Youth, on which *The Bell Curve* principally relies in this regard—to wash out confidently the multifarious consequences of social stratification. Simply controlling for parental income, as these studies typically do, is hardly sufficient. The effects of stratification can work in subtle and indirect ways that persist through momentary parity of income. For instance, the child of a first-generation middle-class black or Puerto Rican family is likely to have fewer social resources—given the effects of ghettoization and discrimination in access to sources of personal capital (mortgages and other bank loans, accumulation of capitalizable home equity, investment opportunities, inherited wealth)—than her white counterpart, and to shoulder an additional burden of everyday racial discrimination. Herrnstein and Murray are crudely, and strategically, insensitive to

154 — EQUALITY & IDEOLOGY IN AMERICAN POLITICS

this level of complexity, as they show when dismissing the possibility that racial discrimination might account for persisting black/white differences in I.Q. scores:

> An appeal to the effects of racism . . . requires explaining why environments poisoned by discrimination and racism for some other groups—against the Chinese or the Jews in some regions of America, for example—have left them with higher scores than the national average.

Second, as Lewontin and Richard Levins (*The Dialectical Biologist*) reflect a consensus among professional geneticists in painstakingly arguing, the attempt to apportion definitively the separate effects of heredity and environment is hopelessly wrongheaded and naïve. I quote them at some length because of the importance of the point:

> All individuals owe their phenotype to the biochemical activity of their genes in a unique sequence of environments and to developmental events that may occur subsequent to, although dependent upon, the initial action of the genes. . . . If an event results from the joint operation of a number of causative chains, and if these causes "interact" in any generally accepted meaning of the word, it becomes conceptually impossible to assign quantitative values to the causes of that individual event. . . . It is obviously . . . absurd to say what proportion of a plant's height is owed to the fertilizer it received and what proportion to the water, or to ascribe so many inches of a man's height to his genes and so many to his environment.

Herrnstein and Murray presume that in measuring patterns of variation in I.Q. scores in a way that neutralizes the effects of selected aspects of environment, they can distill the part played by heredity in determining cognitive ability. Thus they repeatedly invoke the claim that intelligence is at least 40–80 percent determined by inheritance. This presumption and the claim derived from it are plain stupid.

Third, even if we grant their cracker barrel view of causation and variation, their case is defeated by the weight of its own numbers. By their own precious calculations, I.Q. accounts for no more than between 10 and 20 percent of the variation they discover between individuals and "races" on most measures, and usually closer to the lower end. (Howard Gardner makes this point also in his important review of *The Bell Curve* in *The American Prospect*, where he also discusses at length other approaches to theorizing human intelligence that Herrnstein and Murray ignore.) If, as they take as a consensual figure, I.Q. derives 60 percent from genetic inheritance (and what could that statement possibly mean as a practical matter, anyway?), then heredity accounts for no more than 6–12 percent of the total variation they find. Why should the tail wag the dog for all those leaden, deceitful pages?

Fourth, we come to the twin studies. Herrnstein and Murray report that Thomas Bouchard at the University of Minnesota (about whom more later) has found the same strikingly high correlations in I.Q. among his sample of supposedly real twins raised apart that Sir Cyril Burt found among the imaginary twins in his fraudulent "research." (Burt, by the way, was easily the most respected psychometrician of his time, knighted for his accomplishments as a theorist of scientific racial hygiene.) Perhaps, though the possibility that life would so faithfully and dramatically imitate art ought to give pause, particularly considering that few other twin impresarios had ever reported the consistent strength of relationship that Burt claimed. And then there is the troubling issue of what exactly one means by separated twins.

Lewontin, Rose, and Kamin in *Not in Our Genes* examine the samples on which the best-known twin studies prior to Bouchard's were based. They note, first, that pure cases of twins separated at birth and raised completely apart would be exceedingly difficult to locate because they would most likely not know each other's whereabouts or even that either sib was in fact half of a twin set. As it turns out, most of the putatively separated twins lived with close family members, and most of those who didn't lived with nearby family friends. Nearly all lived within a few miles of and had regular, if not constant, contact with each other. According to research notes, one English set lived within a few hundred yards of each other, played together regularly and wanted to sit at the same desk at the school they both attended. Another English set had been separated until age 5, then finished growing up under the same roof and were in continuous contact thereafter until they were interviewed for the study at age 52. A set in a famous Danish study were "cared for by relatives until the age of seven then lived together with their mother until they were fourteen." The research notes indicate that

> they were usually dressed alike and very often confused by strangers, at school, and sometimes also by their stepfather. . . . [They] always kept together when children, they played only with each other and were treated as a unit by their environment.

Such is the twin research that is the hereditarians trump card. (Maybe they can make dog-faced boys the next scholarly frontier.)

Several of *The Bell Curve*'s reviewers have detected a damning empirical flaw in the logic of its case. On the one hand, Herrnstein and Murray contend that I.Q. is largely fixed by nature and cannot be improved. On the other, they note that studies inside their own paradigm have recorded a steady upward trend in test scores across time. They squirm mightily to make those points fit, but they can't. Nor can they face up to the entailments of that contradiction, because the point of the book, like the point of every line that Murray has ever written, as well as every syllable of Herrnstein's I.Q. research, is only to advance a reactionary, racist, and otherwise anti-egalitarian ideological agenda by dressing it with a scientistic patina.

Beneath the mind-numbing barrage of numbers, this book is really just a compendium of reactionary prejudices. I.Q. shapes farsightedness, moral sense, the decisions not to get pregnant, to be employed, not to be a female househead, to marry and to remain married to one's first spouse (presumably the divorced and remarried Murray has an exemption from this criterion), to nurture and attend to one's offspring, and so on.

Simply being stopped—but not charged—by the police becomes evidence of an I.Q.-graded tendency to criminality. White men who have never been stopped have an average I.Q. of 106; those stopped but not booked have to schlep along at 103; those booked but not convicted check in at 101; the convicted but not incarcerated peer dimly from a 100 wattage; and those who go to jail vegetate at 93. Even putting aside the bigotry embedded in their cops' view of the world, this is batty. Not only is the slope of this curve—as with so much of their data—too perfectly straight but the suggestion that minute increments of difference could portend such grave consequences is numerical fetishism gone off the deep end. Two points on an I.Q. test can separate conviction from acquittal!?

Instructively, the authors restrict their analysis of white criminality to a male sample and parenting to a female sample. Parents = mothers. And while they examine abuse and neglect of children (found to be almost the exclusive province of the lower cognitive orders) among this female sample, spousal abuse is mentioned nowhere in the book, much less considered a form of male criminality.

In his review Howard Gardner accuses Herrnstein and Murray of practicing "scholarly brinkmanship." The description is apt. They repeatedly leave themselves enough wiggle room to avoid responsibility either for the frightening implications of the line they advance so insistently or for defending the crackpot pseudoscience on which they ultimately base their interpretation. Just a few examples of the way the authors try to have it both ways: Early in the book—and Murray has repeated this canard ad nauseam in his soft-spoken, carefully measured tones on newschat shows since publication—they announce piously that they want all to understand that "intelligence is a noun, not an accolade." Small matter that the book is entirely an attempt to justify the opposite view. Similarly, they end with an equally pious call to treat every person as an individual and declaim against making judgments about groups, when group difference has been the central organizing principle of their entire argument.

This kind of mendacity is one of their narrative's main tropes. When forced by the logic of their own account to a point at which they would have to declare explicitly as militant hereditarians, they say, Well, it really doesn't matter ultimately whether or not I.Q. is inherited because the environmental changes required to increase I.Q. are impossibly huge. Yet that argument depends completely on the hereditarian justification of inequality that they spend the whole book trying to establish.

\* \* \*

Nowhere is the authors' dishonesty clearer than with respect to race. Their analysis of white variation in I.Q. is ultimately a front to fend off charges of racism. What really drives this book, and reflects the diabolism of the Murray/Herrnstein combination, is its claim to demonstrate black intellectual inferiority. They use I.Q. to support a "twofer": opposition to affirmative action, which overplaces incompetent blacks, and the contention that black poverty derives from the existence of an innately inferior black underclass.

Murray has protested incessantly that he and Herrnstein wanted in no way to be associated with racism, that the book isn't even about race, which is after all the topic of only one of *The Bell Curve*'s twenty-two chapters. But in addition to the infamous Chapter Thirteen, "Ethnic Differences in Cognitive Ability," three others center on arguments about black (and, to varying degrees, Latino) inferiority. The very next chapter, "Ethnic Inequalities in Relation to IQ," is a direct attempt to explain existing racial stratification along socioeconomic lines as the reflection of differences in group intelligence. The other two chapters in Part III seek to pull together claims about racial differences in intelligence and behavior. Those four chapters set the stage for the book's only two explicitly policy-driven chapters, "Affirmative Action in Higher Education" and "Affirmative Action in the Workplace," both of which are about initiatives directed toward blacks, and both slide into stoking white populist racism with "thought experiments" positing poor or working-class whites shunted aside in favor of underqualified, well-off blacks.

Murray's protests do suggest something about his views of race, however; it's apparently a property only some of us have. *The Bell Curve* makes a big deal of restricting the eight chapters of Part II to discussion of whites alone. If we assume that they are no less a "race" than everyone else is, then well over half the book is organized around race as a unit of analysis. Moreover, the theme of racially skewed intelligence and its significance for public policy runs through the entire volume. (In the third chapter the authors speculate about how many billions of dollars the Supreme Court's 1971

*Griggs v. Duke Power Company* decision, striking down the use of all but performance-based tests for employment and promotion, has cost the "American economy," and they argue gratuitously for choosing police by I.Q.) And how could it be otherwise in a book whose punch line is that society is and must be stratified by intelligence, which is distributed unequally among individuals and racial groups and cannot be changed in either?

Despite their concern to insulate themselves from the appearance of racism, Herrnstein and Murray display a perspective worthy of the stereotypical Alabama filling station. After acknowledging that genetic variations among individuals within a given "race" are greater than those between "races," they persist in maintaining that racially defined populations must differ in genetically significant ways because otherwise they wouldn't have different hair texture or skin color. And besides, they say, there must be differences between races because races "are by definition groups of people who differ in characteristic ways."

Despite Murray's complaints that it has been misinterpreted, *The Bell Curve* is committed to *racial* inequality. Admitting that they can't isolate biologically pure racial categories, Herrnstein and Murray opt to "classify people according to the way they classify themselves." But this destroys the possibility that their statistical hocus-pocus does any of the hereditarian work they claim for it. What they describe at most is race as a category of common social experience. Therefore, whatever patterns they find among racialized populations can only reflect that experience.

Most tellingly, however, they attempt quite directly to legitimize J. Philippe Rushton, the Canadian psychologist whose career has centered on demonstrating fundamental, almost species-like, racial difference. They announce self-righteously that "Rushton's work is not that of a crackpot or a bigot, as many of his critics are given to charging." This about a man who presents, in his book, *Race, Evolution, and Behavior*, racial rankings on "Criteria for Civilization" (only "Caucasoids," naturally, consistently meet all twenty-one items on his checklist) and "Personality and Temperament Traits," in addition to erect penis size (by length and circumference, no less), as well as the rest of the stock-in-trade of Victorian scientistic racism, and who computes an "Interbreeding Depression Score" to help clarify his statistical findings!

Rushton is in fact only the tip of the iceberg. *The Bell Curve* is embedded in the intellectual apparatus of the racist, crypto-fascist right. The central authorities on whom Herrnstein and Murray rely for their claims about I.Q., race and heredity are nearly all associated with the Pioneer Fund, an ultrarightist foundation that was formed in the 1930s to advance eugenicist agendas. The Fund boasts of having been almost entirely responsible for funding I.Q. and race and heredity research in the United States since the 1970s, and much of it worldwide. Rushton, along with nearly all those who contribute jacket blurbs for his book, is a major recipient of Pioneer grants. This includes Thomas Bouchard of the Minnesota twins, as well as Richard Lynn, on whom Herrnstein and Murray draw extensively, describing him as "a leading scholar of racial and ethnic differences." Among Lynn's leading scholarship to which they refer are the following articles: "The Intelligence of the Mongoloids," *Personality and Individual Differences* (1987); "Further Evidence for the Existence of Race and Sex Differences in Cranial Capacity," *Social Behavior and Personality* (1993); and "Positive Correlations Between Head Size and I.Q.," *British Journal of Educational Psychology* (1989). In addition, Lynn is editor of *Mankind Quarterly*, the Pioneer Fund's flagship journal.

Herrnstein and Murray take pains to sugarcoat and hedge their more outrageous claims, but their nasty political agenda, always visible in the wings, occasionally comes to center stage. They warn of the "dysgenic" effects for the nation of low-I.Q. women's relatively greater fertility and that the "shifting ethnic makeup" resulting from immigration of low-I.Q., high-breeding populations will "lower the average American I.Q. 0.8 points per generation."

What makes this international vipers' nest of reactionaries so dangerous is that many of its members maintain legitimate academic reputations. Rushton, for instance, as recently as 1988 won a Guggenheim Fellowship. Others routinely do contract research for the U.S. military. Most hold respectable university appointments.

\*    \*    \*

This brings me to the final and perhaps most important point to be made about this hideous book. It is worthwhile to pause for a moment to compare the appearance of *The Bell Curve* to the last significant eruption of pseudoscientific, hereditarian political reaction into American public life. Only two decades ago, the same Herrnstein, Jensen, and Shockley flooded the channels of the public information industry with essentially the same arguments I've been discussing here.

At that time I refused to attend to the controversy, partly out of a conviction that it is both beneath my dignity and politically unacceptable to engage in a debate that treats as an open question that I might be a monkey. Progressive forces were still at least a residual presence in American politics, however, and liberal intellectuals could be counted on to fight the foes of minimal human equality. I am still convinced that having to do what I've done in this review besmirches my dignity. It's a statement about the right's momentum that *The Bell Curve* makes such a splash that *The Nation* (for which this essay was originally written) had to devote so much space to arming our troops against it.

Mainstream racial discourse is dishonest and polluted enough to take the book seriously. Jason DeParle, in his *New York Times Magazine* puff piece, can't decide whether the Charles Murray who burned a cross in his youth, who alleges that the Irish have a way with words, Scotch-Irish are cantankerous, and blacks are musical and athletic, and who proposes a separate but equal world in which "each clan will add up its accomplishments using its own weighting system . . . and, most importantly, will not be concerned about comparing its accomplishments line-by-line with those of any other clan," is a racist. *New Republic* editor Andrew Sullivan opines that "the notion that there might be resilient ethnic differences in intelligence is not . . . an inherently racist belief."

Now liberals of all stripes—and even illiberals like Pat Buchanan, John McLaughlin, and Rush Limbaugh, which should make us wonder what exactly is going on—are eloquently dissenting from Herrnstein and Murray's unsavory racial messages. It's necessary to remind them that more than any other force in American politics, they are responsible for this book's visibility.

Murray has always been the same intellectual brownshirt. He has neither changed over the past decade nor done anything else that might redeem his reputation as a scholar. And it doesn't matter whether he is a committed ideologue or an amoral opportunist. Nazis came in both varieties—think of Alfred Rosenberg and Paul de Man—and in real life the lines separating the two are seldom clear.

We can trace Murray's legitimacy directly to the spinelessness, opportunism, and racial bad faith of the liberals in the social-policy establishment. Although Murray's draconian conclusions seemed unpalatable at first, they have since come to inform common sense about social policy, even in the Clinton White House. Liberals have never frankly denounced Murray as the right-wing hack that he is. They appear on panels with him and treat him as a serious, albeit conservative, fellow worker in the vineyard of truth. They have allowed him to set the terms of debate over social welfare and bend over backward not to attack him sharply.

Many of those objecting to Herrnstein and Murray's racism embrace positions that are almost indistinguishable, except for the resort to biology. Mickey Kaus in his scurrilous tract *The End of Equality* presents a substantive agenda for American politics quite like theirs, minus the I.Q. and explicit hereditarianism. Herrnstein and Murray note the similarities and draw on him for their absurd concluding chapter. Although William Julius Wilson in *The Truly Disadvantaged* criticizes Murray's thesis in *Losing Ground*, he does so only by suggesting alternatives to Murray's interpretation of data. Wilson reserves harsh moral judgment for left-liberals, whom he scolds for not being tough-minded enough about pathologies among the poor. He urges a pre-emptive focus on "ghetto-specific cultural characteristics," thus ceding important ground to Murray's perspective. Many of those so exercised in *The New Republic*'s special feature on *The Bell Curve* have joined Murray in meanspirited bashing of "political correctness" and affirmative action. And many more join him in writing about inner-city poor people as an alien and defective Other, a dangerous problem to be administered and controlled—not as fellow citizens.

I have argued that the difference between racially inflected "underclass" ideology and old-fashioned biological racism is more apparent than real. Racist ideologies in the United States have always come in culturalist and biologistic, and often overlapping, strains. The point is the claim of essential inequality, not the location of its source.

While reading Herrnstein and Murray and the literature of which they draw, I often felt like a mirror image of Julian West, Edward Bellamy's protagonist in *Looking Backward*, who fell unconscious at the end of the nineteenth century and awoke at the end of the twentieth. And indeed, the authors' strategic hedging of their hereditarian claims could presage the return of an updated version of the Lamarckian race theory popular a century ago. As "culture" has increasingly become a euphemism for "race"—an expression of inherent traits—it is only a short step to characterizations of group difference more overtly inflected toward biology, yet avoiding what remains, for the moment anyway, the stigma of biological determinism.

There's not much reason for optimism. Daniel Patrick Moynihan once announced at his Senate Finance Committee hearing on welfare reform that we could be witnessing the processes of "speciation" at work among the inner-city poor. Nodding their agreement were the Secretary of Health and Human Services, Donna Shalala, and her two world-class poverty researcher undersecretaries, Mary Jo Bane and David Ellwood (the originator of the "two years and off" welfare policy, who incidentally shows up in *The Bell Curve*'s acknowledgments). Just how different is that from Rushton or the Aryan Nations or the old White Citizens' Council?

# Part Three

# THE QUESTION
## OF PRACTICE

# —Posing As Politics

C-SPAN and Black Entertainment Television are next to each other on my cable system. So when senators Paul Wellstone and Carol Moseley-Braun were making their valiant stand against the Republicans' 1995 budget bill, I passed an insomniac night flipping back and forth between their filibuster and *Rap City*. The contrast was striking, between both the images projected and the systems of meaning that imbued each with political significance.

A few weeks later, on a panel at a Democratic Socialists of America youth conference, I found myself in the middle of a discussion of hip-hop/house culture and its global dissemination. Cautionary suggestions about exulting too much in this youth movement's undefined, though allegedly great, radical promise produced the session's most passionately argued moments.

Around the same time, I received a list of working papers from the University of Chicago's public policy school, which was then William Julius Wilson's mini Tuskegee. The coauthor of one paper was a graduate student who had previously challenged my skepticism about the large political claims made for inner-city youth culture. The paper was about the "social control" problems that result from a supposed breakdown of intergenerational communication in impoverished black neighborhoods. This is conventional sociology of a decidedly conservative bent; it's a feature of the reigning species of culture-of-poverty ideology, the search for social pathologies that mark a defective urban underclass. Instructively, this student, who had tried to defend the elevation of rap first as political action, then as a necessary precursor to political action, could adopt without qualms the classically depoliticized, victim-blaming frames for talking about inequality and dispossession that have been the stock-in-trade of Chicago sociology since the early twentieth century. That's the beauty of cultural politics; it can coexist comfortably with any kind of policy orientation.

These incidents threw into relief for me the key problem with progressives' current romance with youth culture and cultural politics in general; it rests ultimately on a rejection of the kind of direct political action that attempts to alter the structure and behavior of the institutions of public authority, what used to be called the state. And it ignores the action of the state itself. In both the graduate student's pro-rap and pro–social control arguments, there is no discussion of the government's regressive development policies, tax and foreign policies that reward capital flight and deindustrialization, chronic underfunding of education and housing for poor people, unequal delivery of public services, criminalization of poverty, or legacy of direct and indirect support for racial discrimination in defining impoverished black and Latino Americans' lives. Nor is there space in either formulation for considering the use of government or other political institutions to improve people's lives. The rap videos' projection of flamboyant cynicism, the pose of hard-bitten alienation that masquerades as "real," contrasts as sharply with Wellstone's and Moseley-Braun's focused resolve to fight for humane public policy as the rappers' avant-garde stylishness does with the senators' very straight self-presentation. The DSA advocates of youth culture's strategic importance elevate it as more vital than political work focused on government and public policy.

This dismissal of state-centered politics is a signal weakness of the left. It offers no guide for emancipatory action; rather, it is deeply harmful to the pursuit of progressive interests. It amounts to a don't-worry, be-angry politics of posture. Beneath radical-sounding rhetoric, the shibboleths of academic cultural studies and the presumptions of identity politics come together to celebrate alienation by labeling it "resistance." Alienation is the opposite of politics; it is by definition resignation and quiescence.

There's a perverse logic at work here, taking off from the premise that the MTV generation's disaffection from conventional political action should be accepted on its own terms. This assumes a smug, Reagan-baby disregard for civic engagement as outmoded and boring, yet the irony is that, in the most literal way, there is political activity in the MTV generation. Clinton, after all, used MTV to court young voters, and various pop stars lent their celebrity to the Rock the Vote movement, which got its main media ride on the music channel. MTV spawned its first celebrity political journalist in Tabitha Soren. Of course, it spawned another political celebrity, too: VJ Kennedy, who proudly declared her Republicanism, made teasing references to her virginity, and professed a desire to sleep with Dan Quayle. The point about youth culture is that it's *young*—by definition, naïve, inchoate, impulsive. Rock what vote? For whom? Clinton, Quayle, take your pick; they're both sort of cute.

As for rap, its political profile has stalled at the level of freaking out conservatives with songs about killing cops and peddling the timeworn notion of the outlaw—or in current parlance, "gangsta"—as political avatar. Individual acts of aggression, whether blowing away bank guards or beating up your girlfriend, are a political dead end (or in the latter case, a tactic of male dominance). Anger and self-definition are potential precursors to political action, but they don't constitute political action in themselves. And the politics they predict can be anything, including skinhead-style racism and fascism. Twenty years ago, the left called this sort of thing "adventurism," a distraction from both real politics and *realpolitik*. Today, having suffered decades of intensifying political marginalization, too many of us are prepared to smile gamely and call it revolution.

When I was treated on the DSA panel to the line about how young people all over the world are converging on a potentially explosive collective identity and perspective, I couldn't help asking how this view differs from hippies' fantasies of a transformative counterculture, Alan Freed's dream in the '50s that rock and roll would bring the world together, or even earlier hopes for jazz expressed in besotted soliloquies outside the Cotton Club or in Nancy Cunard's salon. And can we forget that it has been a string of corporate marketing campaigns—from Coca-Cola to Benetton—that has most effectively projected the image of a global youth culture knitted together through music and fashion?

I know, I know; corporate youth culture is inauthentic and co-opted; there's a real one out there about to erupt, tucked away from the eyes of all but the cognoscenti. Contemporary youth culture is

New and Improved — different from, more subversive than, its predecessors. But subversive of what? When all is said and done, defining subversion as avoiding incorporation into the mass market is nothing more than a call for permanent product revolution. This morning's authenticity is in the boutique this afternoon and the Paramus mall tomorrow.

Confronted with the charge that I'm just expressing a generational animus, I like to point out that it was my age cohort that invented the notion of youth as a politically meaningful social category, and I can produce witnesses to verify that I opposed it even then. But the idea of a distinct youth culture is older still; in the 1977 book *The Damned & the Beautiful*, Paula Fass examines its construction — already around a marketing category — in the '20s. Besides, objection to the idea of youth culture as political activism isn't confined to those too old to get in on the fun. Many young people now, as thirty years ago, participate enthusiastically in a shared symbolic world of music and style without imagining themselves to be doing anything of world-historic significance. Many embrace that world lightheartedly and apolitically; others do so zestily while understanding that their political commitments lie in a different domain — one that centers on fighting the balanced budget amendment and cuts in special welfare spending, organizing to preserve and extend antidiscrimination policies and women's reproductive freedom, to cut regressive military spending, and to rebuild labor.

Cultural production can reflect and perhaps support a political movement; it can never generate or substitute for one. There is no politics worthy of the name that does not work to shape the official institutions of public authority that govern and channel people's lives. Anything else is playacting.

# —Ethnic Studies and Pluralist Politics

For those old enough to have lived through the struggles for black studies a generation ago, the wave of campus protests in recent years demanding ethnic studies programs has a déjà vu quality, almost like the opening paragraphs of Marx's *Eighteenth Brumaire*: "And just when they seem engaged in revolutionizing themselves and things, in creating something that has never yet existed, precisely in such periods of revolutionary crisis they anxiously conjure up the spirits of the past to their service and borrow from them names, battle cries, and costumes in order to present the scene of world history in this time-honored disguise and this borrowed language. Thus Luther donned the mask of the Apostle Paul, the Revolution of 1789 to 1814 draped itself alternately as the Roman republic and the Roman empire."

It's certainly understandable that the specter of "the Sixties" haunts student activism. Young activists seem to look over their shoulders, to orient themselves by the standard of that iconic time because the student movement of the 1960s was, after all, the last great outpouring of campus radicalism. But even if they didn't want to think about it, they couldn't avoid doing so. The right, in its Kulturkampf, has apotheosized the Sixties as a catch-all symbol for all that's evilly egalitarian in contemporary life. From a slightly different political direction, baby-boomer neoliberals—like the 1990s leadership of the Democratic party—weave the "excesses of the Sixties" into their tale of how "McGovernism" has discredited liberal politics. And, more to the point, overlapping the two are the oh-so-pious professional defenders of Holy Universalism, whose jeremiads against academic "balkanization" and "tribalism" echo the last generation's self-righteous defenses of Eurocentrism as "intellectual standards" and "objectivity' against early proponents of black studies. Arthur Schlesinger, Jr.'s "common culture"—now as then—is one that demands acceptance of a chauvinist fantasy that

Europe is the *"unique* source" of ideas of "individual liberty, political democracy, the rule of law, human rights and cultural freedom." John Patrick Diggins insists on a *New York Times* op-ed page that commitment to truth and scholarly objectivity must lead both to recognition that American roots stem from John Locke and John Calvin and to embrace of that hoary, settler-colonial vestige "the genius of 'American exceptionalism.'" Sometimes it seems as if nothing has changed at all in the last thirty years.

But things have changed. Thirty years ago, the officially racist restrictions on immigration to the United States had just been lifted; black Americans' citizenship rights had just been reaffirmed and bolstered by Federal Civil Rights and Voting Rights legislation, and the second wave of the women's movement was only beginning to gather steam. As usual, the university reflected the world of which it was a part—a step behind. Nonwhites and women of any sort were almost nonexistent on the faculties of elite universities, and recruitment of black students was just beginning. Standard Americanist curricula took the nation's story to be a procession of white men debating among themselves about big principles and figuring out what to do or think about everyone else here, if the latter entered the scholarly narratives at all. Political scientists celebrated a pluralist model of American democracy that supposedly worked quite well—qualified at most with a passing "except for the Negroes" clause. Sociologists back-slapped through panegyrics on the "affluent society" and fretted over how "Americans" would deal with their Negro problem or absorb minority groups. Henry Steele Commager's *American Mind*, like Wilbur Cash's *Mind of the South*, thought entirely within a white, male head, and of course American literary sensibility was matter-of-factly white and European in its referents.

The movement for black studies not only responded to that Eurocentism; it also emerged within a broader activist stream exposing the sanctimonious pretense that the academy stands outside and above the politics shaping the surrounding world. Struggles at the University of Chicago and Columbia highlighted universities' predatory involvement in local urban renewal activity; thus the imagery of ethereal pristineness melted away to reveal corporate institutions that throw their weight around to displace nonwhite poor people in ruthless pursuit of *lebensraum*. (The *Voice*'s James Ridgeway's 1968 book, *The Closed Corporation*, was an important exposé of the universities' corporate and military connections.) At Duke 400 students moved into the president's house to protest the university's opposition to unionization among its largely black and poor service and maintenance employees, and six miles away in Chapel Hill similar issues erupted into a bitter strike that practically shut down the University of North Carolina. And from one end of the country to the other students mobilized against their universities' complicity in the Vietnam War, either directly, through research for the military, or indirectly, through even more nefarious alliances with corporate weapons contractors like Dow.

The black studies movement reflected as well the university's significance in ethnic pluralist politics. University pedigree had become steadily more important as a criterion for upper middle class status. And — beginning with Jews and others who would come to occupy the label "white ethnics" — representation among faculties and student bodies at elite institutions signalled incorporation into what historian David Hollinger has called "the circle of the 'we.'" Symbolically, such representation indicates that a group's members can attain the highest cultivation and that the group has established itself above the line separating those who count in the society from those seen mainly as problems to be administered. Materially, beachheads in elite universities provide cultural authority for propagandizing the group's image and advancing specific constructions of its interests.

The non-WASPs who first made the university a venue for ethnic validation already had attained whiteness, the privileged status that let them speak credibly in the first person plural about a supposedly common European heritage. Their legitimacy therefore could rest on mastery of the codes of "Western Civilization", a shared racial/cultural tradition that washed over and cleansed previously tainted identities emanating from Ireland or southern and eastern Europe. (Yale Law School Dean Guido Calabrese, Renaissance scholar and Yale president A. Bartlett Giammatti, Daniel Moynihan, Lionel Trilling, Nathan Glazer, and Daniel Bell all rose

on this wave of ethnic incorporation. All exemplify, to paraphrase
Engels's evolutionary metaphor, the part played by Ivy League affiliation in the transition from racial to ethnic difference.) It also presumed and propagated a Eurocentric notion of universality that is
the thread connecting Schlesinger's and Diggins's middle-brow
high-mindedness and Pat Buchanan's thuggishly nativist racism.

Blacks—as the main Other against whom whiteness was
defined—just didn't have similar access to this cultural custodianship; black voices intoning paeans to "our" European heritage
didn't quite convince. The officially universalistic narratives of the
United States were heavily inflected to sanitizing the centrality of
black people's subordination and exploitation in the development
of national culture, and they were equally resistant to recognizing
black civic and intellectual agency as a formative strain of the national experience. Southern exceptionalism rationalized slavery,
and especially slaves, as somehow not really part of the authentic
American saga. An orthodoxy derived ultimately from planters'
apologists and other white supremacists persisted about Reconstruction, as did a view of blacks as basically wards of American
democracy and Western Civilization more broadly—recipients
rather than subjects of meaningful social action. American academics would no more accept blacks as Keepers of the Flame of the West
than as investment counselors or electricians. On the other hand,
postwar decolonization underscored the false, ideological character
of the Western Civilization idea's universalist claim and further im-
pelled a demand for inclusion through revision of prevailing narratives rather than simple absorption into them.

Despite the different stances supporting pursuit of academic incorporation among white ethnics and the black studies movement,
both were embedded in the same larger dynamic. Beneath the language of "contributions," "voices," and the often vaporous, solipsistic rhetoric of identity politics, demands for black studies
programs in the last generation, or Latino or Asian-American studies programs today, are partly also calls for recognizing the particular groups' legitimacy as nodes within the ethnic pluralist system.
Institutionalizing ethnic studies is an element of establishing and
legitimizing ethnic identities appropriate for that system; creation of

Asian-American Studies, for instance, is part of creating a generic Asian-American identity, a category that derives its rationality from the facts of racial discrimination and the logic of American politics rather than from shared properties inherent among people of broadly Asian descent.

As a political phenomenon, perhaps what's significant about this movement is the effects that it may have on the young people engaged in it. For some, of course, this will be only the fleeting instant of activism that will justify self-righteous defense of a subsequent lifetime of cynicism or passivity; for some it may even be the pro forma pretext for a God-that-failed rightist conversion. Some will go on to become race relations technicians either in the university or elsewhere, and be more or less useful and humane, time-serving or obstructionist. Others will develop deeper political consciousness through these struggles and be genuinely radicalized by it. How large that last, from my view most important, group is depends to some extent on how the rest of us respond to their efforts.

The fact that the current wave of demands for recognition in the academy is linked to the status claims of what are sometimes called the "new ethnic groups" outside the university does not suggest that they lack scholarly justification. Intellectually, they are a response to the narrowness that organizes mainstream disciplines — particularly in the study of the United States. A powerful argument for incorporation of ethnic studies (or black studies or women's studies) is that those programs are necessary to set the record straight by providing richer, more complete accounts of the world. Taking race and gender seriously, for example, quite significantly alters the story of American social, political and intellectual life, and not only by introducing different voices or subject matter. Doing so even changes the ways we see conventional texts and subjects.

*Moby Dick* is a different, richer text when read through a lens sensitive to the significance of race in mid-nineteenth century social thought. On arriving in New Bedford, in the second chapter, and after several evocative references to Native Americans, Ishmael has a pregnant encounter with a black congregation; the Pequod's journey illustrates the realities of economic globalization already, and Melville's descriptions of the crew reflect both the era's equivalent of liberal multiculturalism and the racialism from which it emerged. Paying attention to the policy initiatives and programs of the Reconstruction governments deepens our understanding of American political development. The "settlement of the West" is a much different tale if the presence of Asians, Latinos and Native Americans is treated as more than a set of props for a white Herrenvolk triumphalism. Recognizing that as the Federal government was retreating from Reconstruction, it was committing resources to "pacification" of the West informs debate about the extent to which abandonment of black rights in the South reflected inadequate capacity or diminished will and provides a broader picture of the dynamics of national politics.

A less persuasive argument is rooted in the psychologistic language of identity politics. The demand to see oneself in the text easily reduces to narcissistically anti-intellectual twaddle, as anyone who has encountered it as a professor is aware. However, despite movement opponents' tut-tutting that it represents a new barbarianism, this demand is a direct outgrowth of two generations of mainstream race relations scholarship that frames discussion of racial stratification in individualist and attitudinal terms—driven by a language of sensitivity and tolerance—rather than in systemic terms of structured inequality. Similarly, the demand to catalogue the "contributions" of the rest of us, grafted from the Budweiser approach to black history, presumes an even older convention of the academic mainstream—the narrative of the March of Civilization. This narrative, like the idea of "civilization" itself, is bogus, the pure product of the Victorian era's imperialist racism, an arbitrary scoreboard of the human species and a simple justification for global plunder.

The identity politics frame appeals also because it is a vehicle for a bourgeois militancy that doesn't require critical intellectual engagement or, for example, rethinking one's ambition to become a rich investment banker after graduation. Indeed, this frame fits nicely with a corporate multiculturalism by providing a diverse professional and middle management workforce with a shared set of thin, curriculum-based symbols of group "cultures," an essentialist checklist enabling coworkers both to imagine their own uniqueness and to mediate interaction through common rituals of "respect." ("That kente cloth stole goes on well with your suit!"; "I'm so moved by Amy Tan.")

Part of the struggle for ethnic studies must be contestation over what it should mean conceptually, as well as the fight to secure its autonomous institutional base. And both aspects of the struggle must be grounded concretely in an understanding of how those issues work themselves out on the ground in academic processes.

Demands for such programs bear simultaneously on personnel and curriculum. They characteristically, and reasonably, join calls for increased minority representation among faculty ranks with calls for incorporating subject matter bearing on minority group experience. The two focal points obviously overlap, but not completely, and the same goes for the larger objectives they serve. The warrants of each are somewhat different and can indeed conflict.

For example, increasing minority faculty representation usually is held to serve several distinct purposes besides democratizing access to skilled positions in the academic workplace, which is nonetheless an adequate justification in its own right. Diversifying the character of the faculty can broaden the university's intellectual horizons by bringing into its center perspectives and experiences drawn from or identifying with different populations; this applies to the discrete disciplines as well as the university community at large. Doing so is also thought to provide role models for minority students and to make the campus seem less alien to them. Because fellow "X"s are most likely to study the "X", recruitment of minority faculty is a reasonable way to pursue expanding the curriculum in the desired areas.

There are instances where this logic breaks down, and some of those become anecdotal grist for anti-affirmative action or anti-p.c. horror tales of reverse discrimination and academic injustice. Occasionally, a superior non-"X" scholar who works on the "X" will lose out in a job search to an "X" competitor of lesser talent; sometimes the non-"X" loser's work even better advances the larger progressive intellectual agenda of "X" studies. Some such cases stem from racist bad faith; getting an "X" on the faculty roster and into the departmental photo substitutes for taking seriously the intellectual imperatives of "X" studies, skirts meeting the implicit challenge to think carefully about unfamiliar stuff and in new ways about familiar stuff. (My hunch is that, underneath all the throat-clearing and blather, guys like Schlesinger, Diggins, Harvard's Stephen Thernstrom, and others who worry so much about a slide toward barbarism are just ticked off at the implication that they need to tool up in areas they'd never thought about and take stock of literature they'd never recognized.) This bad faith can come dressed up in the garb of identity politics as well as in the raiments of the Old Guard. Some of these cases are more complex; especially in institutions with virtually no minority faculty, the imperative of democratizing the workplace can reasonably take priority. No general rule can govern the trade-offs required to make real decisions of this sort. Every situation is defined by a unique set of needs and constraints; each set of candidates combines unique mixes of strengths and limitations; which are in turn weighted by the idiosyncratic situation and vision of the hiring department or school.

A debate that presumes, on the one side, that hiring "X" faculty and strengthening "X" studies are identical, that the former exhausts the program of the latter, and, on the other, that concerns with expanding curriculum and refocusing the boundaries of scholarly discourses threaten to subvert the intersubjective basis of academic knowledge is wrong-headed and worse than unhelpful. It reproduces the most cartoonish op-ed page puffery, and it misses entirely what is at stake in the effort to secure spaces for what is sometimes derisively called oppression studies.

The most secure mechanism is creation of formal institutional presence, either in academic programs (which typically can appoint faculty or award tenure only jointly with departments, if at all) or departments (which typically have independent appointive powers). Reasonable arguments exist for going in either direction. There is a tension at the core of both options, though. The ultimate intellectual objective of ethnic studies, like black studies and women's studies, must be to alter the conceptual orientation of the "mainstream" disciplines. This means, for instance, changing the ways that all U.S. historians—whether or not their work centers on black studies or ethnic studies subject matter—imagine what America is, refashioning the kinds of questions they ask and where they look for answers. And creation of special programs or departments is a practical necessity for this project of intellectual broadening and enrichment.

Inertia, as well as less benign resistance, disincline existing departments to diversify curriculum and faculty, and possibilities for joint appointments and cross-listed courses with an ethnic studies program, say, offer concrete incentives that reduce resistance. Moreover, academic knowledge is produced through networks of scholars who interact while digging in common fields. Interdisciplinary programs help to incubate and nourish such networks across departmental lines. Yet, as one argument against them notes, formalizing black or ethnic studies could create academic ghettos by allowing mainstream departments to ignore them and the work produced in their scholarly networks, and the isolation born of their colleagues' bad faith can also breed insularity and intellectual pathologies. (Can anyone say "ice people"?) This danger is real, but there's no way to avoid it. Just as with the concern that affirmative action stigmatizes its beneficiaries, the really existing options aren't ghettoized ethnic studies programs or an opening of idealized mainstream departments to the new perspectives and lines of research. Black, female, and Latino firefighters understand that their choices are simply affirmative action or no jobs, and the same goes not just for minority faculty but also for the areas of study that most of them embody.

The only way to negotiate these tensions is to think clearly and practically about them and about the larger purposes that specific initiatives like institutional formalization are intended to serve. Perhaps that's the most useful link to the history of black studies, that it provides raw material for the kinds of concrete pitfalls and possibilities that exist along the way.

# —The Battle
# of Liberty Monument

On September 14, 1874, the Crescent City White League mounted an insurrection against Louisiana's Reconstruction government, then seated in New Orleans. The insurrectionists routed an overmatched, racially integrated militia and metropolitan police force and held sway in the city for three days, until Federal troops arrived to reinstate the elected government.

This attempted putsch, dubbed the "Battle of Liberty Place" by its supporters, instantly became a key moment in the lore of heroic local (white) resistance to the supposedly tyrannical and horribly corrupt Reconstruction regime. In 1891—seven years before Louisiana's Redeemers installed a new, white supremacist constitution so extreme that even Booker T. Washington remonstrated against it—the New Orleans city government embodied its now all-white constituency's fervor by erecting a monument, at ground zero of downtown, to commemorate the 1874 uprising.

Now, more than 100 years later, municipal display of this "Liberty Monument" has provoked a bitter, racially inflected controversy in New Orleans, but the nature and character of that conflict have implications reaching far beyond local concerns. The current Battle of Liberty Monument speaks to the insidious force of white racism in the construction of American historical mythology, as well as to the backhanded and coded ways that force works in contemporary politics. This controversy, like those elsewhere in the South over public display of the Confederate flag, also throws into relief dangerous features embedded in common notions of historic preservation and the overlapping limitations of prevailing forms of "multiculturalism."

The municipal administration's behavior, moreover, gives us an inadvertent lesson (especially important as we suffer the conciliationist liturgy of Clintonism's left apologists) in the folly of attempting to compromise with, or pull a fast one on, evil.

The city of New Orleans removed the Liberty Place monument

and placed it in storage in 1989, ostensibly to make way for construction work on the surrounding streets. Because the monument had been registered as a historic landmark and Federal funds were to be used for removing it, the city first had to obtain permission from the state and Federal historic-preservation agencies. Local officials had to agree to restore the statue to an appropriate, proximate location once the disruption was over.

Negotiations around the removal focused exclusively on technical matters relating to street improvements and historic-preservation guidelines. But the black-led municipal government clearly was alive to other, deeper problems with the monument's display. Along with its request to dismantle the structure temporarily, the administration asked permission to remove racially offensive inscriptions that had been added in 1932. This request rested in part on the argument that because those inscriptions—which lauded the insurrection for having installed a government elected "by the white people" and praised the 1876 election that "recognized white supremacy and gave us our state"—were not part of the original placement, they were "nonhistorical." City officials thus sidestepped the real issue, the inscriptions' odious content, and instead framed the question within an apparently neutral, procedural set of guidelines defining historical "authenticity."

In 1991, the city began requesting extensions of its deadline for restoring the monument and proposed to re-erect it either in a museum or on sites that happen to be less conspicuous than the old location. Again the justifications accompanying these proposals were all technical and procedural. Both state and Federal historic-preservation agencies balked at the city's proposals, setting off a lengthy round of negotiations. Public debate heated up during this period, and it reached boiling point when a local white pharmacist and avid supporter of David Duke brought legal action aimed at forcing the city to restore the monument near its original location.

State historic-preservation officials eventually—significantly, perhaps, after Edwin Edwards's gubernatorial return—endorsed one of the city's proposed sites for relocation, and the structure was re-erected early in 1993. Then militant demonstrations became the main landscape surrounding the monument, and several angry protests and confrontations occurred at city council meetings. The council passed an ordinance that should enable it to declare the "Liberty Monument" a nuisance (among other stipulated conditions, because it "honors, praises, or fosters ideologies which are in conflict with the requirements of equal protection for citizens as provided by the Constitution and the laws of the United States, the State of Louisiana, or the law of the City of New Orleans"). This could finally end a century-long public affront to all citizens who uphold principles of justice. If so, it will be a small but symbolically important victory. (A subsequent compromise led to the monument's placement at an obscure location, adjacent to downtown but isolated from general view and pedestrian traffic.)

The de-facto coalition of historic preservationists and latter-day white supremacists is a reminder that the preservationist impulse is by no means automatically politically progressive. It can come just as easily from a reactionary nostalgia about "tradition" as from models of harmonious, democratic social life. It can reflect privileged people's attempts to protect amenities for themselves at others' expense as much as it can a social democratic concern to limit predatory growth.

Perhaps the ambivalence of the preservationist impulse is clearest in the South, where it is often tied to the romanticized artifacts of an era of unabashed white supremacy. The conceptual gymnastics generated in the Battle of Liberty Monument are instructive.

Throughout the controversy, the monument's supporters have pressed a bizarre distinction between the commemoration of "history," "heritage," "liberty," "tradition," "resistance to tyranny" on the one hand, and the specific content of the objects and events chosen to express those abstractions on the other. Even the insurrection itself is held, as local attorney John Wilkinson claims, to have had "nothing to do with race [and] everything to do with an angry people trying to take their rightful government back from an ignorant and corrupt administration." U.S. Fifth Circuit Court of Appeals Judge John Minor Wisdom (like Wilkinson a descendent of a White League insurrectionist, though himself one of the judicial heroes of the civil rights movement) acknowledged that the White

League actively sought to establish white domination but contends that somehow "that was not the big issue . . . it was more restoration of home and democracy."

This is a curious assessment of a body that presented itself as defenders of a "hereditary civilization and Christianity menaced by a stupid Africanization." Indeed, the League apparently maintained quite high standards of white supremacy. Lawrence N. Powell, a Tulane University historian, notes that the "Italian-American community long regarded Liberty Place as an insult, too, following the 1891 lynching of eleven Sicilians by a mob led by White League veterans intoning the spirit of September 14."

It is understandable, though not exactly laudable, that local officials would choose to justify removal of the obelisk from conspicuous display in ways similarly evasive of the actual history it enshrines. Administrations "get things done" by crafting a compromise rhetoric, a lowest common denominator that depoliticizes issues, often by casting them in technical or incremental terms. The goal is always to bevel off the sharp edges of programmatic or ideological difference that could disrupt the coalitions of interest groups on which elected officials rely.

In this case especially there is the additional factor of pressure on a black-led administration to bend over backwards to show that it does not govern too much in behalf of black interests.

So a 1990 city planning commission report included among its criteria for sites for reinstallation that the monument should be seen "as an urban design element" and that officials should "not engage in the historical/social debate about its merits." The report went on to assess one site favorably in part because it "would be consistent with the idea of the monument as an urban design marker and not a shrine." (Only one member of the commission objected vigorously to the claim that the structure could be disassociated from its racist origins and legacy and opposed all plans for its return to conspicuous display.) Similarly, documents submitted to Federal preservation officials in 1989 had referred obliquely and antiseptically to the monument's historical significance and focused instead on its architectural features.

It may well be that the city administration hoped thus to satisfy

black desires to be rid of the monument without broadly antagoniz-
ing whites. But the city's posture, in effect, conceded white monument supporters' specious claims by not challenging them on
substantive grounds. Moreover, if the monument were about those
airy abstractions, then there should not have been any problem
about its particular location.

The city's evasive tactic failed, but it did prompt the monument's supporters to descend from ethereal abstractions toward
historical truth in their defenses. Jonathan Fricker, the state's director of historic preservation, flatly dismissed the city's effort to define
the obelisk's historic significance as architectural, characterizing it
as "a fairly standard piece of late nineteenth-century commemorative sculpture." He allowed that usually "an object or building
[that] is purely commemorative in nature is not considered eligible
for the National Register." Exception could be made "if the fact that
the monument was erected was significant in its own right historically." He then asserted that "in this case, the erection of the monument . . . was considered significant because it represented the
views, the intellectual views, historical views, ideological views of
the majority of Southerners in the late nineteenth century, that the
Civil War had been a war of northern aggression and those who
rose against Reconstruction government were heroes."

Preservationists argued further that because the monument's
historical significance is "very site-specific," it must, therefore, be
displayed "somewhere within the area of the battle." As usual, truth
emerged in the move from the abstract to the concrete.

In making these arguments, Fricker and others who opposed the
efforts to remove the obelisk admit what city officials boasted of
when they added the 1932 inscriptions and what other racist politicians underscored throughout the 1950s and 1960s when they used
Liberty Place as a backdrop for their segregationist pageants and
showcase for their vicious political offensives. The "heritage" and
"tradition" symbolized in the monument can be nothing other than
white supremacy.

Unfortunately, and ironically, those who would deny or hide
from this brute reality have been abetted by the language of a simple-
mindedly pluralist multiculturalism. Blacks are said to have their

version of the past and whites theirs. For the former, for example, Reconstruction was a period of expanded opportunity and strides toward equality. For white Southerners it was a time of pain and suffering under alien tyranny. These are presented as two separate but equally valid social realities, without hint of connection through politics and social structure.

This rhetoric gives rise to fatuous speculation about the degree to which states' rights and home-rule arguments might have been distilled from their specifically racist content, as if the practical objective of white domination and the savagery acted out on its behalf were in some way ephemeral to a nobler, ideal agenda. That is precisely the purchase on history that white supremacist ideologues have advocated all along.

This perspective is all too compatible with a lazy and ultimately ahistorical cultural pluralism driven by psychobabble about group "voices" and "contributions." David Duke's line compares Liberty Monument to Black History Month in this idiotically tit-for-tat view. Blacks have a commitment to equality, which is fine for them; white racists have a commitment to white supremacy, which deserves equal respect because it is an equally authentic group perspective.

It is this inadequate notion of pluralism that lay beneath the municipal administration's efforts to placate the monument's supporters. The city eventually modified this strategy. The putative disclaimer now accompanying the re-erected structure reads simply: "In honor of those Americans on both sides of the conflict who died in the Battle of Liberty Place. . . . A conflict of the past that should teach us lessons for the future." (This is even more tepid than the previous disclaimer—itself no model of commitment to principle—posted in the 1970s: "The sentiments expressed are contrary to philosophies and beliefs of present-day New Orleans.")

I am convinced that it would have been far more productive if the city had stood firmly on principle all along. The inevitable controversy over removing the monument would have been more honest. And the city would have been able to win the day anyway, as it finally seems to have done now, by galvanizing support of the heavy black electoral majority. Moreover, honest discussion of the heritage of racism would be good for local politics.

As this episode of the Liberty Monument struggle sputtered toward resolution, the verdict in the second Rodney King trial was delivered. That's just a reminder of how deeply embedded and dangerous is the evil extolled in the Liberty Monument and just how high are the stakes in our struggle against it. There is no room for compromise with that evil, no matter what drivel emanates from the Democratic Leadership Council and its acolytes. Harsh? Ultraleftist? Let me leave doubters with a thought experiment. How would all of this look in contemporary Germany, if Jews instead of blacks were on the receiving end of the rhetoric about "heritage" and the police terror?

# —Looking Back at *Brown*

On May 16, 1954, I made my First Communion at a church in downtown Washington, D.C. It seemed like a very big event at the time. The next day, a few blocks away, the Supreme Court announced its ruling in the *Brown v. Board of Education* case, overturning the "separate but equal" mystification that had codified racial segregation since 1896. These two events—one that filled my life with solemnity and anxiety for months, and the other which I only dimly understood—somehow merged in my child's perspective.

I had successfully mastered the fine distinctions of catechistic instruction and the choreography of filing, genuflecting, kneeling, sitting, and rising in unison—all with only a couple of unexpected raps to the knuckles and the back of the head from Sister Anna Maria's feared clicker. Sacramental dry runs and dress rehearsals finally culminated in the actual First Penance and Holy Eucharist. And then my parents and I could walk comfortably into Washington theaters and restaurants that before had been inhospitable.

Of course, the *Brown* decision did not outlaw petty apartheid in the District of Columbia or anywhere else—but it created enough of a stir in the adult environment, apparently, to prompt the lifting of some forms of de facto segregation, and to penetrate the consciousness of a very preoccupied seven-year-old.

*Brown*'s immediate impact was mainly symbolic. It signified a victory in and of principle, and it fueled a sense of possibility. The decision energized and emboldened black Americans, conferring on them a sense of equal membership in the polity.

The ruling's fortieth anniversary in 1994 momentarily focused public attention on *Brown* again and on its significance in American life. At the same time, apparently quite different forces gathered from across the ideological spectrum to support resegregation. This suggests that it's appropriate to consider the meaning of the *Brown* decision and its effects on the larger social order.

Perhaps most significantly, *Brown* boosted (though it certainly also was influenced by) a rising tide of post-World War II black activism challenging segregation. A year and a half after *Brown*, the Montgomery bus boycott signaled a sweeping wave of aggressive political action that continued through the passage of the 1964 Civil Rights and 1965 Voting Rights legislation.

On the other hand the *Brown* decision served to obscure the true nature of racial segregation in America. In the popular view, *Brown* emphasized the harmful psychological effects on black children of separate schools, and defined segregation mainly in terms of attitudes and individual prejudice and discrimination. But racial segregation was a social system, codified and impersonalized by law. Outside the South, it was an ensemble of local ordinances and rules whose purpose was to cordon off and dislocate black Americans not just from physical contact with whites, but also from equal access to the fruits of citizenship. Separate schools, publicly enforced ghettoization, and racially gerrymandered electoral districts not only rested on notions of black inferiority; they were devices for denying blacks an equal claim on public resources and a means of redress.

The South, Jim Crow's natural home, was a regime of white supremacy. After Reconstruction, alliances of Redeemers and New South progressives rewrote one Southern state constitution after another to establish public life on an explicitly white-supremacist basis, and to define race as the elemental foundation of citizenship and social status.

Virtually every Southern state passed laws specifying the fractions of "black blood" that marked the boundaries of whiteness. (Louisiana—where much of the white population's claim to that exalted status could not bear careful scrutiny—was the exception, until 1970 when it adopted the same retrograde standard used in the Old South.)

Nor was this simply a naïve or irrational fixation on racial classification. Being recognized as white was a precondition for everything from being able to sit on a streetcar or try on a hat to being able to escape debt peonage, hold a supervisory job, vote, or expect due process under the law.

In that context, appeals to "interracial cooperation," recognition of common humanity, overcoming bigotry and intolerance, and other efforts to treat racial oppression as the summary result of individual ignorance or character flaws don't just miss the point. They function perniciously to deflect attention away from public institutions. The history of Southern racial liberalism in this century—down to the Confederate Twins of the Clinton Administration—has been driven by precisely such saccharine quietism.

Race—or, more exactly, white supremacy—was a fundamental principle of social organization, a *sine qua non* of political, economic, and cultural life, enforced by state power.

Racial discrimination and enforced inequality have existed in varying degrees throughout the United States. Nowhere, of course, since Emancipation has official racism been so explicitly the foundation of public policy as in the Jim Crow South. Yet it is important to recall that the Jim Crow system could not have existed without the endorsement and direct support of the Federal Government.

This pattern of Federal collusion reached the height of irony when it was woven into the democratic rhetoric justifying the New Deal and World War II. My father and his Army buddies have never stopped marveling at the hypocrisy that exhorted them to fight the racist Nazis in a segregated U.S. Army. Small wonder that my generation produced the slogan "No Viet Cong Ever Called Me Nigger."

No less than Nazi Germany, the Jim Crow system rested on state terror. The system required forcible disfranchisement of black citizens. In Louisiana, for example, more than 100,000 blacks voted in the 1896 election. In 1904, fewer than 1,000 cast ballots. The system relied on official police power and paramilitary entities like the Ku Klux Klan. In that environment, distinctions between vigilante bands and government, between lynch law and trial by jury, are empty scholasticism.

Unlike Nazi Germany, though, Southern segregation was not monolithic. The vagaries of the Federal system allowed for variation, and the terms of racial etiquette differed from place to place. In some cities, blacks were barred from department stores. In others, the races could commingle. In some establishments, black shoppers could try on hats but not shoes. In others, the reverse rule might apply. In pre-boycott Montgomery, blacks entered the front of the bus, paid the driver, got off the bus, and re-entered at the rear. In New Orleans, blacks entered at the front, paid, then sat behind a "For Colored Patrons Only" sign. Unlike some cities, in New Orleans, the signs marking the black section could be moved back and forth.

I recall this variation vividly, from the point of view of a protected and therefore curious child. Going on pilgrimages to New Orleans first from New York, where there was no conspicuous Jim Crow, and then from Washington, which was a sort of intermediate zone, was baffling and fascinating. I remember my grandmother answering my questions on a ferry by explaining assertively that crazy people had to sit on the other side of the chicken wire. I recall her also berating and shaming a white zoo employee who insisted that the pony ride was off limits to my cousin and me. My grandmother's boldness was a bedrock trait of her character. But it also marks the latitude peculiarly available in a big, open city. It would have been a different story in Sunflower County, Mississippi—or in her native Pointe Coupee Parish, Louisiana.

This variation in the enforcement of white supremacy, despite what it might seem to imply about the regime's porousness, actually made life for black people all the more anxious and unpredictable. Going to an unfamiliar locale was fraught with danger, since all blacks were presumed to know the prevailing racial etiquette in complete detail and ignorance was no excuse.

At the same time, the terror required to create and maintain the Jim Crow social order underscores its historical contingency. As a coherent social system, it persisted for only two-thirds of a century or so, depending on location. All of my grandparents were alive and cognizant before the complete erection of the wall of segregation. It was mainly demolished before I could vote.

Black Americans and their allies forestalled Jim Crow for at least two decades after the end of Reconstruction. They challenged it in various ways for its entire duration.

After World War II, those efforts began to resonate with the concerns of elites anxious about American's international image as the

Cold War developed. (University of Southern California professor Mary Dudziak has provided the definitive account of this phenomenon in *Cold War Civil Rights*.) The fact of the Nazi experience made America's official racism finally embarrassing to liberal sensibilities. The *Brown* decision is in part the product of that climate.

There are four more general points to be made in reflecting on *Brown*.

- Government action is not only shaped by broader social forces; it also guides and shapes them. There is no effective politics — for black citizens or anyone else — that does not take account of and contest for the direction of the state.
- Racial subordination is not a constant feature of American life. It has changed in response to pressures from above and below. We might only wonder, for instance, how different this society would be now — indeed, how different the very idea of race would be — if the Hayes-Tilden Compromise had not been struck, if the 1875 Civil Rights Act had not been struck down, or if Justice John Marshall Harlan's dissenting view had prevailed in *Plessy v. Ferguson*.
- It is especially important now to remember that racial segregation was first and foremost a system of state-sponsored racial oppression. Despite contemporary nostalgia, there was no Golden Age of organic black community under Jim Crow. Black Americans did not choose segregation any more than Polish Jews chose to be herded into the Warsaw ghetto. Nor did they experience any greater autonomy in community life.
- It is significant that the *Plessy* decision legitimizing segregation was handed down one year after Booker T. Washington's "Atlanta Compromise" speech that proclaimed black acquiescence to Jim Crow. Now, as underclass rhetoric sweeps over public discourse, justifying one nighmarish social policy after another, and candidates for Booker T. Washington's role are popping up in Cambridge, and elsewhere, we should take heed. We've lived the tragedy, and that should help us avoid an even deadlier farce.

# —Sectarians on the Prowl

I had an enlightening moment at a solidarity march for locked-out workers in Decatur, Illinois. As the marchers approached the auditorium where the rally would be held, we had to run a gauntlet of literature tables staffed by sectarian parties. I noticed that their operatives were scoping out the crowd, looking for flickering signs of interest, and I learned to my dismay that establishing eye contact could be taken as such a sign.

"Have you seen our paper?" was the opener. A woman behind one of the tables was but little affected when I responded that I used to sell it myself for a while more than twenty-five years ago. The encounter proceeded down a well-worn path—invitations to sign up for a mailing list to get news about goings-on in my area, enlistment of support for battles the party was fighting in one place or another (mainly in defense of their own cadres who are described as popular leaders of something or other), suggestions about attending an important meeting soon to be held in Chicago.

The scene reminded me of TV wildlife documentaries that depict predators lurking along the edges of herds of antelope or migrating wildebeest, ready to pluck off the weak and vulnerable.

Although sectarian groups by and large aren't vicious or ill-intentioned, they do prey on the fringes of movements, and with potentially destructive consequences. If they're prominent and militant enough, sectarian groups can obstruct effective action. Their fulsome, arcane debates and idiosyncratic combativeness also can drive away reasonable people who come to movements because they want to pursue concrete political goals.

What remains is a self-propelling spiral of ever-deeper irrelevance and alienation from meaningful political action. Because it reproduces itself like tenured mediocrity in universities, the cycle is almost impossible to break.

For some time now I've been wondering about how exactly to define the terms "sectarian" and "ultraleft." What separates these categories from styles of radical thought and practice that are more credible? Granted, in part the difference is only a matter of choosing sides in a debate: Ultraleftists and sectarians are the people who disagree with you. From that perspective, the difference is something like that between a religious sect and a cult, or between a durable party organization and a political machine.

A good friend remarks that he was raised in a cult in downstate Illinois that believes that God came to Earth in the form of a dove, had sex with a woman who some time later gave birth to the Messiah—a cult called Protestantism. (Just a reminder that all religious groups embrace beliefs that seem wacky to those who don't share them.)

Likewise, liberals committed above all else to reelecting Bipartisan Bill in 1996 frequently castigated as ultraleftists everyone who challenged him from the progressive side. The charge serves as a convenient way to avoid confronting criticisms, and it bears a family resemblance to red-baiting. Characterizing critics as ultraleftist places them beyond the pale of legitimacy, so you don't need to respond to anything they say.

Sectarianism can work in pretty much the same way. No one ever says, "Hi, would you like to join my cult?" or "I came to ask you to vote for the machine," or "I'd like to speak on behalf of my ultraleftist sectarian organization." Still, I suspect that there is a distinct style of politics on the left that most of us would recognize as sectarian.

Here's how the logic works. One's party or organization has the unambiguously correct program, strategy, and line. The purpose of activism, therefore, is to gain adherents for the party. Political struggles are important not so much in themselves, but because they provide a forum for propagating the organization's line and identifying potential recruits. So you go into activities primarily to push your group's agenda. Thus the obligatory ten-minute, five-part question at public meetings.

Ultraleftism is more difficult to define because it depends on some notion of a range of reasonable or appropriate left stances. But it, too, exists.

Ultraleftism is a distinct political tendency. At bottom it is a refusal to take into account the ways that existing political realities limit possibilities for action. Ultraleft politics confuses means and ends, muddles the distinctions among goals, strategy, and tactics. Historically, for instance, ultraleftists have dogmatically opposed participating in coalitions with liberals or mainstream politicians.

This tendency severs the idea of commitment to principle from the need to make realistic assessments of the options that exist in the fluid here-and-now; to analyze tough-mindedly our strengths and weaknesses; to think seriously and instrumentally about how to build a constituency within a social base (to "unite the many to defeat the few," for those nostalgic for old slogans).

Ultraleftism is a maximalist politics. It's much more about taking positions that express the intensity of one's commitments than about organizing or building anything. Rather than crafting language to build broad support for a substantively radical program, for instance, ultraleftists prefer potted rhetoric that asserts their bona fides, without concern for communicating outside the ranks of believers.

Sectarianism and ultraleftism have long histories, dating back even before Lenin's 1920 tract, *"Left-wing" Communism: An Infantile Disorder*. But most recently they have arisen as a response—or nonresponse—to the disappearance of radical activism's apparent social base after the 1960s. The decline of large-scale anti-war activism and black-protest mobilization put radicals in the unsettling position of developing increasingly revolutionary political rhetoric as the constituencies for that rhetoric withdrew.

The result was a turn inward. People who had formed organizing collectives were befuddled by their failure to connect meaningfully with the groups they wanted to organize. The focus shifted to inventing elaborate rituals of collective purification. (I remember being instructed on a 1969 visit to the Fort Dix Coffeehouse Project in the G.I. movement that the staff believed that closing the bathroom door was a sign of petit-bourgeois individualism.)

From there it was only a short step to the wildly esoteric rhetoric and debates—purgers and purgees accusing one another of being "Mensheviks" and the like—and internecine struggles of the late 1970s.

Lack of connection to palpable constituencies makes it possible to convince oneself of all manner of ridiculous fantasies. One such is the claim I've heard that Farrakhan's Million Man March was actually a "one-day general strike."

Indeed, this sort of politics is perhaps predisposed to such bizarre ideas because it isn't rooted in a close analysis of the history that we're living; it tends to be driven by slogans and anachronistic analogies ("When Mao was on the way to Yenan," or "When the Bolsheviks were organizing for power"). To that extent, its practioners don't have a subtle, or even credible, understanding of the world around them.

Relying on formulaic social theory and slogans makes it difficult to connect with the experience of ordinary people. And desperation to forge some kind of connection leads to the pursuit of any alliance, no matter how repugnant to progressive interests. Single-minded focus on an arcane objective makes it possible to rationalize anything. So, for example, trade-union activists who are unable to win rank-and-file workers over to their "revolutionary" programs will apologize for Farrakhan and the protofascist militia movement, soft-pedal opposition to sexism and homophobia, support tax-cut politics, and retreat from support for reproductive freedom and aggressive policy intervention to promote racial and gender equality.

The appeal of such defective politics is understandable. Nevertheless, we need a better politics than this. Instead of an ultimately self-defeating, feel-good approach, we need a politics that rests on careful, nuanced analysis of the social conditions we live in, grounded on and shaped by a concrete project of advancing the struggle for progressive social transformation.

We need, that is, a politics that proceeds from a subtle form of what used to be called historical materialism.

# —"Fayettenam," 1969:
# Tales from a G.I. Coffeehouse

## A NEW CHALLENGE FOR A
## YOUNG ORGANIZER

In the fall of 1969 I left Chapel Hill, North Carolina, where I'd been in college and involved in antiwar, student, and labor organizing activity, to go to Fayetteville as part of a group intending to set up a G.I.-organizing project. I had just been involved in a long, grueling and very intense strike by non-academic employees at the university, during the course of which I was among a number of people arrested and convicted for our strike-support activity. After the strike, I felt that it was time for me to leave campus organizing, as did the North Carolina authorities. (The terms of my two-year probation included a prohibition on engaging in any "disruptive" activity on the campus of any public educational institution.)

At the same time, though, I had become friends with a grad student who earlier had helped set up the Oleo Strut at Ft. Hood, Texas, and the UFO at Ft. Jackson, two of the first G.I. antiwar coffeehouses. Through him I got to know Howard Levy, a dermatologist who had been court-martialed and imprisoned for his political activities—including his refusal to train Green Berets in dermatological torture techniques. They talked to me about a plan originating from the United States Servicemen's Fund, the group that funded and raised money for antiwar coffee houses, to recruit people to begin a project at Ft. Bragg, and they asked me to consider being part of the group.

I hadn't been thinking about doing anything remotely like G.I. organizing. However, I had done a great deal of antiwar work and had some experience with "Fayettenam," as it was commonly called. A year earlier I was part of a group that got arrested passing out antiwar leaflets on post. So I'd already had an up-close and personal encounter with the 503rd MPs, seen the inside of the stockade, been permanently banned from the base, tried before the U.S.

Commissioner, and threatened with being sent to Federal prison, escorted to the county line by state troopers, and tailed and threatened on the highway by either Klansmen or military intelligence.

## WHAT BETTER PLACE TO FIGHT AGAINST THE WAR?

As I thought it over, going to Fayetteville made more and more sense. What better place to fight against the Vietnam war than Ft. Bragg? It was at that time the largest military installation in the world with a permanent party (counting Pope Air Force Base that served it) of 83,000, and it was home to the 82nd Airborne Division, 18th Airborne Corps, Special Forces, and the JFK School of Special Warfare. In addition, the 503rd did riot duty up and down the East Coast, and Bragg was a basic training center.

Also, I knew the other people who were going to be part of the project and considered them good friends and comrades. We had all worked together frequently, were all serious, level-headed, and experienced organizers. We all trusted and respected one another and generally got along well. Trust and respect were more important than friendship, though I think it was a common experience that those with whom one became really friendly were those whose judgment one trusted. We were all in the middle of a dynamic movement that had a real constituency to be accountable to, with formidable adversaries who weren't afraid of violence and sabotage.

### BUILDING THE COFFEEHOUSE

We decided to organize into two direct but closely coordinated projects, one focused on working with black troops, the other on white troops. Our thinking, with which organizers at several other coffee houses disagreed, was that at that point it didn't make sense to try to organize black and white soldiers into the same organization, at least not at Bragg. Racial polarization on post was intense, and black troops had formed an independent black power group. I suspect, though, that what was true at Bragg was true more generally and that activists elsewhere didn't want to acknowledge the fact.

For instance, organizers from the Camp Pendleton project used to travel around with a black marine and a white marine to show off "interracial proletarian solidarity," but these marines always seemed rather like props.

Before we moved to Fayetteville, a few of us visited the Ft. Dix coffeehouse in New Jersey to see how a functioning project operated. Everyone was security conscious; the Ft. Dix coffeehouse had been firebombed recently. We made up a cover story that we were thinking about setting up a project at Ft. Polk in Louisiana, just to try to misdirect military intelligence for long enough to acquire leases in Fayetteville.

In retrospect, they probably knew anyway, but the intelligence apparatus's inefficiency may have given us some operating room. Once we got to town, however, we experienced constant surveillance and petty intimidation from city and county law enforcement agencies as well as the military.

We were able to get set up in Fayetteville and pretty much hit the ground running. One of the organizers with the white project had been working in the city for some time with the Fayetteville Area Poor People's Organization (FAPPO). Both G.I.s United Against the War (the white group) and the smaller Black Brigade (later the Black Servicemen's Union) had been meeting for a time at the Quaker House, a center for antiwar and progressive activities in the city.

### BRIDGES BETWEEN BLACK G.I.s AND BLACK CIVILIANS . . .

Not long after getting more intimately involved with black troop life, we realized that it would be tactically necessary and politically interesting to link G.I. organizing efforts with the work going on in the city's black community. Black soldiers and black Fayettevillians were alien to each other in ways that at first impeded organizing on both sides.

G.I.s tended to repair to black Fayetteville for R & R, a sort of more familiar, local version of Thailand. When they were in that mode, they were both uninterested in local issues and often hostile to any serious undertakings like rallies, meetings, political discussions, or demonstrations. To the extent that they maintained relationships with—and exerted depoliticizing pressure on—women in town, this attitude was a source of tension with FAPPO, which worked almost exclusively in black communities and whose most active participants were female.

On the other side of the ledger, we hoped that joint organizing would help to humanize G.I.s in the minds of the townspeople and, ideally, build antiwar, antimilitarist and anti-imperialist consciousness among FAPPO's main constituencies and in black Fayetteville at large. At its height, FAPPO had a membership of over 2000 and was well known as a center of black activism in the area. They organized the local chapters of the National Welfare Rights Organization and the National Tenants Organization.

After some time, the Black Servicemen's Union gained representation on FAPPO's governing council, and the groups worked closely in planning and executing projects. For instance, when Rep. Ron Dellums came through on his tour of the stockades, he addressed a FAPPO mass meeting in a housing project. Not only did this address prompt a new wave of infiltrators from Military Intelligence but it almost got Dellums arrested, when he couldn't find his congressional immunity badge after upbraiding a racist cop who had harassed the occupants of the car taking him to the meeting.

### . . . IN COMBINED COMMUNITY ORGANIZING

We found ways to involve G.I.s in community issues, which in turn provided a basis for their broader political education. And linking the role the military played in Vietnam to the role it played in Fayetteville helped broaden the focus and perspective of community activists.

An early, unsuccessful effort to get the Army to pave unpaved streets in the city's poor, black neighborhoods was a nice educational vehicle, especially for youth organizing. (I had mixed emotions about this initiative because of the counterproductive implications of a possible victory. The Army certainly would have treated it as part of is domestic public relations work. They were already dropping in Green Berets to do service work in isolated, rural communities in the mountains and on the coast.) Actually, FAPPO's reputation and practice were such that it wasn't necessary to designate special youth initiatives. When young people—for example, in a controversy growing out of racial injustice in meting out discipline at a local high school—began to consider political activism, they naturally sought out FAPPO's assistance and guidance.

## REAL WAR STORIES?

Another virtue of the joint G.I.-community focus was that it was a counterweight to the militarist and adventurist rhetoric to which many G.I.s were disposed. First-timers at meetings often would express impatience with a notion of politics less flamboyant or more elaborate than "picking up the gun." I remember one such, who went off on a diatribe about how the racist Russians were giving the Vietnamese guns to "kill brothers."

I've wondered over the years whether he really had such wacky politics or if he was just a too enthusiastic agent. Some people were just looking for something to attach themselves to, the simpler and more formulaic the better. I recall cases of guys who went from the Black Panthers to the Nation of Islam to other sects and maybe back again in the span of a few months; this was no different from what one saw on campuses. The Black Panthers, who—on the East Coast, at least—related to the G.I. movement in a decidedly opportunistic way, fueled this kind of rhetoric and created all sorts of openings for provocateurs.

One of the most bizarre cases I encountered was of a guy who just materialized in town, alleging to be a Panther, and made contacts with a group of black Special Forces NCOs. This was already weird because very few NCOs supported political work, and Special Forces troops, unsurprisingly, had been not at all receptive. Fayetteville's town center revolved around a former slave market, which had been restored—rebuilt, actually, because Sherman's troops had blown it up on their way through town during the Civil War—and preserved, supposedly, as a symbol of town pride.

Groups of black people in the city had talked off and on since the
1940s about blowing it up again, and this kind of musing was common in the late 1960s and early 1970s. This "Panther," though, had
a different idea. His plan was to rip off an arms room in the Special
Forces area, move into the slave market and proclaim the revolution. The black community supposedly would rise spontaneously
in support to boycott all white businesses and provide a cover of
disruption for the guerrilla band to withdraw to the countryside to
begin systematic guerrilla warfare. We were able to defuse that
scheme at a very tense meeting in a trailer park, and the supposed
Panther vanished just as suddenly as he had shown up.

### THE SEEDS WE PLANTED

I wish that I could report more dramatic and inspiring successes.
We had small, finite accomplishments—like winning victories for
individual soldiers against arbitrary and unjust punishment and dis-
criminatory treatment, and creating a climate in which several
troops refused to do riot duty for the Panther trial in New Haven
and planned to refuse mobilization when they were put on alert to
go to Jordan in 1970. There were more in the community organizing
as well.

Our main victories, however, were in developing the politics of
those who were involved in the efforts. This applies not only to the
organizers and activists themselves; in later years I've come across
people who were adolescents and preteens in Fayetteville during
that period and report being shaped in their politics by our work
and presence in the area.

All these small victories, both concrete and otherwise, are tiny
pieces of a much bigger movement. Most immediately, they were
our contribution—along with many, many other people's bigger
and smaller ones—to ending the Vietnam war by cultivating dissent
and creating a climate that threatened to raise the cost of maintaining domestic social peace if it continued. In the longer view, we
helped to develop a cadre of activists who've gone on from there to
engage in struggles elsewhere for decades.

I know that I found some of my closest friends and comrades in that activity; intense political struggles confer a particular kind of enduring trust and mutuality upon those who participate intimately in them. And that is a basis for building subsequent political relationships. At the same time, however, I returned to Fayetteville at the dawn of the Reagan era after several years absence, and it was too easy to find my old FAPPO coworkers. They still lived on the same unpaved streets, still worked the same unrewarding jobs. That's a sobering reminder that we didn't win. There's still a great deal of work to be done.

# —The Longer March

O n the Saturday after the AFL-CIO election that installed the "New Voice" leadership, I attended a daylong conference of shop stewards from Service Employees International Union Local 73. Sitting in the packed auditorium on the Illinois Institute of Technology campus that morning, I was struck by contrasts with the Million Man March that had taken place less than two weeks earlier.

Of course, this gathering wasn't a massive production like Farrakhan's spectacle, and it didn't invite oceanic absorption within the throng. And yes, it was a different kind of event, a meeting of the already organized and mobilized. So comparing them may seem not quite fair. Yet both meetings were called to inform and to stimulate action, and both drew powerfully on black Americans' political energies and concerns.

The difference in the groups' compositions first sparked comparison. A solid majority of attendees at the stewards' conference were nonwhite, and they were largely, if not predominantly, black. But Latinos and Asian Americans were also prominent in numbers, as were whites. The group in the auditorium was rather like street life in the Rogers Park neighborhood on Chicago's far North Side; each of the major food groups in the American ethnoracial stir-fry, as clever multiculturalists have described it, was sufficiently represented so that no cohort overwhelmed and none seemed like a minority.

The white people there appeared to fit the profile of the now famous Reagan Democrats; several of those who spoke even displayed Southern accents, from the city's Uptown/Appalachia connection or from downstate Illinois, which unfolds toward the old Confederacy. No doubt many of them would vote Republican but for their union experience, and for that matter, some probably still haven't accepted the fact that they shouldn't.

Men and women were present in roughly equal numbers, both on the program and in the audience. No one seemed to notice, nor to care enough to be either put off by or rhapsodic about the gender parity, though I'm sure that some men of all groups would bond in the bathroom around varying levels of sexist grousing.

Let me hasten to point out that this is not a cue to roll out the pieties about interracial solidarity and join hands to sing "We Shall Overcome" and "We Are the World" in the round. A chief affliction of American politics is mistaking surface for substance, and identification with the left hardly confers immunity. Putting together a diverse array of people for a photo op is no big deal; ad agencies do it every day. Moreover, elevating interracialism as a political goal in itself is at best hollow-headed liberalism, the stuff of the morality plays on Saturday morning cartoons. Worse, it is often just a high-minded cover for either white ethnocentrism or calls to soft-pedal antiracist politics. Playing the interracialist card as likely as not reduces blacks' and others' concerns to the issue of what they think about whites, and ever since the abolition movement, backsliders and moderates have invoked the need for interracial solidarity to argue against direct assaults on bastions of white privilege. The setting I've described is more the instrument and effect of a kind of politics than its source.

Just as at the nonprotest in Washington, speakers talked a lot about unity, but with a significant difference. The unity extolled at the stewards' conference was concrete and strategic. It was celebrated as a tool that had demonstrated its effectiveness for making people's lives better; it was not an abstract slogan or a romantic wish. In every utterance, this unity was tied to getting specific things done: organizing shops, winning contract negotiations, electing candidates, agitating against NAFTA, supporting locked-out workers from three unions in Decatur, Illinois, campaigning for legislation, commiserating about common work situations and life circumstances. Joe Iosbaker, a steward from the University of Illinois-Chicago Medical Center, put it succinctly: "Solidarity begins with our own experiences." People spoke from their shared experiences as health care workers, tollway workers, security guards, and employees of the Chicago Housing Authority and Illinois Secretary of State's Office.

Most of the speakers were stewards themselves, drawn from the rank and file. The luminaries on Farrakhan's stage spoke in the first-person plural, but their "we" was a royal one and ultimately didactic. The stewards also spoke in the first-person plural, no less enthusiastically or informatively, but intimately and without distancing artifice. And there was none of the rhetoric of collective self-deprecation, none of the victim-blaming underclass ideology tricked out in a kente cloth of psychobabble.

After the morning session, we broke up into workshops. In one, stewards focused on organizing outside their own workplaces, and then went out to make home visits to workers from a shop where the local was conducting an organizing campaign. Attendees also mobilized to do grassroots organizing around the assault on health care as well as with the Chicago Jobs With Justice Coalition's Living Wage campaign, which is pressuring local government neither to hire nor contract with any firm that starts workers at less than $7.60 an hour. Other workshops stressed leadership development for stewards.

Real politics can be very complicated. Almost certainly, the black people at the conference supported the Million Man March and took pride in it. I suspect that most of the others there supported it as well. Yet the model of politics that they enacted could hardly be more at odds with Farrakhan's and the symbolic crusade conducted in Washington. This is a cautionary note about the shallowness of public opinion and its distance from the ways that people actually order their lives.

I'm not bidding to be a bargain-basement John Reed for the awakening giant of labor. Being active in a union is no magic elixir; it doesn't necessarily cure racism and sexism or instill decency, wisdom, and political principle. Serious struggles, some of them ugly, go on within the union movement at every level. I also recognize that in its commitment to progressive politics and internal participatory democracy, Local 73 is a particularly good local in one of the better, most aggressive unions. And esprit was running especially high because SEIU's president, John Sweeney, had just been elected head of the AFL-CIO.

The diversity among its stewards reflects the union's conscious efforts more than spontaneous "proletarian solidarity." In unions as elsewhere in life, openness and unity are always fraught with tension and exist only through constant negotiation—among rank and file, between the latter and union leadership, and within leadership itself. Moreover, the virtue of practical commitment to real constituencies pushes any union, no matter how progressive, towards parochialism and opportunistic alliances that strain against the commitment to larger political agendas.

Nevertheless, for all the limitations of the labor movement and of the individuals who comprise it, there's no place else where the left's political concerns gain a hearing and have a constituency outside the coffee shops, cultural studies programs, and sectarian hutches. There's no place else where we can find the kind of force that we'll need to win the struggle for a just United States in a just world. And there is no place else for us to seek hints about what that world will look like when we win it.

# —Building Solidarity

Solidarity is a key notion on the left. It pops up a lot in leaflets and speeches, in calls to mobilize for demonstrations, attend forums, or participate in boycotts. We call on ourselves to express solidarity with striking workers, with victims of child labor and sweated labor, with Sandinistas, Zapatistas, French transit workers, East Timorese, or the African National Congress.

For all its moral urgency, this notion of solidarity is a member of the same conceptual family as *noblesse oblige*. It exhorts *us* to go do something that shows our support for some *them*, and typically a them someplace else.

I don't mean to dump on this kind of support work; it's important and should be done. It can realize victories that advance progressive interests everywhere, and it can be an indispensable tool for political education. It is also, though, a kind of passive or second-hand politics. It encourages people to respond to injustices committed by the U.S. government and U.S.-based corporations against others, not themselves.

I got to see this aspect of the left's rhetoric of solidarity at the Labor Party Founding Convention, where it stood in stark contrast to a different notion of solidarity historically associated with the labor movement. Labor solidarity rests on a more pragmatic foundation. Building solidarity in this context is about constructing and maintaining a *we* to fight in concert for common objectives.

The slogan "An Injury to One Is an Injury to All" isn't just an ethical statement about how we should understand our relations to others. It's a prescription for action: We must treat an injury to any one of us—even those we don't like—as harmful to all if we intend to maintain the unity we need to reach our common goals.

This is the symbolic power of the "Solidarity Forever" lyric, "the union makes us strong."

Workers in a particular shop are in the same basic position and share the same basic interests relative to their employer. Recognizing these common interests is the essence of union, the foundation from which the bargaining unit, the trade-union local, the international, the federation of internationals, and the party, arise.

Because its glue is concrete objectives, union solidarity necessarily requires negotiation, compromise, and toleration of difference. It's no accident that trade unions are the most racially
integrated voluntary associations in American life. People don't always overcome their prejudices, but they have to learn to accommodate each other. That necessary accommodation, and the
pragmatic, mutual interests it serves, can subsequently break down
racist, sexist, nativist, or homophobic tendencies.

The labor movement has by no means always lived up to this
potential. That's one of the reasons it has fallen on such hard times.
Business unionism and willing participation in the system of racial
and gender hierarchy have led to defining the boundaries of the
"we" too narrowly, even to the point of actively organizing to preserve white, male privilege. Too often, unions have upheld a false
distinction between "economic" and "social" issues to avoid challenging racial and gender injustice. Nevertheless, the model of
union solidarity is our only path to building the kind of mass movement we need to realize a progressive national and global agenda.

The processes through which the Labor Party's program and
constitution were developed and adopted gave an object lesson in
the power of union solidarity. The committees that drafted the two
documents each worked as a collective.

The program committee, of which I was a member, over a three-
day period constructed a program document based on more than
160 resolutions submitted by chapters and individual members, results of research and workshops conducted by the Labor Institute
with several thousand unionized workers, and intense deliberation
among ourselves. We made all our decisions through deliberation
and consensus, talking through each section until we agreed on its
substance and language unanimously.

Once the program committee had generated a consensual draft,
we met with the constitution committee, made up of representatives
of five of the major endorsing union bodies, to receive their suggestions and concerns. Although the committees differed seriously on
certain issues, we struggled, negotiated, and compromised until we
all could unite comfortably around each section of the program

document. Everyone on the committee came away proud of what we had accomplished and enriched by the process.

I know that I'll be grateful forever for the experience of working with a truly exemplary group of colleagues: Howard Botwinick of the Central New York Labor Party Advocates (LPA) chapter; David Campbell of the Oil, Chemical, and Atomic Workers, Local 1-675; Kit Costello of the California Nurses Association; Linda Jenkins of the Communications Workers of America, Local 1180; Cathy King of the Northern New Jersey LPA chapter; Don DeMoro of the East Bay LPA chapter; Les Leopold and Mike Merrill of the Labor Institute; and Calvin Zon of the United Mine Workers. I treasured the opportunity to partake of their insight, good judgment, principle, and comradeship, and to be part of what may turn out to have been a historic moment with them.

The committees recognized that supporting each other's work without reservation was necessary for moving the convention's agenda along. We also understood that such support could emerge only from a participatory process in which we negotiated consensus on our proposals for the larger body and then explained the consensual positions—including the negotiations and compromises reflected in them—to the constituencies represented. This in turn was the basis for building a wider solidarity, as the union delegations caucused among themselves and determined whether and how to operate as a coherent bloc on the convention floor.

The importance of this solidarity-based democracy was clearest in the debate about electoral politics. A joint proposal from the program and constitution committees prohibited Labor Party entities from running or endorsing candidates for office at least until the 1998 convention. (At the 1998 convention we adopted a strategy that lays out guidelines and thresholds governing eventual electoral action.) This proposal went to the major union delegations just as the program and constitution drafts had.

One major union delegation, the International Longshoremen's and Warehousemen's Union (ILWU), dissented from the larger union consensus and introduced an amendment from the floor that would have permitted state and local entities to run and endorse candidates. After considerable, lively debate, the amendment was defeated, largely (but not exclusively, since many LPA chapter delegates also voted against it) on the strength of the other unions' bloc voting.

The debate about participation in electoral politics underscored two quite distinct conceptions of politics among the general delegation. On the one hand was an idea of political action that is ultimately a form of bearing witness, taking a public moral stand as a self-justifying act. In this view the most important criteria shaping the positions and strategies that we adopt are existential, primarily a matter of indicating who we are and what we stand for and believe.

On the other hand was a view of politics as an incremental organizing activity. From that perspective, positions and strategies must be tempered by the need to appeal to people who don't already agree with us on all points but who can understand that we address their interests as no one else does.

The practical principle is to try to create a program and vision that can reach and educate the broadest possible base without sacrificing a working-class agenda for governance. This is the mindset, for instance, that shaped the program's emphasis on the economic and class content of what are often characterized as "social issues."

The idea is to build a coalition on the model of union solidarity; developing a base, consolidating it, expanding it, consolidating again, and so on. This is what the joint committee's political-action statement meant by an "organizing model of politics," a strategy based on intensive, issue-based organizing of the old-fashioned shop-to-shop, door-to-door technique. The paramount objective is to reach out to people who aren't already mobilized in left politics, to begin a conversation that builds a movement.

Proponents of the witness-bearing approach came disproportionately—though again not exclusively—from the at-large and chapter delegations, and the union delegations were most solidly rooted in the organizing approach, though many people from the chapters also supported the organizing view. I suspect that the nature of trade-union work imposes a practical and strategic discipline often lacking these days on the left.

These two fundamentally different notions of politics underlay the convention's electoral politics debate. No one who argued for running candidates responded directly on the convention floor to the several, very practical opposing arguments. These were: 1) opting for an electoral strategy would by law cut off access to the trade-union treasury funds needed to finance the Party; 2) a number of key international unions and locals that have endorsed the Labor Party would withdraw their support if we were to enter electoral politics at that point; 3) other unions that would consider endorsing us wouldn't do so if we were to go the electoral route prematurely; 4) we don't have the strength to be successful electorally, and running losing campaigns only demoralizes our base and drains resources because political candidacies are an ineffective vehicle for organizing; and 5) if we were to win some offices, we aren't strong enough to keep officeholders in line, to keep them from—or help them avoid—rolling over for corporate interests.

The responses to these very concrete and practical points were uniformly abstract and evasively moralistic—the stuff, that is, of bearing witness. (And when did engaging in electoral politics get to be a litmus test for the left anyway? Did I forget to set my watch ahead one morning and miss a big shift?)

The failure of disciplined strategic thinking on the left is a serious problem. It reflects and stems from the extreme demoralization and isolation that has plagued us for two decades. We'll never be able to build the kind of movement we need unless the left can find its moorings and approach politics once again as an instrumental, more than an expressive, activity. Emulating the model of union solidarity would be a big step in the right direction.

Printed in the USA
CPSIA information can be obtained
at www.ICGtesting.com
JSHW082200140824
68134JS00014B/341